7th Workshop on Linked Data in Linguistics (LDL-2020)

Marseille, France
11 – 16 May 2020

Editors:

Maxim Ionov
John P. McCrae
Christian Chiarcos

Thierry Declerck
Julia Bosque-Gil
Jorge Gracia

ISBN: 978-1-7138-1265-4

LREC 2020 Workshop
Language Resources and Evaluation Conference
11–16 May 2020

**7th Workshop on Linked Data in Linguistics
(LDL-2020)**

PROCEEDINGS

Editors:
Maxim Ionov, John P. McCrae, Christian Chiarcos, Thierry
Declerck, Julia Bosque-Gil, Jorge Gracia

Proceedings of the LREC 2020
7th Workshop on Linked Data in Linguistics
(LDL-2020)

Edited by:
Maxim Ionov, John P. McCrae, Christian Chiarcos, Thierry Declerck, Julia Bosque-Gil, and Jorge Gracia

The 7th Workshop on Linked Data in Linguistics was supported by the European Union's Horizon 2020 research and innovation program under grant agreement no. 825182 through the Prêt-à-LLOD project, the German Ministry for Education and Research (BMBF) through the project Linked Open Dictionaries (LiODi, 2015-2020) and the COST Action CA18209, NexusLinguarum: European network for Web-centred linguistic data science.

For more information:
European Language Resources Association (ELRA)
9 rue des Cordelières
75013, Paris
France
http://www.elra.info
Email: lrec@elda.org

7th Workshop on Linked Data in Linguistics (LDL-2020). Building tools and infrastructures

Past years have seen a growing interest in the application of knowledge graphs and Semantic Web technologies to language resources, and their publication as linked data on the Web. As of today, a large amount of language resources were either converted or created natively as linked data on the basis of data models specifically designed for the representation of linguistic content. Examples are wordnets, dictionaries, corpora, culminating in the emergence of a Linguistic Linked Open Data (LLOD) cloud (`http://linguistic-lod.org/`).

Since its establishment in 2012, the Linked Data in Linguistics (LDL) workshop series has become the major forum for presenting, discussing and disseminating technologies, vocabularies, resources and experiences regarding the application of semantic technologies and the Linked Open Data (LOD) paradigm to language resources in order to facilitate their visibility, accessibility, interoperability, reusability, enrichment, combined evaluation and integration. The LDL workshops contribute to the discussion, dissemination and establishment of community standards that drive this development, most notably the OntoLex-lemon model for lexical resources, as well as standards for other types of language resources still under development.

The workshop series is organized by Open Linguistics, founded 2010 as a Working Group of the Open Knowledge Foundation[1] with close involvement of related communities, such as W3C Community Groups, and international research projects. It takes a general focus on LOD-based resources, vocabularies, infrastructures and technologies as means for managing, improving and using language resources on the Web. As technology and resources increasingly converge towards a LOD-based ecosystem, this year we particularly encouraged submissions on Linked-Data Aware Tools and Services and Linked Language Resources Infrastructure, i.e. managing, curating and applying LLOD technologies and resources in a reliable and reproducible way for the needs of linguistics, NLP and digital humanities.

After ten years of community work, a critical mass of LLOD resources is already in place, yet, there is still a need to develop a robust ecosystem of tools that consume linguistic linked data. Recently started research networks and European projects are working in the direction of building sustainable infrastructures around LRs, with linked data as one of the core technologies. LDL-2020 is thus supported by the COST Action "European network for Web-centred linguistic data science" (NexusLinguarum) and two Horizon 2020 projects, the European Lexicographic Infrastructure (ELEXIS), and Prêt-à-LLOD, which focuses on providing an infrastructure for linguistic data to be ready to use by state-of-the-art technologies.

With a focus on building tools and applications, the *7th Workshop on Linked Data in Linguistics (LDL-2020)* was organized in conjunction with the 12th Language Resource and Evaluation Conference (LREC-2020). We received a total of 23 submissions out of which 12 were accepted (acceptance rate 52%). Due to Covid-19, LDL-2020 was not taking place as a physical meeting, but as a virtual event[2]. Presentations of the accepted papers were organized in three groups with four presentations each, on modelling, applications and lexicography, respectively.

---

[1] `https://groups.google.com/forum/#!forum/open-linguistics`
[2] Details and the program are available at `http://ldl2020.linguistic-lod.org/program.html`

Modelling

In *Towards an ontology based on Hallig-Wartburg's Begriffssystem for Historical Linguistic Linked Data* Tittel et al. compare two strategies for the LOD modelling of a conceptual system that is used in historical lexicography and lexicology, based on SKOS and OWL, respectively, and with examples from medieval Gascon and Italian.

In *Transforming the Cologne Digital Sanskrit Dictionaries into Ontolex-Lemon*, Mondaca and Rau evaluate two strategies for transforming TEI/XML data into OntoLex-Lemon, the enrichment of TEI XML with RDFa data, and a native RDF modelling. This evaluation tackles an important issue for applications in Digital Humanities as the TEI does not provide commonly accepted specifications for interfacing traditional XML-based workflows and Linked Open Data technologies.

In *Representing Temporal Information in Lexical Linked Data Resources*, Khan describes recent developments on his extension of the OntoLex-Lemon vocabulary with diachronic lexical information with examples from the Oxford English Dictionary and an etymological dictionary.

In *From Linguistic Descriptions to Language Profiles*, Shafqat Mumtaz Virk et al. introduce the concept of language profiles as structured representations of various types of knowledge about a natural language, they describe how to semi-automatically construct such data from descriptive documents and they develop a language profile of an example language.

Applications and Infrastructures

While overarching linked data-based infrastructures are only emerging, numerous applications of this technology are being reported.

With *Terme-à-LLOD: Simplifying the Conversion and Hosting of Terminological Resources as Linked Data*, Maria Pia di Buono et al. simplify the transformation and publication of terminology data by virtualization: A preconfigured virtual image of a server can thus be used to simplify installation of transformation and hosting services for terminological resources as linked data.

Frank Abromeit et al. introduce *Annohub – Annotation Metadata for Linked Data Applications*, a dataset and a portal that provides metadata about annotation and language identification for annotated language resources available on the web. Annohub builds on metadata repositories to identify language resources, on automated routines for classifying languages and annotation schemes, a broad range of transformers for various corpus formalisms and human curation for quality assurance.

Salgado et al. address *Challenges of Word Sense Alignment* for Portuguese Language Resources and report on a comparative study between the Portuguese Academy of Sciences Dictionary and the Dicionário Aberto. Word sense alignment involves searching for matching senses within dictionary entries of different lexical resources and linking them, implemented here by means of Semantic Web technologies.

In *A Lime-Flavored REST API for Alignment Services*, Fiorelli and Stellato describe a REST API to enable the participation of downstream alignment services an orchestration framework for ontology alignment. Using explicit metadata about the input ontologies, other resources and the task itself, a report is produced that summarizes characteristics and alignment strategies. For the lexical content of the input ontologies and external language resources, the report uses the Lime module of the OntoLex-Lemon model.

Lexicography

Abgaz describes on-going work on *Using OntoLex-Lemon for Representing and Interlinking Lexicographic Collections of Bavarian Dialects*, comprising two main components, a questionnaire with details about questions, collectors, paper slips etc., and a lexical dataset which contains lexical entries (answers) collected in response to the questions. The paper describes how the original TEI/XML format is transformed into Linguistic Linked Open Data to produce a lexicon for Bavarian Dialects.

With Linguistic Linked (Open) Data and, especially, the OntoLex vocabulary now being widely adapted throughout lexicography, there is a demand for tools, both for exploiting linked lexical data and for creating a user-friendly access to it. In *Involving Lexicographers in the LLOD Cloud with LexO, an Easy-to-use Editor of Lemon Lexical Resources*, Bellandi and Giovannetti describe LexO, a collaborative web editor of OntoLex-Lemon resources.

As for tools for lexicography, Gun Woo Lee et al. describe *Supervised Hypernymy Detection in Spanish through Order Embeddings*, based on a hypernymy dataset for Spanish built from WordNet and the use of pretrained word vectors as input.

Finally, Nielsen reports on *Lexemes in Wikidata*, i.e., the way that Wikidata records data about lexemes, senses and lexical forms and exposes them as Linguistic Linked Open Data and the growth and development of this data set since its first establishment in 2018.

Organizers:

Maxim Ionov, Goethe University Frankfurt (Germany)
John P. McCrae, National University of Ireland, Galway (Ireland)
Christian Chiarcos, Goethe University Frankfurt (Germany)
Thierry Declerck, DFKI GmbH (Germany) and ACDH-ÖAW (Austria)
Julia Bosque-Gil, University of Zaragoza (Spain)
Jorge Gracia, University of Zaragoza (Spain)

Program Committee:

Paul Buitelaar, Insight (Ireland)
Steve Cassidy, Macquarie University (Australia)
Philipp Cimiano, University of Bielefeld (Germany)
Gerard de Melo, Rutgers University (USA)
Francesca Frontini, Université Paul-Valéry (France)
Jeff Good, University at Buffalo (USA)
Dagmar Gromann, Vienna University (Austria)
Yoshihiko Hayashi, Osaka University, Waseda University (Japan)
Fahad Khan, ILC-CNR (Italy)
Bettina Klimek, University of Leipzig (Germany)
Elena Montiel-Ponsoda, Universidad Politécnica de Madrid (Spain)
Steve Moran, Universität Zürich (Switzerland)
Roberto Navigli, "La Sapienza" Università di Roma (Italy)
Sebastian Nordhoff, Language Science Press Berlin (Germany)
Petya Osenova, IICT-BAS (Bulgaria)
Antonio Pareja-Lora, Universidad Complutense Madrid (Spain)
Laurent Romary, INRIA (France)
Felix Sasaki, Cornelsen Verlag GmbH Berlin (Germany)
Andrea Schalley, Karlstad University (Sweden)
Gilles Sérasset, University Grenoble Alpes (France)
Armando Stellato, University of Rome, Tor Vergata (Italy)
Marieke van Erp, KNAW Humanities Cluster (The Netherlands)
Piek Vossen, Vrije Universiteit Amsterdam (The Netherlands)

Table of Contents

Proceedings of the 7th Workshop on Linked Data in Linguistics (LDL-2020), pages 1–10
Language Resources and Evaluation Conference (LREC 2020), Marseille, 11–16 May 2020
© European Language Resources Association (ELRA), licensed under CC-BY-NC

Towards an Ontology Based on Hallig-Wartburg's *Begriffssystem* for Historical Linguistic Linked Data

Sabine Tittel, Frances Gillis-Webber, Alessandro A. Nannini
Heidelberg Academy of Sciences and Humanities, University of Cape Town, University of Vienna
Heidelberg, Germany, Cape Town, South Africa, Vienna, Austria
sabine.tittel@urz.uni-heidelberg.de, fran@fynbosch.com, alessandro.alfredo.nannini@univie.ac.at

Abstract

To empower end users in searching for historical linguistic content with a performance that far exceeds the research functions offered by websites of, e.g., historical dictionaries, is undoubtedly a major advantage of (Linguistic) Linked Open Data ([L]LOD). An important aim of lexicography is to enable a language-independent, onomasiological approach, and the modelling of linguistic resources following the LOD paradigm facilitates the semantic mapping to ontologies making this approach possible. Hallig-Wartburg's *Begriffssystem* (HW) is a well-known extra-linguistic conceptual system used as an onomasiological framework by many historical lexicographical and lexicological works. Published in 1952, HW has meanwhile been digitised. With proprietary XML data as the starting point, our goal is the transformation of HW into Linked Open Data in order to facilitate its use by linguistic resources modelled as LOD. In this paper, we describe the particularities of the HW conceptual model and the method of converting HW: We discuss two approaches, (i) the representation of HW in RDF using SKOS, the SKOS thesaurus extension, and XKOS, and (ii) the creation of a lightweight ontology expressed in OWL, based on the RDF/SKOS model. The outcome is illustrated with use cases of medieval Gascon, and Italian.

Keywords: Historical Linguistics, Linked Open Data, Ontology Authoring

1. Introduction

As the most solid grounding of the Semantic Web, the Linked Data (LD) paradigm is used to represent and inter-link structured data on the web. The standard proposed by the W3C for representing LD (LOD respectively, with 'O' symbolising open access) is the graph data model *Resource Description Framework* (RDF) that represents data in the form of triples with subject, predicate, and object, each identified through URIs that are accessible via HTTP (Cyganiak et al., 2014). There are many advantages to representing linguistic resources in RDF, and applying LD principles to them, such as structural and conceptual interoperability, uniform access through standard Web protocols, and resource integration and federation (Chiarcos et al., 2013). Representing dictionary data as Linguistic Linked Open Data (LLOD) is a very promising approach, especially as it allows for interoperability among different lexicographic resources through the use of common vocabularies that have emerged for the modelling of linguistic data. The OntoLex-*lemon* vocabulary (Cimiano et al., 2016) has been established as the *de facto* standard RDF data model for LLOD; it provides the framework for the representation of language data such as lexical entries, their written representations, and their meanings. The data modelled with OntoLex-*lemon* can easily be integrated by linking to external resources, such as ontologies for linguistic annotations (e.g., LexInfo[1]), and extra-linguistic information, such as place names (e.g., TGN[2]). We point out that the typical scenario of (historical) linguistic research is characterised by poor data accessibility through searching for *words* and their formal representations across resources of different languages and language stages. This scenario hampers semantic driven research of the *meanings* of the words, par-

ticularly for historical language data with non-standardised word spelling. To facilitate access independent from the *words* and their formal representations, the data modelling must, hence, also be enriched by semantic mapping (of entries, senses, concepts) to appropriate ontologies that depict the 'real world' (DBpedia[3], AGROVOC[4], AAT[5], etc.). The use of an external extra-linguistic ontology as a cross-mapping hub for linguistic resources, especially for historical resources, is able to overcome the typical, word-form driven research scenario. This is facilitated by OntoLex-*lemon* and its "principle of semantics by reference in the sense that the semantics of a lexical entry is expressed by reference to an individual, class or property defined in an ontology" (Cimiano et al., 2016, 2.1). One such ontology—in the philosophical meaning of the term—is the so-called Hallig-Wartburg (HW), first published in 1952 ([2]1963): *Begriffssystem als Grundlage für die Lexikographie* (Hallig and von Wartburg, 1963). In this paper, we focus on the use of HW by linguistic resources and on its transition from a printed book to an LOD resource in order to facilitate its use by linguistic resources on the Semantic Web.

The remainder of the paper is structured as follows: In section 2., we describe the role of HW for linguistic resources of historical language stages that have been or intend to be modelled as LOD. In section 3., we discuss an attempt to convert HW from the original book, via an XML digitisation, into an LOD resource that can be used for semantic mapping. In light of the requirements of the LOD paradigm, we first evaluate a thesaurus-like RDF/SKOS model in section 3.1.; in section 3.2., we discuss its further conversion to an ontological model, and we show its practical application with the use case of data from two historical

---

[1] https://lexinfo.net/ [12-02-2020].

[2] https://www.getty.edu/research/tools/vocabularies/tgn/index.html [12-02-2020].

[3] https://wiki.dbpedia.org/ [12-02-2020].

[4] http://agrovoc.uniroma2.it/agrovoc/agrovoc/en/ [13-02-2020].

[5] https://www.getty.edu/research/tools/vocabularies/aat/ [12-02-2020].

dictionaries, DAG and LEI, in section 4. Our approach reveals difficulties and shortcomings both with respect to a re-engineering of the ontological model and to the conceptual scheme of HW itself, which we discuss in section 5.

2. Onomasiological Lexicography and the use of Hallig-Wartburg's *Begriffssystem*

Traditional lexicography either follows a semasiological approach in presenting dictionary data, i.e., the data is ordered by the *words*, or an onomasiological approach, i.e., the data is ordered by the *meaning* of the words. For an onomasiological approach, a thesaurus-like categorisation of the world is needed as a structuring means. Resources referred to as thesauri include the *Historical Thesaurus of the Oxford English Dictionary* (HTOED) (Kay, 2009), Roget's *Thesaurus of English words and phrases* (first edition London 1852, Davidson (2002)), and Dornseiff's *Der deutsche Wortschatz nach Sachgruppen* (Dornseiff, 1934). Possibly the best-known example of a thesaurus-like categorisation of the world used within Romance philology and the reference work of the discipline is Hallig-Wartburg.

2.1. Structure of Hallig-Wartburg

Hallig's and Wartburg's *Begriffssystem*—German for 'system of concepts'—is a conceptual scheme in that it is a controlled vocabulary with a hierarchically structured set of concepts. At first glance, it seems to be a thesaurus-like resource. However, ISO 25964 defines a thesaurus as a "controlled and structured vocabulary in which concepts are represented by terms, organized so that relationships between concepts are made explicit, and preferred terms are accompanied by lead-in entries for synonyms or quasi-synonyms", a term being a "word or phrase used to label a concept" and a concept being a "unit of thought" (International Organization for Standardization, 2011). The terms come from the vocabulary of one or several natural language(s) meaning that they are lexicalised in that language and typically expressed with equivalence relationships (synonyms, quasi-synonyms or antonyms) in the thesaurus (Kless et al., 2012a; Kless et al., 2012b); cp. also Helou et al. (2014) on ontology entities expressed in natural language by associating them with terms. The lexicalisation of the labelling terms is the decisive factor for the classification of HW as not compliant with ISO 25964. HW does not provide lexicalised terms in a natural language. HW, unlike thesauri such as HTOED, Roget, and also the thesaurus-like, lexical database WordNet (Fellbaum, 1998), does not spring from a list of words of a natural language (the 'terms'), e.g., of a (semasiologically structured) dictionary, word list or similar source. Instead, it is meant to be a resource for the use of, e.g., onomasiologically structured dictionaries: It is an *extra-linguistic* reference system of the real world reflecting the model of thought of a 'talented average person' (HW 12), independent from language and with an a priori character ("ein empirisches, aus sprachlichen Allgemeinbegriffen bestehendes, [...] auf phänomenologischer Grundlage beruhenden Gliederungsprinzipien gestaltetes außersprachliches Bezugssystem", ib. 21). HW contains approx. 1675 non-lexicalised concepts ordered in a nine-level hierarchy.

It is clear that a concept must be communicated by a sign, and, indeed, the HW concepts are denoted by *words* of the French language. However, these words are only vehicles and, thus, arbitrary: HW makes it explicit that the words, e.g., 'La mer', are mere symbols of the concepts and not to be misunderstood as lexemes of the French lexicon (ib. 16; 72). This can be illustrated by, e.g., *périodique* (periodical) and *quotidien* (daily) that are both sub-concepts of the concept of *fois* (time [occasion]), not of 'period' and 'day', respectively (ib. 17). As a consequence, concepts may occur several times (with cross-references), e.g., 'fishing' both as an occupation and a sport (ib. 73). The authors of HW were aware of possible misunderstandings and point out that a particular identification of the emblematic character of the French words, e.g., through square brackets, would have been useful but that they refrained from this for the sake of readability (ib.).

The concepts of the upper six levels of the hierarchy are denoted by French non-lexicalised categories, e.g., 'L'univers', 'Le ciel et l'atmosphère', and 'Le ciel et les corps célestes', and, additionally, the concepts are identified by a system of capital letters between A and C, followed by Roman numerals, Arabic lower case letters, etc.: 'A', 'A I', 'B II h', etc. This six-level hierarchy forms the 'Plan' with 524 concepts, the outline with the logical abstraction of concepts representing broader, conceptual fields, cf. HW 101–112 (Fig. 1).

k) Les besoins de l'être humain	140a
1. L'alimentation	140a
aa) Généralités	140a
bb) Les repas	141a
cc) Les aliments	141a
1. La viande	141a
2. Le pain, la pâtisserie	141a
3. Les œufs	141b
4. Les laitages	141b
5. La préparation des aliments	141b
6. Les assaisonnements, le sucre, etc.	141b
7. Les mets	142a
8. Les boissons	142a
dd) Le tabac	142b
2. La vie sexuelle	142b

Figure 1: The 'Plan' (extract), HW 103.

In HW 113–229, the six conceptual levels of the 'Plan' are then further extended by another, up to three-level hierarchy of approx. 1,150 finer-grained concepts for "lexicography proper as represented by the 'words' classified in its application" (Orr, cited by HW 20, footnote 4), which we will refer to as 'Application' in the following (Fig. 2). These concepts are not consecutively numbered.

k) Les besoins de l'être humain	repu
	jeûner
besoin, *v. aussi p. 158b.*	jeûne
	rompre le jeûne
	approvisionner
1. L'alimentation	ration
	provision, *v. aussi p. 188b.*
aa) Généralités	
affamé	frugal
faim	glouton
être à jeun	gourmand
famine	gourmet
appétit	friand
nourrir	délicat

Figure 2: Finer-grained 'Application' (extract), HW 141.

Thesauri (and this applies to a conceptual scheme such as

HW as well) establish hierarchical relationships and associative relationships between concepts. The hierarchical relationships can be generic, a whole-part relation, and a concept-instance relation; the associative relationships exist between hierarchically unrelated but semantically or conceptually related concepts (Kless et al., 2012a, 135f.). HW contains hierarchical (both generic and whole-part relations) and also associative relationships between the concepts (HW 18); neither cyclic hierarchical relationships nor orphans. HW prioritises the hierarchical over the associative classification but deliberately prefers the latter in cases where an association seems more 'natural' (ib.), particularly in fields where the concepts are closely connected to specialised domains, such as house building and hunting. With this approach to classification, HW wants to take account of the fact that every language has its own peculiar interpenetration of systematics and non-systematics, which is reflected in the linguistic interpretation of the world (ib.) E.g., the concept 'construire' (to construct) is neither hierarchically allocated to 'L'action' (B II h 3) [together with 'faire' (to make) and 'créer' (to create)], nor to 'L'espace' (space, C I e) [together with 'assembler' (to assemble)]. Instead, it is associated to the concept of house building, i.e., 'La construction' (B III b 7 bb, sub 'L'habitation, la maison'). The concept 'miette' (crumb) is logically a sub-concept of 'morceau' (part, sub-concept of C I d 'Le nombre et la quantité') but associated to the concept 'Le pain, la pâtisserie' (bread, patisserie, B I k 1 cc 2), and 'saumure' (brine) is a concept associated to 'La viande' (meat, B I k 1 cc 1). An example for a hierarchical, whole-part relation is the relation of the concept 'les narines' (nostrils) to its superordinate concept 'Le corps et les membres' (the body and its parts).

The concepts and their classification reveal problematic congruencies, wrong hierarchisation, and inconsistencies[6]:

1. On levels 1-6, we find the identical concept 'Généralités' 27 times, semantically disambiguated through its place in the hierarchy, e.g., as a sub-concept of 'Les arbres'; these concepts can be suppressed since one could simply refer to the respective superordinate concept. On levels 7-9, 'esp.' (abbreviating *espèces*, sub-species, e.g., of the apple) occurs.

2. On levels 8 and 9, we find the string 'etc.' as a concept denomination.

3. On levels 7-9, some concepts are followed by references to homonymic concept denominations (printed in italics, separated by a comma), e.g., 'port, *v. aussi p. 197a*'.

4. On levels 7-9, some concept denominations are specified through German definitions. In some cases, this aims at the semantic disambiguation of homonymic concept denominations within the same superordinate concept, e.g., 'beau-père "Schwiegervater"' (father-in-law) / 'beau-père "Stiefvater"' (stepfather).

5. C II a 17 'La phonétique' is on the same hierarchy level as C II a 18 'La linguistique' but should be a sub-concept of the latter.

6. We find 'alchimie' falsely classified under A II e 'Les métaux' which is a sub-concept of the top concept A 'L'Univers'. However, this top concept should contain only sub-concepts related to organic and inorganic nature, and not to human activities (HW 89).

7. Similarly, under A IV 'Les animaux' we find 'Les animaux fabuleux' (fabulous beasts) and its sub-concepts 'phénix' (phoenix) and 'dragon' (dragon), concepts that cannot be separated from human conception and should, thus, rather be associated to B II e 'L'imagination'.

8. A classification inconsistency is the presence of the sub-concept 'Le tabac' (tobacco, B I k 1 dd) under 'Les aliments' (food, B I k 1), as if tobacco were food.

2.2. Lexicographical and Lexicological Resources using Hallig-Wartburg

HW has been chosen by numerous lexicographical and lexicological works as a means of semantic structure. The most comprehensive *Französisches Etymologisches Wörterbuch* (FEW) (von Wartburg, since 1922) is a dictionary of the Galloromance languages and dialects covering the period from the middle ages until today, structured by the alphabetical order of the etyma of the treated word families. The words of unknown or uncertain origin are treated in vol. 21–23 where they are grouped onomasiologically, ordered by the HW concepts. The HW concepts form the structural backbone of the dictionaries *Dictionnaire onomasiologique de l'ancien occitan* (DAO) (Baldinger, 1975 to 2005) and the *Dictionnaire onomasiologique de l'ancien gascon* (DAG) (Baldinger, since 1975): both follow HW to structure the editing and publishing of the dictionary entries (Glessgen and Tittel, 2018, 805). Semantic criteria are used in the *Lessico Etimologico Italiano* (LEI) (Pfister, since 1979) to build the structure of very complex articles, as in the FEW 21–23 (Tancke, 1997, 466); in these cases, the lexicographical sections are ordered by semantic categories (in Italian language) that closely recall those of HW. Recently, the online edition of the *Dictionnaire de l'occitan médiéval* (DOM) (Stempel, 1996 to 2013) started evaluating the introduction of HW concepts to align the entries to those of DAG*él*.[7] The *Dictionnaire étymologique de l'ancien français* (DEAF) (Baldinger, since 1971) follows a semasiological approach but inherits HW categories when it refers to entries of FEW 21–23. The *Mittelhochdeutsche Begriffsdatenbank* (MHDBDB[8]) creates an onomasiological database for Middle High German, building on HW (Hinkelmanns, 2019): the HW categorisation has been further developed with the application on the lexis of Middle High German *Frauendienst* by Ulrich von Lichtenstein (1255) and of *Lanzelet* by Ulrich von Zatzikhoven (after 1193) (Schmidt, 1980; Schmidt, 1988; Schmidt, 1993). Also, many onomasiologically structured lexicological studies on medieval until 16th century French, Italian, Spanish, Gascon and Occitan resources (literary texts, architecture, Bible, etc.), use HW concepts, e.g., Bevans (1941) on the Old French vocabu-

---

[6]Naturally, concepts that reflect the zeitgeist of the time of HW's creation, e.g. 'Les costumes nationaux et pittoresques', are to be found as well.

[7]Personal communication by Maria Selig, DOM.
[8]http://mhdbdb.sbg.ac.at/ [06-02-2020].

lary of Champagne[9], Keller (1953) on the vocabulary used by Wace (* approx. 1110 – † after 1174), de Man (1956) on the Brabant language in archival sources 1300-1550, etc. (Baldinger, 1959, 1091f.).

2.3. Hallig-Wartburg in Linked Open Data resources

As a contribution to the emerging linguistic LOD cloud and to expand the inadequately represented historical linguistic resources, efforts to model these lexicographic resources as Linked Data have been initiated: The FEW is currently digitally available as bitmap images[10] but a digitisation by means of XML is underway (Renders, 2015), and Renders (2019) announces a study on how to model etymological data of the FEW as LOD. For the electronic version of the LEI, LEI-Digitale (Prifti, 2019), the LEI editors carry out feasibility studies on LOD modelling and semantic mapping to HW or to a taxonomy based on HW (Nannini, in progress). Tittel and Chiarcos (2018) created a RDF data model for the electronic version of the DEAF (DEAF*él*) and Tittel (in progress) for DAG*él*, the electronic complement to the DAG (Glessgen, since 2014). The relaunch of the MHDBDB (planned for 2020) will include an RDF version of the data (Hinkelmanns, 2019).

3. From the *Begriffssystem* to an Ontology

The representation of HW in RDF, and SKOS or as an ontology, achieves compatibility with other Semantic Web technologies and is thought to facilitate interoperability across linguistic resources applying HW as their onomasiological framework. This helps to establish the word-form and language-independent access to these resources: a pivotal motivation to model them as LOD and to include references to the HW concepts. A potential reuse both of HW and of the linguistic resources using HW is also thought to be promoted by the fact that the HW RDF graph is easy to be referenced by other bigger, more comprehensive and more detailed LOD resources, independent from a natural language. Also, recall one of the main principles of the LD paradigm: to provide useful information (in RDF) that is returned when navigating to a URI, i.e., provide dereferenceable URIs.

However, the native format of the HW is a book publication which, thus, needs to be converted into a format compliant with the LOD paradigm. For the digital editing of the DAG*él*, the 524 numbered concepts (the 'Plan', Fig. 1) of HW (second edition 1963) have been digitised in 2014 using DAG's dictionary writing system (Glessgen and Tittel, 2018). The finer-grained approx. 1,150 concepts of the 'Application' (Fig. 2) were excluded from the digitisation because the DAG*él* uses only the concepts of the 'Plan' as its framework. As a first step towards an RDF graph based on HW, we exported the data as XML from the DAG*él*'s database. The XML structure is based on rows with a single XML element `field` and one attribute with two possi-

ble contents, as shown in List. 1. Alas, it does not contain information that can easily be exploited for a future hierarchical representation of the category levels, as visualised in Fig. 3.

```
1  <?xml version="1.0"?>
2  <resultset
3   xmlns:xsi="http://www.w3.org/2001/
4   XMLSchema-instance">
5  <row>
6   <field name="identifier">B I k 1 cc 1</field>
7   <field name="concept">La viande</field>
8  </row>
9  <row>
10  <field name="identifier">B I k 1 cc 2</field>
11  <field name="concept">Le pain, la pâtisserie</field>
12  </row>
13  </resultset>
```

Listing 1: Extract of XML data.

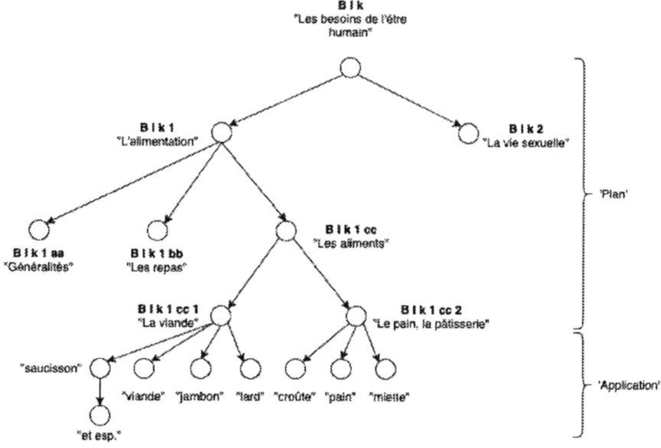

Figure 3: Hallig-Wartburg concept hierarchy.

3.1. Hallig-Wartburg in RDF and SKOS

HW is represented in a standard format of a Knowledge Organisation System (KOS), a system to represent classification schemes, thesauri, taxonomies and similar structures. The W3C has defined the *Simple Knowledge Organization System* (SKOS) which provides a data model and vocabulary for expressing KOSs in RDF (Miles and Bechhofer, 2009). Two types of semantic relations are distinguished by SKOS: hierarchical and associative. The hierarchical relation is typically represented by the 'narrower' and the 'broader' property, an associative relation is indicated by the use of 'related'. However, the specific nature of concept relations cannot be expressed. The ISO 25964 SKOS extension (Miles and Brickley, 2004) distinguishes finer-grained semantic relations between the concepts and aims at providing better interoperability between SKOS and the thesaurus standard. It is ideal to explicitly express hierarchical generic and whole-part relationships through the SKOS-Thes properties 'broaderGeneric' and 'broaderPartitive' respectively. The associative relation expressing a partitive relationship between concepts can be expressed through the more specific property 'relatedPartOf'. *Extended Knowledge Organization System* (XKOS) was developed to extend SKOS for statistical classification, and one of its features, comparable to the SKOS-thesaurus extension, is to refine SKOS' semantic properties (Cyganiak

---

[9]Draws on the *Questionnaire*, the dialectal recordings made by Rudolf Hallig as a preparation for HW (Christmann and Böckle, 1983, 398).

[10]https://apps.atilf.fr/lecteurFEW/ [accessed 05-02-2020].

et al., 2017). XKOS is a public working draft of a potential specification and therefore we chose to use the SKOS-thesaurus extension to express the semantic relations, although the properties of the latter are still classified as 'unstable'. Nevertheless, XKOS offers possibilities to define the classification levels of a KOS which we deem valuable for our approach. The representation of HW's hierarchical and associative relationships is thus straightforward. However, the respective relations are not explicitly expressed in the original source, and a representation in SKOS must comprise a manual assessment of the relations.

We converted the XML data into RDF and SKOS (including extensions), applying the following rules:

1. Since the HW is concept-based according to ISO 25964, all HW concepts can be represented as SKOS concepts.

2. To define the hierarchy levels and their respective members, we include XKOS 'ClassificationLevel'.

3. We define the three concepts of the top level, A 'L'univers', B 'L'homme', and C 'L'homme et l'univers', as top concepts of the concept scheme (List. 2, l. 7).

4. We utilize the content of XML `<field name="concept">` as the concept denomination: to emphasize the symbolic character of the denomination by capitalising all characters, eliminating French accents and replacing spaces, punctuation marks, and apostrophes with an underscore, e.g., L_HOMME_ET_L_UNIVERS.

5. We also utilize said content to add a SKOS 'scopeNote' providing information about the scope of the concept. Aiming at removing possible ambiguity or misunderstanding of the non-lexicalised information (erroneously as 'terms') we deem a scope note the accurate 'translation' of the information given in HW.

6. In SKOS, preferred and alternative lexical labels can be used for "generating or creating human-readable representations of a knowledge organization system" (Miles and Bechhofer, 2009); it is consistent with SKOS to assign (multiple) alternative lexical label(s) but no preferred lexical label to a resource. SKOS does not specify whether a resource with none of the two lexical labels is consistent with the SKOS data model, however, it is said to be advised to include a lexical label "in order to generate an optimum human-readable display" (ib.). Considering this advice and the *de facto* missing terms in HW that could naturally become lexical labels, we propose to misuse the concept denominations: We allocate an additional function to the French words used as arbitrary symbols by Hallig and Wartburg interpreting them as 'terms' expressed through `skos:altLabel`, e.g., "Les besoins de l'être humain". This design decision aims to compensate for the missing terms but refrains from declaring preferred labels.

7. For backwards compatibility, we preserve the consecutive numbers of the upper six levels as contained in XML `<field name="identifier">`, using the SKOS 'notation' property; we define the string literal by a particular HW specific identification scheme `<hwIdentificationScheme>`.

8. We eliminate concepts denominated by 'etc.', assuming that the linguistic resources using HW as a reference do not classify lexemes under a concept 'etc.' (approved by the editorial team of the DAG*él*).

9. Hierarchical generic relations are expressed through `skos-thes:broaderGeneric`, e.g., the relation between 'La viande' and 'Les aliments' (List. 2, l. 40), hierarchical whole-part relations through `skos-thes:broaderPartitive`, e.g., the relation between 'les narines' and 'Le corps et les membres' (List. 2, l. 51), and associative relations through `skos-thes:relatedPartOf`, e.g., the relation between 'miette' and 'Le pain, la pâtisserie' (List. 2, l. 46). To enable navigation from the top concept level down into the hierarchy, we include the SKOS 'narrower' property (l. 27; 41).

10. We distinguish homonymic concepts within the same superordinate concept, that are, thus, not disambiguated by their respective, different superordinate concepts, as follows: We add a number to the concept denomination and preserve the German definitions that are used for the semantic disambiguation as a SKOS 'editorialNote', e.g., sub B III a 1 aa 3 ('La parenté'), 'beau-père': `:BEAU_PERE_1 skos:scopeNote "beau-père"@fr skos:editorialNote "Schwiegervater"@de` and `:BEAU_PERE_2 skos:scopeNote "beau-père"@fr skos:editorialNote "Stiefvater"@de`. We chose `editorialNote` over the ostensibly obvious SKOS property `definition` to be able to use the latter for a further knowledge enrichment with accurate genus-differentiae sense definitions.

11. We eliminate references to pages with homonymic concepts assuming that this information won't be of value for semantic integration.

The result is shown in List. 2, the data is provided in Turtle syntax (Prud'hommeaux and Carothers, 2014).[11]

```
1  @prefix     : <http://example.org/hallig-wartburg#> .
2
3  :HW a skos:ConceptScheme ;
4    skos:prefLabel "HW classification scheme"@en ;
5    xkos:numberOfLevels 9 ;
6    xkos:levels ( :HW_Level1 ... :HW_Level9 ) ;
7    skos:hasTopConcept :L_HOMME , :L_UNIVERS , ... .
8
9  :hwIdentificationScheme a rdfs:Datatype ;
10   rdfs:comment "HW concept identification scheme" ;
11   owl:oneOf (
12     "B"^^xsd:string
13     "B I k 1 cc 1"^^xsd:string
14     "B I k 1 cc 2"^^xsd:string ... ) .
15 :HW_Level1 a xkos:ClassificationLevel ;
16   xkos:depth 1 ;
17   skos:member :L_UNIVERS , :L_HOMME ,
18   :L_HOMME_ET_L_UNIVERS .
19 :L_HOMME a skos:Concept ;
20   skos:altLabel "L'homme"@fr ;
21   skos:scopeNote "L'homme"@fr ;
22   skos:notation "B"^^:hwIdentificationScheme;
23   skos:inScheme :HW ;
24   skos:topConceptOf :HW ;
```

27 ______________________________

[11]For the sake of brevity, we suppress (lines of) code that do not add substantial value, and standard namespaces are assumed defined the usual way, also in List. 3, 5 and 6.

```
25    skos:narrower :L_HOMME_ETRE_PHYSIQUE .
26  :L_HOMME_ETRE_PHYSIQUE a skos:Concept ;
28    skos:altLabel "L'homme, être physique"@fr ;
29    skos:scopeNote "L'homme, être physique"@fr ;
30    skos:notation "B I"^^:hwIdentificationScheme ;
31    skos:inScheme :HW ;
32    skos-thes:broaderGeneric :L_HOMME ;
33    skos:narrower :LE_SEXE , :LA_RACE , ... .
34  :LA_VIANDE a skos:Concept ;
35    skos:altLabel "La viande"@fr ;
36    skos:scopeNote "La viande"@fr ;
37    skos:notation "B I k 1 cc 1"^^:hwIdentificationScheme ;
38    skos:inScheme :HW ;
39    skos-thes:broaderGeneric :LES_ALIMENTS ;
40    skos:narrower :VIANDE , :JAMBON , :LARD ... .
41  :MIETTE a skos:Concept ;
42    skos:altLabel "miette"@fr ;
43    skos:scopeNote "miette"@fr ;
44    skos:inScheme :HW ;
45    skos-thes:relatedPartOf :LE_PAIN_LA_PATISSERIE .
46  :LES_NARINES a skos:Concept ;
47    skos:altLabel "les narines"@fr ;
48    skos:scopeNote "les narines"@fr ;
49    skos:inScheme :HW ;
50    skos-thes:broaderPartitive :LE_CORPS_ET_LES_MEMBRES .
```

Listing 2: Extract of RDF data.

We have considered including the Lemon-tree vocabulary into the modelling. Lemon-tree has specifically been designed to model lexicographical thesaurus-like resources as LD, bridging SKOS and the OntoLex-*lemon* vocabulary (Stolk, 2019). Yet, for the modelling of HW, following the examples given by Lemon-tree, only SKOS and XKOS would be used, hence the advantage would not be obvious.[12] The MHDBDB has created a SKOS model of the onomasiological framework (extending HW) that structures the data.[13] However, its design differs significantly from the result of our attempt: The model excludes both the original HW identifiers and the French concept denominations. Instead, concept denominations have been translated to German and English, and they are treated as lexical terms, expressed through the SKOS property 'prefLabel'. The model expresses the relationships solely as hierarchical generic through SKOS 'broader' (not using the inverse relation 'narrower', resulting in the fact that a navigation from a top level down is not possible). In any case, it has become clear that an LOD compliant model of HW presents a desideratum in the discipline of historical linguistic data.

3.2. Towards an Ontological Model

The HW RDF/SKOS model is compliant with the LOD paradigm but it is a representation close to the book published in 1953. With the means of a KOS, it lacks of conceptual abstraction, nuanced semantic relations, and information integration for interoperability (cp. Soergel et al. (2006)). The Web Ontology Language (OWL) (Bechhofer et al., 2004) is a popular W3C recommended format to express ontologies, offering an alternative means for porting KOSs to the Semantic Web. The next step is, thus, to construct an ontological model of the HW in OWL on the basis of the RDF/SKOS model. This will allow for more ex-

---

[12]A linguistic resource could, however, use Lemon-trees's object property isSenseInConcept to relate a "lexical sense to a concept that captures its meaning to some extent (that is, partially or even fully)" (Stolk, 2019).

[13]We thank Peter Hinkelmanns, MHDBDB, for making the model available to us and for sharing thoughts on how to model HW in SKOS.

pressivity and descriptiveness than offered by SKOS relations, also preparing for future extension. The result will be a lightweight ontology, i.e., an RDF document serialised in OWL, its benefit over the RDF/SKOS model being better interoperability and the potential for a extra-linguistic cross-mapping hub for the (historical) linguistic resources using HW concepts as their onomasiological architecture: A lightweight ontology based on HW provides a possibility for resources such as DAG*él*, LEI, DEAF, and MHDBDB to create instances of the HW classes.

The HW concepts meet the requirement of reflecting universal categories and the SKOS concepts (instances in SKOS) can thus be represented as classes in OWL (cp. Baker et al. (2013, 38); Kless et al. (2012b, 406-409)). This is a viable approach for creating an ontology in OWL Full but its result of course does not have inferencing qualities. Adding the expressive capabilities to allow for reasoning over the ontological model requires a re-engineering of the SKOS model into a formal ontology expressed with OWL DL, which we will discuss shortly in section 5.

The syntactic conversion from the SKOS model into OWL Full is not straightforward. The fact that thesauri-like KOSs express concept relations through basically two kinds of relationships only (hierarchical and associative) makes them underspecified from the perspective of an ontological model (Kless et al., 2012b). At the same time, the aligning of specific relationships in a thesaurus to relationships in an ontological model is not obvious and lacks of corresponding relata, in particular, associative relationships rarely find their matches (ib. 412). In this paper, we demonstrate the approach of adopting the relationships expressed by SKOS and its thesaurus extension (ib. 422): The conversion of the concepts ordered hierarchically by the generic relation into class/sub-class relations (expressed by means of RDFS 'subClassOf') (Brickley and Guha, 2014) is obvious; `skos-thes:broaderPartitive` will be preserved for the hierarchical whole-part relationship, and `skos-thes:relatedPartOf` for the associative relationship. The lexical label can be expressed through RDFS 'label', the SKOS properties 'scopeNote' and 'notation' will be preserved. We conducted a small study representing sample data of HW as an ontological model, see List. 3.

```
 1  <rdf:RDF xmlns="https://example.org/hallig-wartburg-
 2   ontology#">
 3
 4  <owl:Ontology rdf:about="https://example.org/hallig-
 5   wartburg-ontology#">
 6   <dct:title xml:lang="en">Hallig-Wartburg Ontology
 7   </dct:title>
 8   <vann:preferredNamespacePrefix>hw
 9   </vann:preferredNamespacePrefix>
10   <dct:description xml:lang="en">Ontology based on ...
11   </dct:description>
12   <owl:versionInfo rdf:datatype="http://www.w3.org/
13   2001/XMLSchema#string">1.0.0
14   </owl:versionInfo>
15  </owl:Ontology>
16
17  <!-- datatype properties -->
18  <owl:DatatypeProperty rdf:about="https://lod.academy/
19   hw-onto/ns/hw#hwIdentificationScheme">
20   <rdfs:label xml:lang="en">HW Identification Scheme
21   </rdfs:label>
22   <rdfs:range>
23     <rdfs:Datatype>
24      <owl:oneOf>...</owl:oneOf>
25     </rdfs:Datatype>
26   </rdfs:range>
27  </owl:DatatypeProperty>
```

6

```
28 <!-- classes -->
29 <owl:Class rdf:about="https://example.org/hallig-
30   wartburg-ontology#LA_VIANDE">
31   <skos:scopeNote xml:lang="fr">La viande</skos:scopeNote>
32   <skos:notation rdf:datatype="https://lod.academy/
33   hw-onto/ns/hw#hwIdentificationScheme">
34   B I k 1 cc 1</skos:notation>
35   <rdfs:label xml:lang="fr">La viande</rdfs:label>
36   <rdfs:subClassOf rdf:resource="https://example.org/
37   hallig-wartburg-ontology#LES_ALIMENTS"/>
38 </owl:Class>
39 <owl:Class rdf:about="https://example.org/hallig-
40   wartburg-ontology#MIETTE">
41   <skos:scopeNote xml:lang="fr">miette</skos:scopeNote>
42   <rdfs:label xml:lang="fr">miette</rdfs:label>
43   <rdfs:subClassOf rdf:resource="https://example.org/
44   hallig-wartburg-ontology#HWCat"/>
45   <skos-thes:relatedPartOf rdf:resource="https://example.
46   org/hallig-wartburg-ontology#LE_PAIN_LA_PATISSERIE"/>
47 </owl:Class>
48 <owl:Class rdf:about="https://example.org/hallig-wartburg-
49   ontology#LES_NARINES">
50   <skos:scopeNote xml:lang="fr">les narines</skos:scopeNote>
51   <rdfs:label xml:lang="fr">les narines</rdfs:label>
52   <rdfs:subClassOf rdf:resource="https://example.org/
53   hallig-wartburg-ontology#HWCat"/>
54   <skos-thes:broaderPartitive rdf:resource="https://example.
55   org/hallig-wartburg-ontology#LE_CORPS_ET_LES_MEMBRES"/>
56 </owl:Class>
57 </rdf:RDF>
```

Listing 3: Extract of OWL ontology (RDF/XML syntax).

4. Practical Application

With the use cases of Old Gascon *bacon* (ham), entry of DAG*él*, and of Italian *cantuccino* (a twice-baked almond biscuit), entry of LEI, we demonstrate how—through the interlinking of linguistic resources via the OntoLex-*lemon* vocabulary   the integration of a reference to a concept of the HW ontology can be integrated into an LOD resource.

Old Gascon *bacon*. The conversion of DAG*él* dictionary entries into RDF is an automated process, broadly similar to the conversion of DEAF (Tittel and Chiarcos, 2018). To automatically insert a mapping of a sense definition to the correct HW concept is straightforward, given that a reference from each sense to HW is part of the XML resource data, as shown in List. 4.

```
1 <m:definition>viande de porc sal&#xE9;e afin de
2   la conserver</m:definition>
3 <m:cat-onomas cat="B I k cc 1">B I k 1 cc 1 /
4   La viande</m:cat-onomas>
```

Listing 4: XML resource data of a DAG*él* entry (extract).

The content of the XML element `<cat-onomas>` can be transformed into `hw:LA_VIANDE`, to which we can refer through OntoLex-*lemon*'s object property `isConceptOf`, as shown in List. 5, l. 14.

```
1 @prefix dag: <http://dag.adw.uni-heidelberg.de/
2              lemme/> .
3 @prefix hw:  <http://example.org/hallig-wartburg-
4              ontology#> .
5
6 dag:bacon a ontolex:LexicalEntry ;
7   ontolex:sense dag:bacon_sense ;
8   ontolex:evokes dag:bacon_lexConcept ;
9   ontolex:canonicalForm dag:bacon_form .
10 dag:bacon_form a ontolex:Form ;
11   ontolex:writtenRep "bacon"@oc-x-40000006 .
12
13 dag:bacon_lexConcept a ontolex:LexicalConcept ;
14   ontolex:isConceptOf hw:LA_VIANDE ;
15   ontolex:definition "viande de porc salée afin de la
16   conserver"@fr ;
17   ontolex:lexicalizedSense dag:bacon_sense .
```

Listing 5: Minimal example of DAG*él* data (RDF/Turtle).

We point out that a finer-grained concept for the Old Gascon lexeme *bacon* is available, i.e., JAMBON (ham). However, DAG*él* only uses the numbered concepts of HW's 'Plan' (Fig. 1) and thus refers to the super-concept LA_VIANDE. As a consequence, a manual post-processing should include replacing LA_VIANDE by JAMBON. Please note that, in List. 5, l. 11, we use the language tag for Old Gascon `oc-x-40000006`, a shortened form that expands to `oc-x-02q35735-241050--1500` using the Web application for generating and decoding language tags at `https://londisizwe.org/language-tags/` [07-02-2020].[14]

Italian *cantuccino*. The digitisation of the LEI and its modelling as LOD is still work in progress. We can, however, show a manually created example of entry *cantuccino* (LEI 10,1458,32) in List. 6.

```
1 @prefix     lei: <http://www.lei-digitale.org/> .
2
3 lei:cantuccino a ontolex:LexicalEntry ;
4   ontolex:sense lei:cantuccino_sense ;
5   ontolex:evokes lei:cantuccino_lexConcept ;
6   ontolex:canonicalForm lei:cantuccino_form .
7 lei:cantuccino_form a ontolex:Form ;
8   ontolex:writtenRep "cantuccino"@it .
9
10 lei:cantuccino_lexConcept a ontolex:LexicalConcept ;
11   ontolex:isConceptOf hw:LE_PAIN_LA_PATISSERIE ;
12   ontolex:definition "un pezzetto, un ritaglio di pane
13   dolce mandorlato"@it ;
14   ontolex:lexicalizedSense lei:cantuccino_sense .
```

Listing 6: Minimal example of LEI data (RDF/Turtle).

HW ontology as cross-mapping hub. The integration of references to the HW ontology is a model to be followed by other resources, where word-sense units refer to the same HW concepts, thus, installing the HW lightweight ontology as a cross-mapping hub and an access point to semantic-driven, language- and word-form independent research. E.g., a database search for the string 'pâtisserie' within the sense definitions of all DEAF*él* entries produces 46 results: *friolete* f. "pâtisserie légère", *fromagie* f. "pâtisserie faite de fromage et d'œufs", etc. In DAG*él*, we find the lexeme *habanhas* m. "pâtisserie semi-sucrée à base de fèves".[15] A mapping of these lexemes to the corresponding HW concept LE_PAIN_LA_PATISSERIE could thus be integrated into the LOD versions of DEAF and DAG in an automated way, leading, in this example, to a semantically driven, extra-linguistic cross-linking of LEI, DAG, and DEAF.

5. Discussion and Future Work

In this paper, we have argued that the modelling of HW as an LOD resource is an important step towards resource integration and cross-language accessibility of historical linguistic resources. The lightweight ontology based on HW provides a model for external resources, facilitating references for semantic mapping. However, moving from

---

[14]ISO 639 does not provide a language code for Old Gascon and we thus follow the pattern to create a unique and decodable language tag described by Gillis-Webber and Tittel (2020).

[15]A search for the HW concept 'B I k 1 cc 2' produces 21 lexemes but is less precise, leading also to lexemes denoting flour, sieving flour, etc.

the RDF/SKOS format towards an ontology should include adding knowledge that enriches the model through additional concepts, relationships, terms, and descriptive metadata. This means adding labels in other languages, and scholastic genus–differentia definitions to help grasp the concepts, e.g., LA_VIANDE: "flesh of animals (including fishes and birds and snails) used as food" (useful resources, i.e., dictionaries, WordNet, etc., for this task need to be evaluated considering conceptualisation incongruences and translation problems [cp. Bizzoni et al. (2014) on the Ancient Greek WordNet]; a cooperation with MHDBDB seems promising in this regard). As a first step, we have published the identification scheme used in Hallig-Wartburg (as shown in List. 3), available at `https://lod.academy/hw-onto/ns/hw#`.

Re-engineering the Model into a Formal Ontology. To enable reasoning over the HW ontology (that is not possible with the OWL Full model demonstrated above) and to introduce more expressive semantic relations for this purpose requires the SKOS model to be re-engineered into a formal ontology. The disjointness condition between OWL classes and individuals (the SKOS concepts) must hold true for OWL DL, thus, any SKOS and SKOS-THES relations will need to be removed. However, to align the relationships expressed through SKOS / SKOS-THES properties with OWL DL is clearly not obvious (Keet and Artale, 2008; Kless et al., 2012b; Baker et al., 2013; Adams et al., 2015). It involves finding equivalences for hierarchical whole-part (spatial, structural, etc.) relationships, associative relationships (e.g., action and action instrument / results / participant / target / etc. (Kless et al., 2012b, 422f.), and coining custom relation properties for relating nuanced same-level and cross-level relations. Using the re-engineering of the AGROVOC thesaurus as an example (Baker et al., 2019), the cost-benefit ratio of a presumably very time-consuming task must be considered. We thus identify a feasibility analysis of (i) re-assessing the relationships expressed in the original HW resource, (ii) making them explicit and (iii) expressing them through relations in OWL as future work.

Insufficient Scope and Granularity of HW concepts. HW shows significant shortcomings that hamper an accurate semantic mapping, reducing its relevance as an extra-linguistic cross-mapping hub. The scope and granularity of HW's categories do not suffice when modelling the lexical units of an entire language: HW is little appropriate for the mapping of the so-called small words (e.g., pronouns, articles). The differentiation is inadequate: HW is primarily geared to general language and lacks any kind of technical precision, e.g., in fields like 'L'astronomie' and 'La biologie' that are reduced to one single concept, respectively.

Insufficient Possibilities for Depicting Historical Life. Regional and cultural imprints through time go hand in hand with semantic shift. The HW, like other extra-linguistic conceptualisations of the world such as DBpedia, depicts modern reality. To map Old Italian *àghila* to HW 'aigle' or DBpedia 'Eagle'[16] is straightforward. However, with language change and semantic shift, many problems arise that make the semantic mapping from a lexeme in a

(medieval) historical linguistic resource to an entity of a conceptual model of the modern world difficult: (i) *things* (abstract or real) denoted by medieval words do not exist anymore, (ii) *words* are extinct and, thus, the concepts denoted by them are hard to identify in a modern world ontology, e.g., Old French *jaonoi* m. "gorse-covered terrain", DEAF J 398,30, (iii) *meanings* of words are extinct, and their modern equivalence is not obvious, e.g., Old French *jambe* f. ("leg", and also:) "post that serves as a support (for a door lintel, a mantelpiece, a vault, etc.)", DEAF J 94,15, and (iv) *meanings* have undergone semantic shift and the underlying concept is clearly different from the one of symbolized by the modern corresponding word. E.g., the veine was considered a sort of blood vessel that transports the 'nourishing blood' from the liver to each part of the body, and the sperm designated both the male and the female generative cell, etc.[17] Hence, a mapping to the modern concepts of 'veine' and 'sperm' is not possible without causing semantic discrepancies. We refer to this circumstance as the *Historical Semantic Gap*. Khan et al. (2014) address the issue of modelling semantic shift with extending the OntoLex-*lemon* vocabulary by adding a time interval to capture different concepts of one lexeme through time. This approach is a major enhancement from the point of view of historical linguistics. However, it does not solve the problem of semantic mapping to an extra-linguistic conceptual model where the historical concept is not represented.

To stabilise HW's role as an onomasiological reference system for historical (linguistic) resources, it must be elaborated in two ways: The net of concepts must be refined and concepts with historically appropriate content must be added. We call the latter process the *historicisation* of HW. To prepare for a future extension towards historicised content, we foresee a class `HistCat` and a symmetric (object) property `hasModernCounterpart`, cf. List. 7.

```
1 <owl:SymmetricProperty rdf:about="https://example.org/
2   hallig-wartburg-ontology#hasModernCounterpart">
3   <rdfs:label xml:lang="en">has modern counterpart
4   </rdfs:label>
5 </owl:SymmetricProperty>
6
7 <owl:Class rdf:about="https://example.org/
8   hallig-wartburg-ontology#HistCat">
9   <rdfs:label xml:lang="en">historicised concept
10   </rdfs:label>
11 </owl:Class>
```

Listing 7: Added property and class to HW ontology.

HW presents few categories that mirror the specification of historical times: Only four concepts include the notion of 'ancient', e.g. 'Les armes anciennes' (early weapons, next to 'Les armes modernes') and 'Les bâtiments de guerre anciens' (early warships, next to 'Les bâtiments de guerre modernes'). With the added class and object property, e.g., the class `LES_ARMES_ANCIENNES` can be defined a subclass of `HistCat` and refer to `LES_ARMES_MODERNES` through the property `hasModernCounterpart`. This would, thus, support the use of HW as an onomasiological framework by both historical and modern resources.

---

[17]DEAF*pré* VEINE[1], `https://deaf-server.adw. uni-heidelberg.de/lemme/veine1`; ESPERME `.../lemme/esperme` [25-02-2020].

6. Acknowledgements

The work of Frances Gillis-Webber was financially supported by Hasso Plattner Institute for Digital Engineering.

7. Bibliographical References

Adams, D., Jansen, L., and Milton, S. (2015). A content-focused method for re-engineering thesauri into semantically adequate ontologies. *Semantic Web*, 09.

Baker, T., Bechhofer, S., Isaac, A., Miles, A., Schreiber, G., and Summers, E. (2013). Key choices in the design of Simple Knowledge Organization System (SKOS). *Journal of Web Semantics*, 20:35 – 49.

Baker, T., Whitehead, B., Musker, R., and Keizer, J. (2019). Global agricultural concept space: lightweight semantics for pragmatic interoperability. *npj Science of Food*, 3, 12.

Baldinger, K. (1959). *s.v.* Romanistik. *Deutsche Literaturzeitung*, 80:1090–1093.

Baldinger, K. (1975 to 2005). *Dictionnaire onomasiologique de l'ancien occitan – DAO* (fondé par Kurt Baldinger, rédigé par Inge Popelar, puis Bernard Henschel, puis Nicoline Hörsch/Winkler et Tiana Shabafrouz). Niemeyer [Heidelberger Akademie der Wissenschaften / Kommission für das Altokzitanische und Altgaskognische Wörterbuch], Tübingen.

Baldinger, K. (since 1971). *Dictionnaire étymologique de l'ancien français – DEAF*. Presses de L'Université Laval / Niemeyer / De Gruyter, Québec/Tübingen/Berlin. [continued by Frankwalt Möhren, and Thomas Städtler; DEAF*él*: https://deaf-server.adw.uni-heidelberg.de].

Baldinger, K. (since 1975). *Dictionnaire onomasiologique de l'ancien gascon – DAG* (fondé par Kurt Baldinger, dirigé par Inge Popelar, puis Nicoline Hörsch / Winkler et Tiana Shabafrouz, sous la direction de Jean-Pierre Chambon, puis Martin Glessgen). De Gruyter [Heidelberger Akademie der Wissenschaften / Kommission für das Altokzitanische und Altgaskognische Wörterbuch], Tübingen / Berlin.

Bechhofer, S., van Harmelen, F., Hendler, J., Horrocks, I., McGuinness, D. L., Patel-Schneider, P. F., and Stein, L. A. (2004). OWL Web Ontology Language. Reference. W3C Recommendation 10 February 2004. URL: https://www.w3.org/TR/2004/REC-owl-ref-20040210/ [accessed: 09-02-2020].

Bevans, C. (1941). *The Old French vocabulary of Champagne. A descriptive study based on localized and dated documents*. University of Chicago Libraries, Chicago.

Bizzoni, Y., Boschetti, F., Diakoff, H., Gratta, R. D., Monachini, M., and Crane, G. (2014). The Making of Ancient Greek WordNet. In *Proceedings of the Ninth International Conference on Language Resources and Evaluation (LREC'14)*, pages 1140–1147, Reykjavik, Iceland. European Language Resources Association (ELRA).

Brickley, D. and Guha, R. (2014). RDF Schema 1.1. W3C Recommendation 25 February 2014. URL: https://www.w3.org/TR/rdf-schema/ [accessed: 13-02-2020].

Chiarcos, C., McCrae, J., Cimiano, P., and Fellbaum, C. (2013). Towards Open Data for Linguistics: Lexical Linked Data. In Alessandro Oltramari, et al., editors, *New Trends of Research in Ontologies and Lexical Resources: Ideas, Projects, Systems*, pages 7–25. Springer, Berlin, Heidelberg.

Christmann, H. and Böckle, K. (1983). Bespr. von Schwake, Der Wortschatz des *Cliges*. *Zeitschrift für romanische Philologie*, 99:397–403.

Cimiano, P., McCrae, J. P., and Buitelaar, P. (2016). Lexicon Model for Ontologies: Community Report, 10 May 2016. Final Community Group Report 10 May 2016. URL: https://www.w3.org/2016/05/ontolex/ [accessed: 10-02-2020].

Cyganiak, R., Wood, D., and Lanthaler, M. (2014). RDF 1.1. concepts and abstract syntax: W3C recommendation 25 February 2014. URL: https://www.w3.org/TR/2014/REC-rdf11-concepts-20140225/ [11-02-2020].

Cyganiak, R., Gillman, D., Grim, R., Jaques, Y., and Thomas, W. (2017). An SKOS extension for representing statistical classifications, ed. F. Cotton, Unofficial Draft, 1 January 2017. URL: http://www.ddialliance.org/Specification/XKOS/1.0/OWL/xkos.html [accessed: 07-02-2020].

Davidson, G. (2002). *Roget's thesaurus of English words and phrases*. (150th anniversary edition). Penguin Books, London.

de Man, L. (1956). Bijdrage tot een systematisch glossarium van de Brabantse oorkondentaal. Leuvens Archief van circa 1300 to 1550. *Deel*, I.

Dornseiff, F. (1934). *Der deutsche Wortschatz nach Sachgruppen*. de Gruyter, Berlin.

Fellbaum, C. (1998). *WordNet: An Electronic Lexical Database*. MIT Press, Cambridge, MA.

Gillis-Webber, F. and Tittel, S. (2020). A Framework for Shared Agreement of Language Tags beyond ISO 639. In *Proceedings of LREC 2020 [accepted paper]*, N.N.

Glessgen, M. and Tittel, S. (2018). Le *Dictionnaire électronique de l'ancien gascon* (DAG*él*). In Roberto Antonelli, et al., editors, *Atti del XXVIII Congresso internazionale di linguistica e filologia romanza (Roma, 18-23 luglio 2016)*, volume 1, pages 805–818. Société de Linguistique Romane / Éditions de linguistique et de philologie ELiPi, Bibliothèque de Linguistique Romane 15,1.

Glessgen, M. (since 2014). Dictionnaire de l'ancien gascon – DAGél. (en collaboration avec Sabine Tittel) URL: https://dag.adw.uni-heidelberg.de/ [accessed: 02-02-2020].

Hallig, R. and von Wartburg, W. (1963). *Begriffssystem als Grundlage für die Lexikographie / Système raisonné des concepts pour servir de base à la lexicographie*. Akademie-Verlag, Berlin. [first edition 1952].

Helou, M., Jarrar, M., Palmonari, M., and Fellbaum, C. (2014). Towards building lexical ontology via cross-language matching. In *GWC 2014: Proceedings of the 7th Global Wordnet Conference*, pages 346–354.

Hinkelmanns, P. (2019). Mittelhochdeutsche Lexikographie und Semantic Web. Die Anbindung der 'Mittelhochdeutschen Begriffsdatenbank' an Linked Open Data. *Das Mittelalter*, 24(1):129–141.

International Organization for Standardization. (2011). International Standard ISO 25964-1:2011, Information and documentation – Thesauri and interoperability with other vocabularies – Part 1: Thesauri for information retrieval, Part 2: Interoperability with other vocabularies. URL: https://www.iso.org/standard/53657.html.

Kay, C. (2009). *Historical thesaurus of the Oxford English dictionary*. Oxford University Press, Oxford.

Keet, C. and Artale, A. (2008). Representing and reasoning over a taxonomy of part-whole relations. *Applied Ontology*, 3:91–110.

Keller, H.-E. (1953). *Etude descriptive sur le vocabulaire de Wace*. Akad. der Wiss. Berlin, Veröffentl. Inst. für Rom. Spr.wiss. 7, Berlin.

Khan, F., Frontini, F., and Boschetti, F. (2014). Using lemon to Model Lexical Semantic Shift in Diachronic Lexical Resources. In *Proceedings of the 3rd Workshop on Linked Data in Linguistics: Multilingual Knowledge Resources and Natural Language*, Reykjavik, Iceland.

Kless, D., Jansen, L., Lindenthal, J., and Wiebensohn, J. (2012a). A method for re-engineering a thesaurus into an ontology. *Frontiers in Artificial Intelligence and Applications*, DOI 10.3233/978-1-61499-084-0-133:133–146.

Kless, D., Milton, S., and Kazmierczak, E. (2012b). Relationships and Relata in Ontologies and Thesauri: Differences and Similarities. *Applied Ontology*, 7:401–428, 11.

Miles, A. and Bechhofer, S. (2009). SKOS Simple Knowledge Organization System reference: W3C recommendation 18 August 2009. URL: https://www.w3.org/TR/2009/REC-skos-reference-20090818/ [accessed: 07-02-2020].

Miles, A. and Brickley, D. (2004). SKOS Extensions Vocabulary Specification. URL: www.w3.org/2004/02/skos/extensions/spec/2004-10-18.html [20-02-2020].

Nannini, A. (in progress). La mappatura semantica del Lessico Etimologico Italiano (LEI). Doctoral thesis.

Pfister, M. (since 1979). *Lessico Etimologico Italiano – LEI*. Reichert, Wiesbaden. [2001– together with W. Schweickard, 2018– W. Schweickard together with E. Prifti].

Prifti, E. (2019). Lo stato della digitalizzazione del LEI. Un resoconto. In Lino Leonardi et al., editors, *Italiano antico, italiano plurale. Testi e lessico del Medioevo nel mondo digitale*, page [in print]. N.N., Firenze.

Prud'hommeaux, E. and Carothers, G. (2014). RDF 1.1 Turtle: Terse RDF Triple Language. W3C Recommendation, 25 February 2014. URL: http://www.w3.org/TR/turtle/ [accessed: 07-02-2020].

Renders, P. (2015). *L'informatisation du Französisches Etymologisches Wörterbuch. Modélisation d'un discours étymologique*. ELIPHI, Strasbourg.

Renders, P. (2019). Integrating the Etymological Dimension into the Onto-Lex Lemon Model: A Case of Study. In *Electronic lexicography in the 21st century (eLEX 2019). Book of Abstracts*, pages 71–72.

Schmidt, K. (1980). *Begriffsglossare und Indices zu Ulrich von Lichtenstein*. Indices zur deutschen Literatur 14/15. Kraus International Publications, München.

Schmidt, K. (1988). Der Beitrag der Begriffsorientierten Lexikographie zur systematischen Erfassung von Sprachwandel und das Begriffswörterbuch zur Mhd. Epik. In Wolfgang Bachofer, editor, *Mittelhochdeutsches Wörterbuch in der Diskussion. Symposion zur mittelhochdeutschen Lexikographie, Hamburg, Oktober 1985*, pages 35–49, Tübingen. Niemeyer.

Schmidt, K. (1993). *Begriffsglossar und Index zu Ulrich von Zatzikhoven Lanzelet*. Indices zur deutschen Literatur 25. Niemeyer, Tübingen.

Soergel, D., Lauser, B., Liang, A., Fisseha, F., Keizer, J., and Katz, S. (2006). Reengineering Thesauri for New Applications: the AGROVOC Example. *Journal of Digital Information*, 4(4).

Stempel, W.-D. (1996 to 2013). *Dictionnaire de l'occitan médiévale – DOM*. Niemeyer / De Gruyter, Tübingen/Berlin. [continued by Maria Selig; electr. version: http://www. dom-en-ligne.de].

Stolk, S. (2019). Lemon-tree. Document 30 March 2019. Latest editor's draft. URL: https://ssstolk.github.io/onto/lemon-tree/index.html [accessed: 07-02-2020].

Tancke, G. (1997). Note per un avviamento al Lessico Etimologico Italiano (LEI). In Günter Holtus, et al., editors, *Italica et Romanica. Festschrift für Max Pfister zum 65. Geburtstag*, pages 457–487. Niemeyer, Tübingen.

Tittel, S. and Chiarcos, C. (2018). Historical Lexicography of Old French and Linked Open Data: Transforming the Resources of the *Dictionnaire étymologique de l'ancien français* with OntoLex-Lemon. In *Proceedings of the Eleventh International Conference on Language Resources and Evaluation (LREC 2018). GLOBALEX Workshop (GLOBALEX-2018), Miyazaki, Japan, 2018*, pages 58–66, Paris (ELRA).

Tittel, S. (in progress). Integration von historischer lexikalischer Semantik und Ontologien in den Digital Humanities. Habilitation thesis.

von Wartburg, W. (since 1922). *Französisches Etymologisches Wörterbuch. Eine darstellung des galloromanischen sprachschatzes – FEW*. ATILF. [continued by O. Jänicke, C.T. Gossen, J.-P. Chambon, J.-P. Chauveau, and Yan Greub].

Proceedings of the 7th Workshop on Linked Data in Linguistics (LDL-2020), pages 11–14
Language Resources and Evaluation Conference (LREC 2020), Marseille, 11–16 May 2020

Transforming the Cologne Digital Sanskrit Dictionaries into Ontolex-Lemon

Francisco Mondaca[1], Felix Rau[2]

[1]Cologne Center for eHumanities - University of Cologne
[2]Data Center for the Humanities - University of Cologne
Albertus-Magnus-Platz, 50923 Cologne, Germany
{f.mondaca, f.rau}@uni-koeln.de

Abstract

The Cologne Digital Sanskrit Dictionaries (CDSD) is a large collection of complex digitized Sanskrit dictionaries, consisting of over thirty-five works, and is the most prominent collection of Sanskrit dictionaries worldwide. In this paper we evaluate two methods for transforming the CDSD into Ontolex-Lemon based on a modelling exercise. The first method that we evaluate consists of applying RDFa to the existent TEI-P5 files. The second method consists of transforming the TEI-encoded dictionaries into new files containing RDF triples modelled in OntoLex-Lemon. As a result of the modelling exercise we choose the second method: to transform TEI-encoded lexical data into Ontolex-Lemon by creating new files containing exclusively RDF triples.

Keywords: tei, ontolex-lemon, lexicog, rdfa, sanskrit

1. Sanskrit Lexicography

Sanskrit (ISO 639-3 san) is a classical language from South Asia. It is the liturgical language of Hinduism and some branches of Buddhism and was the literary and scientific language of South Asia well into modern times. As a consequence, Sanskrit has a 4000 year long history.

Sanskrit belongs to the Indo-Aryan branch of the Indo-European language family and it is the only attested form of Old Indo-Aryan. Based on internal diachronic developments, it is conventionally divided into Vedic Sanskrit (early Old Indo-Aryan, 2000 BCE–600 BCE) and Classical Sanskrit (later Old Indo-Aryan) after the Vedic period (Masica, 1991).

As the oldest attested form of Indo-Aryan, Sanskrit constitutes one of the oldest attested Indo-European laguages and is central to our understanding of this language family. From the 19th century onward, philological research produced a vast array of Sanskrit text editions, grammatical descriptions, and dictionaries. In particular, the Große Petersburger Wörterbuch (Böhtlingk and Roth, 1855) and Monier-Williams' Sanskrit-English Dictionary, (Monier-Williams, 1899) are among the most important bilingual lexicographical works of the 19th century, if not in general. The corpus of scientific Sanskrit dictionaries consist of over thirty-five works and includes mono- and bilingual general dictionaries as well as more specialised thematic works. Some of these work, such as Grassmann's dictionary (Grassmann, 1873), are specific to one text. Others are covering only one specific variety of Sanskrit. For example, the Buddhist Hybrid Sanskrit Dictionary (Edgerton, 1953) covers the distinct variety of Sanskrit used in some early schools of Buddhism (Burrow, 2001). Other dictionaries aiming at covering the whole lexical range of 4000 years of language history, resulting in lexicographical challenges modern Sanskrit lexicography still has to address (Lugli, 2018).

The entries in the more extensive dictionaries – in particular in the Große Petersburger Wörterbuch (Böhtlingk and Roth, 1855) and Monier-Williams' Sanskrit-English Dictionary, (Monier-Williams, 1899) – are highly structured and complex. These lexicographical microstructures pose a challenge to all attempts of developing general schemes and vocabularies for entry structures and are good test cases for whether a model can cover complex bilingual, multi-writing system entries.

2. About the Cologne Digital Sanskrit Dictionaries (CDSD)

2.1. Overview

The Cologne Digital Sanskrit Dictionaries[1] is the most prominent collection of digitized Sanskrit dictionaries available on the Internet. This project was initiated in 1994 when XML did not exist yet and Sanskrit had no proper Unicode support. Sanskrit is traditionally written in a variety of local scripts, but is now generally printed in Devanagari, a the North Indian script that is most prominently used to write Hindi and Nepali. While support for Devanagari was already included in Unicode 1.0.0 in 1993, full coverage of the characters needed to encode Sanskrit texts and lexicographic resources was only achieved in 2009 when the Vedic Extensions were added with Version 5.2. to the Unicode standard. As a consequence, an ASCII-based encoding scheme was developed in 1994 specifically for this collection, in order to encode strings in Devanagari, or to encode its Roman script transliteration (later standardized as ISO-15919). In 2003, when XML and Unicode were already part of the technologies available for serializing language resources, the CDSD offered different web applications for accessing its dictionaries. The CDSD collection consists of more than thirty-five Sanskrit dictionaries, mostly bilingual dictionaries covering different modern European languages. The CDSD web portal offers different web applications to access each dictionary. Also from the CDSD web portal each dictionary can be downloaded. The

---

[1]https://www.sanskrit-lexicon.uni-koeln.de

dictionaries can be accessed on GitHub[2] in their source format. Their XML-encoded versions can also be accessed via web APIs[3] provided by the API framework Kosh [4].

2.2. Searching for Sustainability and Interoperability

During the LAZARUS project (2013-2015)[5] in order to provide a sustainable and interoperable format for the CDSD collection, a common TEI-P5[6] schema[7] was developed. Three dictionaries were transformed into TEI-P5: the two most complex dictionaries both from a content and a layout perspective (Monier-Williams, 1899; Böhtlingk and Roth, 1855) and one English-Sanskrit dictionary (Apte, 1884). During the VedaWeb project (2017-2020)[8], four dictionaries of the CDSD collection (Apte, 1890; Edgerton, 1953; Grassmann, 1873; Macdonell and Keith, 1912) have been transformed into TEI-P5 employing the schema developed during the LAZARUS project. VedaWeb offers a digital edition of the Rigveda, the most ancient Indo-Aryan text. VedaWeb is an API-driven project. On the one hand, the project offers its textual data through a REST API [9]. On the other hand, the project offers its lexical resources via REST and GraphQL APIs[10]. One of the main features of VedaWeb is that each token of the Rigveda points to an entry in Grassmann's dictionary (Grassmann, 1873). This Sanskrit-German dictionary has been specially compiled for the Rigveda with the goal of defining every token present on it. The VedaWeb app calls the Grassmann GraphQL API and displays its respective information.

3. Transforming TEI-encoded dictionaries into Ontolex-Lemon

3.1. Where to start?

Taking into account the experiences gained during the projects LAZARUS and VedaWeb, we decided to begin the transformation of the available TEI-P5 dictionaries into OntoLex-Lemon (McCrae et al., 2017) with the most complex Sanskrit-English dictionary: Monier-Williams (Monier-Williams, 1899). This Sanskrit-English dictionary is considered to be the most detailed Sanskrit dictionary compiled in the English language. It is also a constant reference for Sanskrit scholars. For these reasons it was chosen to be the basis for creating a TEI-schema that would be applied to other dictionaries of the collection. And it will be the basis of this new transformation scenario.

3.2. Existing transformation methods

There are two main approaches for transforming TEI-encoded data into a Ontolex-Lemon compliant version. The first approach consists in extracting the lexical data contained in the TEI file and create a new file with this data modelled in Ontolex-Lemon. This method has been applied previously to the *Dictionnaire étymologique de l'ancien français* (Tittel and Chiarcos, 2018). Tittel and Chiarcos employ XSLT Stylesheets for the transformation. The same technology is applied at the tei2ontolex GitHub repository[11] developed by the European Lexicographic Infrastructure Project (ELEXIS) (Declerck et al., 2019), where researchers John P. McCrae and Laurent Romary, experts in Ontolex-Lemon and TEI respectively, have worked together.

To create new files modelled in Ontolex-Lemon would be less verbose, because it would leave the TEI file with its tags and attributes as it was originally encoded. But this method would also duplicate the amount of files containing lexical data to be curated. It would also require to synchronize both the TEI and Ontolex-Lemon serialized versions. A second approach consists in employing RDFa within the source TEI file (Chiarcos and Ionov, 2019), i.e. modelling TEI and Ontolex-Lemon within the same file. This method would simplify at first sight the task of encoding the existent lexical data with Ontolex-Lemon. However, an issue to consider when applying RDFa within TEI files is that while this method is W3C-compliant it is not TEI-endorsed (Chiarcos and Ionov, 2019).

Another issue that arises when modelling digitized dictionaries with Ontolex-Lemon derives from the constraint that it allows a single part-of-speech (POS) per entry. In this regard TEI-P5 and TEI-Lex0 [12] are flexible because they allow multiple POS per lexical entry. Consequently, the structure of a printed dictionary is respected in TEI. On the contrary, in OntoLex-Lemon the lexicographic structure must be split when an entry contains more than one POS. This is a negative aspect when modelling and encoding digitized dictionaries because it makes a transformation scenario more complex and verbose than necessary.

This issue is addressed by the Ontolex-Lemon Lexicography Module (lexicog) [13]. Lexicog does respect the structure of a digitized dictionary. However, it achieves this basically from a layout perspective. It does create a parallel structure linked to Ontolex-Lemon core's module where the lexicographic information, e.g. POS, is encoded. Complexity and verbosity are thus not reduced.

The terms complexity and verbosity are here employed from the perspective of a human that reads a file and seeks to elucidate the model behind it. While XML is the most verbose of all RDF serializations (Cimiano et al., 2020), the same applies to Turtle or other RDF serializations when modelling digitized dictionaries in Ontolex-Lemon. In our opinion the complexity and verbosity that emerges when modelling digitized dictionaries in Ontolex-Lemon has its

---

[2]https://github.com/sanskrit-lexicon/csl-orig/tree/master/v02

[3]https://cceh.github.io/kosh/docs/implementations/cdsd.html

[4]https://kosh.uni-koeln.de

[5]https://cceh.uni-koeln.de/lazarus

[6]https://tei-c.org/guidelines/p5

[7]https://github.com/cceh/c-salt_dicts_schema

[8]https://vedaweb.uni-koeln.de

[9]https://vedaweb.uni-koeln.de/rigveda/swagger-ui.html

[10]https://cceh.github.io/c-salt_sanskrit_data

[11]https://github.com/elexis-eu/tei2ontolex

[12]https://dariah-eric.github.io/lexicalresources/pages/TEILex0/TEILex0.html

[13]https://www.w3.org/2019/09/lexicog

origin in establishing that an entry can have only a single part-of-speech.

3.3. Modelling Ontolex-Lemon with RDFa

As seen in the previous section the two presented methods for converting TEI-encoded data into Ontolex-Lemon consist in creating new files containing exclusively RDF triples or in applying RDFa within the same TEI file.

Figure 2 shows an entry in Monier Williams that has been partially modelled in RDFa using Ontolex-Lemon. Figure 1 shows the entry as it has been modelled in TEI-P5. The first problem that arises in figure 2 is that morphosyntactic information encoded as part-of-speech (POS) in Ontolex-Lemon can not be related to an `ontolex:LexicalSense`. This must be related to an `ontolex:LexicalEntry`. A possible solution for applying RDFa would be to modify the existent XML-TEI structure, i.e. create new XML nodes.

Another issue when applying RDFa and Ontolex-Lemon relates to choose an external ontology or vocabulary for encoding POS. When encoding lexical data with Ontolex-Lemon, usually the lexinfo[14] ontology is employed. In figure 2, the POS 'mfn.' means 'masculine, feminine and neutral'. There is no such category in `lexinfo:partOfSpeech` for this POS. A possible solution would be to create a vocabulary containing the POS to be found in all the Sanskrit dictionaries of the collection and later map the values of this vocabulary to existing values of `lexinfo:partOfSpeech`.

4. Conclusion

At first sight RDFa seemed to tackle our requirements better than creating new files containing RDF triples when transforming TEI source files into Ontolex-Lemon. But a brief modelling exercise showed that employing RDFa required adding new elements into the TEI source files. These structural modifications to the TEI files would unnecessarily complicate the maintenance of these files over time. Therefore, the method to follow will be to create completely new files modelled in Ontolex-Lemon. To this end, we will follow the experiences made during the transformation of the *Dictionnaire étymologique de l'ancien français* (Tittel and Chiarcos, 2018) into Ontolex-Lemon, as well as the current development of the tei2ontolex[15] repository.

5. Bibliographical References

Apte, V. S. (1884). *The Student's English-Sanskrit Dictionary*. Arya Bhushana, Poona.

Apte, V. S. (1890). *The Practical Sanskrit-English Dictionary*. Shiralkar, Poona.

Burrow, T. (2001). *The Sanskrit Language*. Motilal Banarsidass Publ.

Böhtlingk, O. and Roth, R. (1855). *Sanskrit Wörterbuch. Herausgegeben von der kaiserlichen Akademie der Wissenschaften, bearbeitet von Otto Böhtlingk und Rudolph Roth*. Eggers, St-Petersburg.

Chiarcos, C. and Ionov, M. (2019). Linking the TEI. Approaches, Limitations, Use Cases. Digital Humanities 2019, July.

Cimiano, P., Chiarcos, C., McCrae, J. P., and Gracia, J. (2020). *Linguistic Linked Data: Representation, Generation and Applications*. Springer, Cham, Switzerland.

Declerck, T., McCrae, J., Navigli, R., Zaytseva, K., and Wissik, T. (2019). ELEXIS - European Lexicographic Infrastructure: Contributions to and from the Linguistic Linked Open Data.

Edgerton, F. (1953). *Buddhist Hybrid Sanskrit Grammar and Dictionary*. Yale Univ. Press, New Haven.

Grassmann, H. G. (1873). *Worterbuch zum Rig-veda*. O. Harrassowitz, Wiesbaden.

Lugli, L. (2018). Drifting in Timeless Polysemy: Problems of Chronology in Sanskrit Lexicography. *Dictionaries: Journal of the Dictionary Society of North America*, 39(1):105–129, August.

Macdonell, A. A. and Keith, A. B. (1912). *Vedic Index of Names and Subjects*. J. Murray, London.

Masica, C. (1991). *The Indo-Aryan Languages*. Cambridge University Press, Cambridge.

McCrae, J. P., Bosque-Gil, J., Gracia, J., Buitelaar, P., and Cimiano, P. (2017). The OntoLex-Lemon Model: Development and Applications. In *Electronic lexicography in the 21st century. Proceedings of eLex 2017 conference*.

Monier-Williams, M. (1899). *A Sanskrit-English dictionary*. The Clarendon Press, Oxford.

Tittel, S. and Chiarcos, C. (2018). Linked open data for the historical lexicography of old french. In *Proceedings of the Eleventh International Conference on Language Resources and Evaluation (LREC 2018)*, Paris, France, may. European Language Resources Association (ELRA).

---

[14]`https://lexinfo.net`

[15]`https://github.com/elexis-eu/tei2ontolex`

```
<entry ana="H1" xml:id="lemma-aSrAta" xmlns="http://www.tei-c.org/ns/1.0">
    <form>
        <idno ana="hc3">110</idno>
        <orth ana="key1" xml:lang="san-Latn-x-SLP1">aSrAta</orth>
        <idno ana="hc1">1</idno>
        <hyph ana="key2" xml:lang="san-Latn-x-SLP1-headword">a-SrAta</hyph>
    </form>
    <sense>
        <gramGrp>
            <gram ana="lex">mfn.</gram>
        </gramGrp>uncooked
        <cit type="literary_source">
            <bibl xml:lang="san-Latn-x-CSDL">
                <ref target="#auth-RV_">RV.</ref>
                x, 179, 1.</bibl>
        </cit>
        <note>
            <unclear ana="mul"/>
            <idno type="MW">014422</idno>
            <ref target="#page-0114" type="facs">114,2</ref>
            <idno ana="L" xml:id="monier_19802">19802</idno>
        </note>
    </sense>
</entry>
```

Figure 1: Entry 'aSrata' in Monier Williams modelled in TEI-P5

```
<entry typeof="ontolex:LexicalEntry" xml:id="lemma-aSrAta" ana="H1">
    <form property="ontolex:lexicalForm">
        <idno ana="hc3">110</idno>
        <orth property="ontolex:writtenRep" ana="key1" xml:lang="san-Latn-x-SLP1">aSrAta</orth>
        <idno ana="hc1">1</idno>
        <hyph property="ontolex:writtenRep" ana="key2" xml:lang="san-Latn-x-SLP1-headword">a-SrAta</hyph>
    </form>
    <sense typeof="ontolex:lexicalSense">
        <gramGrp>
            <gram property="lexinfo:partOfSpeech" ana="lex">mfn.</gram>
        </gramGrp>
        uncooked
        <cit type="literary_source">
            <bibl xml:lang="san-Latn-x-CSDL">
                <ref target="#auth-RV_">RV.</ref>
                x, 179, 1.
            </bibl>
        </cit>
        <note>
            <unclear ana="mul"/>
            <idno type="MW">014422</idno>
            <ref target="#page-0114" type="facs">114,2</ref>
            <idno ana="L" xml:id="monier_19802">19802</idno>
        </note>
    </sense>
</entry>
```

Figure 2: Entry 'aSrata' in Monier Williams modelled in TEI-P5 and partially with errors in Ontolex-Lemon with RDFa

Proceedings of the 7th Workshop on Linked Data in Linguistics (LDL-2020), pages 15–22
Language Resources and Evaluation Conference (LREC 2020), Marseille, 11–16 May 2020
© European Language Resources Association (ELRA), licensed under CC-BY-NC

Representing Temporal Information in Lexical Linked Data Resources

Anas Fahad Khan

CNR-Istituto di Linguistica Computazionale "A. Zampolli"
Pisa, Italy
fahad.khan@ilc.cnr.it

Abstract

The increasing recognition of the utility of Linked Data as a means of publishing lexical resources has helped to underline the need for RDF-based data models with the flexibility and expressivity to be able to represent the most salient kinds of information contained in such resources as structured data; this includes, notably, information relating to time and the temporal dimension. In this article we describe a perdurantist approach to modelling diachronic lexical information which builds upon work which we have previously presented and which is based on the ontolex-lemon vocabulary. We present two extended examples, one taken from the Oxford English Dictionary, the other from a work on etymology, to show how our approach can handle different kinds of temporal information often found in lexical resources.

Keywords: linguistic linked data, diachronic lexical data, perdurantism

1. Introduction

The difficulties of representing relationships that change with time – also referred to as *fluents* or *diachronic relations* in the literature – in RDF have been by now well-rehearsed (Welty et al., 2006). The core problem here, of course, is that the RDF framework does not allow us to simply add an extra temporal parameter to binary and unary properties: something that would otherwise make modelling diachronic relations fairly straightforward. A number of different 'workarounds' have been proposed to deal with this situation[1]. There is, however, no single one size fits all solution that will work in every case and different solutions are better suited to different use cases. In this article our focus will be on lexical data, and in particular data that derives from legacy resources including dictionaries and scholarly works on meaning change. In the course of the article we will look at some of the different ways in which such data can carry a temporal dimension, including indirectly, through the use of citations and attestations. We will then propose the use of a perdurantist design pattern for representing this temporal information. Our intention with this submission is to rouse interest in the perdurantist approach to modelling lexical change in light of the work which is going on both in the W3C Ontolex community and in a number of projects and use cases which have recently arisen, and to elicit feedback from the Linguistic Linked Data community in order to help determine the variety of use cases which the approach is able to handle well and those which it cannot.

2. Temporal Information in Lexical Datasets

The increasing recognition of the utility of Linked Data as a means of publishing lexical resources – thanks in large part to projects such as ELEXIS (Krek et al., 2018) and LiLA (Passarotti et al., 2019) – has helped to underline the need for RDF-based data models with the flexibility and expressivity to be able to represent the most salient kinds of information contained in such resources as structured data: this includes, notably, information relating to time and the temporal dimension. Time is a central concern of certain kinds of lexical resource, this is most obviously true of etymological and historical dictionaries, but the inclusion of temporal information in lexical resources is by no means limited to such specialist works, and etymologies in particular are found in a wide range of dictionaries and lexical datasets. In previous related work we have looked at how to represent etymologies, viewed as hypotheses about word histories, explictly both in RDF (Khan, 2018) and in the Lexical Markup Framework (Khan and Bowers, 2020). However, temporal information is not always explicitly included in the form of an etymology. For instance, it is also common for resources to list the senses in each lexical entry in some order of temporal precedence[2]. Other resources include descriptions of the semantic shift processes which led from temporally antecedent senses to subsequent senses; yet others mark senses (or forms, etc) as obsolete and/or give some basic information on the time period in which a sense or form (or grammatical construct) was in use or was most commonly in use. In fact, in these and in other contexts, one frequently finds reference to a particular historical stage of a language, such as Old French or Middle English, something which also helps to group together lexical phenomena in time. Many lexical resources, especially more authoritative or scholarly dictionaries, also give citations for separate senses and even of forms (or, in fact, for any interesting or salient lexical information which has changed over time, such as verb transitivity or the historic existence of now obsolete noun declensions). These citations help to locate senses (and forms etc) in time, and one of the central aims of the current work is to show how such information can be efficiently integrated into the RDF encoding of an entry. It is worth noting that the information originating from citations also tends to be less vague than

---

[1]See for instance `https://www.w3.org/TR/swbp-n-aryRelations/`

[2]For instance the Oxford English Dictionary describes its entries as being "structured to show the evolution of senses and uses over time". cite `https://public.oed.com/how-to-use-the-oed/glossary/`

other kinds of temporal data present in lexical resources, as will be illustrated by the examples which we will present below. It is a hallmark of most lexical temporal data that it tends to be vague, sometimes very vague (for instance in the case of proto-languages with no written testimony). In the majority of cases it is hard to pinpoint the year, or even the century, that a certain sense or form or word began to be used and/or stopped being used. In other cases it is hard to fix the historical periods in which entire languages were spoken. If we are going to potentially reason with such data we need an approach that takes into consideration the vague nature of such data. We discuss this further and propose a solution in Section 3.1..

2.1. Previous Work

The work in this paper builds upon, and in many cases presents in altered form, ideas and proposals which we have published previously. We initially presented the idea of extending the *lemon* (McCrae et al., 2011) and afterwards the *ontolex lemon* (McCrae et al., 2017) models using perdurants in order to represent temporal information in (Khan et al., 2014) and (Khan et al., 2016), using the resulting model to encode a linguistic dataset dealing with the evolution of emotion terms in Old English in (Khan et al., 2018)[3]. Many of the properties and classes in that version have been modified as a result of working on modelling various different lexical datasets. We have also worked on the more specific case of modelling etymologies as linked data (Khan, 2018). However the current work focuses much more on the representation of time and temporal intervals than those previous works, developing our approach by focusing on two extended examples.

2.2. Case Studies

2.2.1. The word *girl*

For our first case study we will look at the Oxford English Dictionary (OED) entry for the word *girl* (OUP, 2008). We chose the OED because of its status as an authoritative work of descriptive, historical lexicography and because of the comprehensive, and therefore challenging (from the modelling point of view), nature of its entries. The OED epitomizes the type of the historical reference dictionary in which individual forms and senses are attested with reference to a historical corpus of citations. In the current case we have chosen the word *girl* because of the somewhat surprising fact (regularly cited in books on etymology, at least in the English language), that it was originally used to refer to a "child of either sex; young person" and not just, as is often the case today, to "a young or relatively young woman". The OED entry starts by giving the standard pronunciation of *girl* in IPA in both British and American English. Next a list of forms is given, we will come back to this shortly. Following this, frequency, origin and etymological information is listed (the etymology of the word is especially obscure and its origin is given as unknown). Then twelve separate senses for the word are given; these are classified into two

groups. The first group is labelled as being "[s]enses relating to a person", and the second group (containing only two senses) is labelled as "other senses". Finally a list of phrases and derivatives is presented. Note that the senses are listed in historical order, although in some cases a sense may have a more recent subsense listed immediately below it and before other historically later senses. The forms are listed as follows in the entry:

> ME **garl**, ME **geerl**, ME **gerl**, ME (18– chiefly *Irish English* and *nonstandard*) **gurl** , ME–15 **gerle**, ME– 16 **girle**, ME–16 **gyrle**, 15 **gierle**, 15 **gurle**, 15 **gyrll**, 15–16 **guirle**, 15–16 **gyrl**, 15– **girl**, 16 **garle**, 16 **gerreld**; *Caribbean* 19– **gyal**, 19– **gyul**.

Here ME stands for Middle English, a time period which the OED describes as running from 1150 CE to 1500 CE[4]. The numbers 15, 16, 18, and 19 refer to the 1500s (i.e., 1500-99)[5], the 1600s (i.e., 1600-99), etc. The senses are listed under numbers and, in the case of subsenses, lower case roman letters. Each sense starts with a definition and some other related information before presenting a list of historical citations for that sense. Below we give the first sense in full:

1. Chiefly in *plural*. A child of either sex; a young person. Now *Irish English (Wexford)*. **knave girl** *n*. a boy.

   *C*1300 *St. Thomas Becket* (Laud) 76 in C. Horstmann *Early S.-Eng. Legendary* (1887) 108 (*MED*) þe Amirales douȝter was In þe strete þare-oute, And suyþe gret prece of gurles and Men comen hire al-a-boute.

   *C*1400 (→a1376) W. LANGLAND *Piers Plowman* (Trin. Cambr. R.3.14) (1960) A. XI. 132 (*MED*) Gramer for girles [*v.rr.* gurles, gerles, childeryn] I garte ferst write, And bet hem wiþ a þaleis but ȝif þei wolde lerne.

   *C*1400 (→?a1300) *Kyng Alisaunder* (Laud) (1952) 2798 (*MED*) Men miȝtten seen þere hondes wrynge..Wymmen shrikyng, gyrles gradyng.

   *C*1405 (→c1387–95) G. CHAUCER *Canterbury Tales Prol.* (Hengwrt) (2003) l. 664 In daunger hadde he at his owene gyse The yonge gerles of the diocise, And knew hir conseil, and was al hir reed.

   *a*1475 *Bk. Curtasye* (Sloane 1986) l. 328 in *Babees Bk.* (2002) I. 308 Ne delf þou neuer nose thyrle With thombe ne fyngur, as ȝong gyrle.

---

[3]Ours was not of course the first attempt to model diachronic lexical or etymological information in linked data. See for instance (Moran and Bruemmer, 2013), (De Melo, 2014). (Khan, 2018) presents a fuller overview of related work.

[4]https://public.oed.com/blog/middle-english-an-overview/

[5]https://public.oed.com/how-to-use-the-oed/key-to-symbols-and-other-conventions/

?a1475 *Ludus Coventriae* (1922) 171 (*MED*) Here knaue gerlys I xal steke.

a1827 J. POOLE *Gloss.* in T. P. Dolan & D. Ó . Muirithe **Dial. Forth & Bargy** (1996) 49 *Gurl, gurlès*, a child, a girl.

1996 T. P. DOLAN & D. Ó. MUIRITHE **Dial. Forth & Bargy** 25 *Gurl*, a child of either sex.

Note that the *C* before a date means 'circa', *approximately*, and *a* means 'antes', *before* or *prior to*. The question mark indicates an uncertain date. In cases where there are two dates, one after the other, with the second in parenthesis following an arrow symbol, e.g.,*C*1400 (→*a*1376), the first date refers to the dating of a manuscript, and the second, the date of composition[6].

2.3. *Sad*

The next example which we will model is adapted from the etymology for the word *sad* given in Philip Durkin's *Oxford Guide to Etymology* (Durkin, 2009). We have chosen this example in order to illustrate how to use our approach to model historical sense shifts (although it can be easily adapted to show the evolution of forms as well for instance). The example regards the meaning shift undergone by the English word *sad* which originally meant 'satisfied' or 'full' in Old English and now has the principal meaning of 'sorrowful, mournful' (this meaning is recorded, as Durkin points out, in a source dated *a*1300). Durkin hypothesises a process of semantic shift that takes place in three stages, via an intermediate sense meaning 'weary or tired of something', as follows:

satisfied, having had one's fill (of something)

[metaphorized and narrowed] > weary or tired (of something)

[broadened] > sorrowful, mournful.

3. Our Approach

In this section we will outline and motivate our particular approach to modelling diachronic lexical data in RDF. The idea, in a nutshell, is twofold: firstly, we propose the use of *qualitative* intervals to model temporal vagueness in lexical data; then, secondly, we define a 'perdurantist' version of certain classes in the ontolex-lemon model in order to allow lexical entries, senses, etc, to each have a 'lifespan' as well as temporal parts.

3.1. Introduction to Qualitative Temporal Intervals and Allen Relations

One way of dealing with the kinds of temporal vagueness which we have previously mentioned is to work with so called qualitative constraints and to focus on the relative temporal positions of different points and intervals on a given timeline, that is, in addition to leveraging whatever exact quantitative information that we might also actually possess. In this case we can make use of Allen relations between temporal intervals (Allen, 1983) in order to reason over such data, and fortunately for us these relations are already encoded within the popular temporal ontology OWL-time[7], see Figure 1. Furthermore there already exists a set of SWRL rules which allow for reasoning over data that describes intervals qualitatively using these relations (Batsakis et al., 2017).

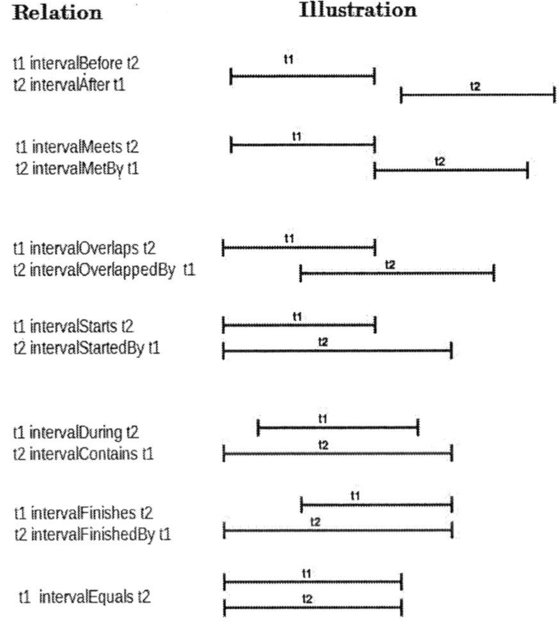

Figure 1: Allen relations used in OWL-time.

As well as defining, or (in cases when they already exist) re-using, standard temporal intervals such as the *13th Century CE* or *1066* with OWL-time[8] we can also define language specific intervals such as *Middle-English* whose definitions are much more subject to variation across different sources: in our case, for Middle-English, we use the definition given by the OED of *(1150, 1500)*. So, for instance, we can define the 14th century, or rather the 1300s as, running from 1300-1399 using the OWL-time vocabulary as follows.

Listing 1: Definition of 13

```
:13 a owl-time:Interval ;
   owl-time:hasBeginning [
     a owl-time:Instant ;
     owl-time:inXSDDateTimeStamp
     "1300-01-01T00:00:00Z"^^xsd:dateTimeStamp
   ];
   owl-time:hasEnd [
     a owl-time:Instant ;
     owl-time:inXSDDateTimeStamp
     "1399-12-31T23:59:59Z"^^xsd:dateTimeStamp
   ] ;
   owl-time:intervalMeets :14 ;
   owl-time:intervalMetBy :12 ;
   rdfs:label "(1300-1399)"@en.
```

---

[6] https://public.oed.com/blog/dating-middle-english-evidence-in-the-oed/

[7] https://www.w3.org/TR/owl-time/

[8] We are using OWL-time but any other temporal vocabulary/ontology with similarly defined properties and classes can also be used.

Note that we have defined the interval both in terms of its beginning and end points (using the xsd:dateTimeStamp datatype property) as well as by relating it to two other intervals using the object properties intervalMeets and intervalMetBy. In addition we can also define the time interval, ME, mentioned in the OED entry and corresponding to the time interval in which Middle English was spoken, by specifying its start and end years and its relationships with other (named) intervals. So in this case we state that it overlaps the interval 11 (the 10th century), contains the interval 12 (the 11th century), and is finished by the interval 13.

Listing 2: Definition of the Middle English interval

```
:enm_interval a owl-time:Interval ;
   owl-time:hasBeginning
      [ a owl-time:Instant ;
      owl-time:inXSDDateTimeStamp
      "1150-01-01T00:00:00Z"^^xsd:dateTimeStamp
      ] ;
   owl-time:hasEnd
      [ a owl-time:Instant ;
      owl-time:inXSDDateTimeStamp
      "1399-12-31T23:59:59Z"^^xsd:dateTimeStamp
      ] ;
   rdfs:label "Middle English (1150-1300)"@en ;
   owl-time:intervalOverlappedBy :11 ;
   owl-time:intervalContains :12 ;
   owl-time:intervalFinishedBy :13 .
```

We can, on the basis of these prior 'building block' intervals, once again use Allen relations to define further interval combinations and thereby capture other salient intervals such as, for instance, the interval ME-16 mentioned in the list of historical forms given above for *girl*.

Listing 3: Definition of ME-16

```
:ME-16 a owl-time:Interval;
   owl-time:intervalContains :12 , :13 ,:14 , :15 ;
   owl-time:intervalFinishedBy :16 ;
   owl-time:intervalStartedBy :enm_interval .
```

The case of the interval 18- above is a little bit trickier in that it requires the specification of one point as the present. Here we have chosen a point in the current year (although the point in question could be the date of the publication of the resource being modelled for instance).

Listing 4: Setting a present point

```
:present a owl-time:Instant;
owl-time:inDateTime [
   a owl-time:DateTimeDescription ;
   owl-time:unitType owl-time:unitYear ;
   owl-time:year "2020"^^xsd:gYear ;
   ] ;
rdfs:comment "The Present"@en .
```

Assuming then that we have already defined the intervals 18, 19, and 20, we can define 18- as in interval that is started by the 17th century, contains the 19th century and is overlapped by the 21st century.

Listing 5: Modelling *18-*

```
:18- a owl-time:Interval ;
   owl-time:hasEnd :present ;
   owl-time:intervalContains :19 ;
   owl-time:intervalStartedBy :18 ;
   owl-time:intervalOverlaps :20 ;
   rdfs:label "(1800-)"@en .
```

One of the biggest challenges in the present context relates to the use of the preposition 'circa' as in *C1300* or *C1400*, which obviously is used to codify 'fuzziness'. The essential thing, however, is to pick a modelling approach and to remain with it consistently throughout a dataset. For instance the option which we have chosen is to model Cd, where d is a date, as being contained in an interval of 10 years before and after d.

Listing 6: Modelling *circa*

```
:circa_1300 a owl-time:Interval ;
   owl-time:intervalContains [
   a owl-time:Interval ;
   owl-time:hasBeginning [
      a owl-time:Instant ;
      owl-time:inXSDDateTimeStamp
      "1290-01-01T00:00:00Z"^^xsd:dateTimeStamp ];
   owl-time:hasEnd [
      a owl-time:Instant ;
      owl-time:inXSDDateTimeStamp
      "1310-01-01T00:00:00Z"^^xsd:dateTimeStamp ];
   ].
```

It will also be useful to define an interval EnglishInterval corresponding to the time during which the English language was spoken and which is ended by the present and 'contains' other, previously defined, intervals such as enm_interval; every English lexical entry in the resource can then be interval contained by EnglishInterval. We can further temporally locate this interval by adding statements to the effect that English language was spoken *after* proto-Germanic, while also taking into account an intervening proto-English period by defining the appropriate intervalBefore Allen relation.

4. Perdurantism v. Endurantism

Although the perdurantist approach has recently become popular amongst computer scientists and knowledge engineers for reasons that are in large part practical, it has its basis in a well established philosophical theory. *Perdurantism*, also known as *four dimensionalism* (in its most common formulations), argues that time should be treated analogously to the spatial dimensions so that objects can have temporal extension just as they can have length, breadth, and width: this means that they can have (spatio-)temporal parts in the same way that we usually describe them as having spatial parts. Naturally the notion of *temporal part* is fundamental to the perdurantist approach; we will use the following definition, given by (Sider, 1997).

> x is a **temporal part** of y during interval $T =_{df}$ (i) x is a part of y at every moment during T; (ii) x exists during T, but only during T; and for any sub-interval t of T, x overlaps every part of y at t.

Perdurantism by treating people, animals, and things in general like processes, only parts of which exist at different times, has the clear shortcoming that it can be unintuitive and difficult to understand. For a perdurantist, the temporal part of a person that *perdured* (to use the technical term) through, say, the month of January, is a part of them in the same or in an exactly analogous way as their limbs or their organs, things which constitute a physical part of them. However, the vast majority of people simply don't think in this way about the world. Perdurantism constrasts with the philosophical approach known as *endurantism*, or *three dimensionalism*, and which many philosophers argue is a more natural way of thinking about existence through time. Indeed, according to most endurantist acccounts, things, objects, etc, instead of being only partially present at one single point of time, are wholly present at each instant of their existence[9] (Sider, 1997). The perdurantist approach, however, has other features which compensate for its relative conceptual oddity. Most importantly, it helps to resolve a number of longstanding metaphysical conundrums relating to change over time. In addition, it provides a very useful way of modelling vagueness, and is also able to meet several of the challenges raised against more traditional theories of time and change by the theory of special relativity (Effingham, 2012). Note that although the names 'three-dimensionalism' and 'four-dimensionalism' might suggest that we are only dealing with 'concrete' objects, namely those that occupy a continuous physical portion of space, this is not in fact the case and perdurantism has in fact been applied to musical works (Caplan and Matheson, 2006) and institutional objects (Hansson Wahlberg, 2014). Our proposal in this work is to apply it to language and linguistic phenomena. We can explain the precise kind of perdurantist approach which we take in this paper through the provision of a simple (non-linguistic) example.

The relation capitalCity, which links together an urban location with a state, can be modelled as a diachronic relation or fluent since it can change over time, i.e., a country can have different capital cities at different points in time. Indeed this is the case with the nation of Italy which has had three separate capital cities, or seats of government, since its unification in 1861. These were/are: Turin from 1861 to 1865 (period t1), Florence from 1865 to 1871 (the period t2), and Rome from 1871 to the current day (the interval t3). One perdurantist approach to modelling this situation (and indeed the one which we will propose for lexical data below) is the following:

- We define separate time slices (or temporal parts) TurinCapital, FlorenceCapital, RomeCapital of each of the Italian cities mentioned above, Turin, Florence, Rome respectively. Note that each of these time slices are also typed as cities, e.g., city(Turin) and city(TurinCapital)

- We relate the temporal parts of these cities together with their wholes using the property temporalPartOfwhich relates a perdurant together with another perdurant of which it is a temporal part, i.e., temporalPartOf(TurinCapital, Turin), temporalPartOf(FlorenceCapital, Florence), and temporalPartOf(RomeCapital, Rome)

- Each of these timeslices is associated with its lifespan using the temporalExtent property which relates a perdurant together with the interval during which it exists, i.e., temporalExtent(TurinCapital, t1), temporalExtent(FlorenceCapital, t2), temporalExtent(RomeCapital, t3).

- We also create time slices of Italy for each of these

periods, Italyt1,Italyt2 and Italyt3 where: temporalExtent(Italyt1,t1),temporalExtent(Italyt2,t2), and temporalExtent(Italyt3,t3)

- Finally we relate these timeslices of Italy using the capitalCity relation: capitalCity(TurinCapital,Italyt1), capitalCity(FlorenceCapital,Italyt2), capitalCity(RomeCapital,Italyt3).

This is a version of the kind of perdurantist approach initially proposed for RDF in (Welty et al., 2006); our version is more directly based on (Krieger, 2014). However it should be noted that when it comes to creating diachronic versions of relationships between a lexical entry and its lexical senses and forms we can make a simplification. These latter are usually defined as being dependent on lexical entries, not least in the ontolex-lemon model where a form or a lexical sense cannot be shared by more than one entry. That is although the relation sense which relates a lexical entry together with each of its senses is a diachronic relation, each of the senses in question is parasitic on that entry, that is, the lifespan of a sense is necessarily contained in the lifespan of an entry, and similarly with forms. Our proposal then is, when it comes to perdurants versions of these classes, to define sense as holding between lexical entries and senses (and form as holding between lexical entries and forms) rather than timeslice of these, as in the case of capitalCity.

4.1. First Definitions

Our first definitions are, as anticipated, perdurantist subclasses of the ontolex-lemon classes Lexical Entry, Lexical Sense, and Lexical Form; these are pLexical Entry, pLexical Sense, and pLexical Form respectively.

$$\text{pLexical Entry} \sqsubseteq \text{Lexical Entry}$$

$$\text{pLexical Sense} \sqsubseteq \text{Lexical Sense}$$

$$\text{pLexical Form} \sqsubseteq \text{Lexical Form}$$

In order to define these classes we will make use of the new object property mentioned above, temporalExtent, whose range is the owl-time class time:Interval, and whose purpose is to relate a perdurant to its temporal dimension; thereafter we impose the restriction that each member of the p- classes is related to exactly one time:Interval individual via the property temporalExtent.

$$\text{pLexical Entry}, \text{pLexical Sense}, \text{pLexical Form}$$
$$\sqsubseteq\ = 1\ \text{temporalExtent}.(\text{time:TemporalEntity})$$

$$\exists \text{temporalExtent}.\top \sqsubseteq \text{time:Interval}$$

4.1.1. Modelling the *girl* Example

In this section we will model the OED entry for *girl* using the classes and properties just defined. Note that for reasons of space and clarity of explanation we will focus on those parts of the entry that show the use of our new classes and properties rather than giving a comprehensive encoding of the entry using elements already available in

---

[9]The standard approach to ontology modelling and knowledge engineering can be described as endurantist.

the ontolex-lemon module and the recently published lexicographic extension of the latter[10](Bosque-Gil et al., 2017) (so for instance we leave out the canonical form and phonetic forms below).

We start by defining the entry as a pLexicalEntry with an associated temporal extent (girl_time) and relating the entry with its forms using the (non-fluent) ontolex-lemon property lexicalForm

Listing 7: The entry *girl* and its forms.

```
:girl rdf:type :pLexicalEntry ;
    :temporalExtent :girl_time;
    ontolex:lexicalForm :garl_form ,
                :garle_form ,
                :geerl_form ,
                :gerl_form ,
                :gerle_form ,
                :gerreld_form ,
                :gierle_form ,
                :girle_form ,
                :guirle_form ,
                :gurl_form ,
                :gurle_form ,
                :gyal_form ,
                :gyrl_form ,
                :gyrle_form ,
                :gyrll_form ,
                :gyul_form .
```

Note that each form is contained within the temporal extent of the entire entry girl_time.

The first two forms which we will look at from the list given in Listing 7 are *garl* and *girle*, the first of which the OED tells us was in use during the Middle English period and the second of which was in use from the Middle English period through to the 15th century. We model these two as in Listing 8: that is after we introduce them as elements of type pForm we thereafter associate them with a given temporal interval using the property temporalExtent. In this case the two periods are those defined above, namely emn_interval and ME-16.

Listing 8: The forms *garl* and *girle*

```
:garl_form rdf:type :pForm ;
   ontolex:writtenRep "garl";
        :temporalExtent :enm_interval .

:girle_form rdf:type :pForm ;
   ontolex:writtenRep "girle";
   :temporalExtent :ME-16 .
```

In the case of the forms *gurl*, *gyal*, and *gyul* we have extra dialectal and geographical information to take into consideration, that is alongside the purely temporal information which has been provided. Indeed the form *gurl* has two separate temporal parts. The first part perdures over the ME period; the second part, which perdures over an interval which starts in the 18th century and ends in the present, is described as being "chiefly *Irish English* and *nonstandard*"). In order to model cases such as the latter, we have added a new datatype property hasUsageNote to our model; this allows for the encoding of geographical and dialectal constraints on the usage of a lexical element as free text. Our choice in this regard was informed by the fact that such information is often difficult to encode as structured data using formalisms such as RDFS and OWL (for instance in the present case how would we

encode the adverb *chiefly* in the description of the form *gerl*? It would be tricky to come up with a general way of encoding such descriptions that would please everyone). However this also leaves the door open to encoding such information in other ways and using other properties, for instance when it comes to purely geographical variations (a specific case which we plan to look at in future work). In Listing 9, therefore, we model the temporal interval associated with gurl_form as consisting of two separate temporal part: relating it to the interval enm_interval using intervalStartedBy and the interval 18- using intervalFinishedBy.

Listing 9: *gurl*

```
gurl_form a :pForm ;
   :hasTemporalPart :gurl_form_IEN , :gurl_form_ME ;
   :temporalExtent [
      a owl-time:Interval;
      owl-time:intervalStartedBy :enm_interval;
      owl-time:intervalFinishedBy :18-;
      ];
   ontolex:writtenRep "gurl"@en .

:gurl_form_ME a :pForm ;
   :temporalExtent :enm_interval .

:gurl_form_IEN a :pForm ;
   :temporalExtent :18- ;
   :hasUsageNote
   "chiefly Irish English and nonstandard"@en .
```

Now we will move onto the temporal modelling of the information contained in the senses of the entry[11]. We can use this information to delimit the temporal interval associated with the sense in time. In what follows we focus on the first sense of the word, the one with the definition '[a] child of either sex; a young person. Now *Irish English (Wexford)*.' This usage of the word is attested in texts such as *Piers Plowman* and the *Canterbury Tales* and the 13th century text *Ludus Conventriae*. The entry for this sense also identifies a temporal part of this sense with a particular quality not shared by the whole: that of being limited to a certain geographically defined dialect (Irish English, or more precisely the dialect of Wexford). And in fact this sense continues to be used up till the present day. We can model this as in Listing 10.

Listing 10: First *gurl* sense

```
:girl ontolex:sense :sense_I1 ,
   :sense_I1_irish_english .

:sense_I1 a :pLexicalSense ;
   :hasTemporalPart :sense_I1_irish_english ;
   :temporalExtent :sense_I1_interval .

:sense_I1_irish_english :pLexicalSense ;
   :temporalExtent :sense_I1_irish_english_interval ;
   :hasUsageNote "Irish English (Wexford)"@en .
```

This brings us to the question of how to integrate the temporal information included in the illustrative examples in the OED entry. Note that in this article we will not discuss how to model the bibliographic information included with each illustrative example – something which we can do using pre-existing vocabularies as well as potentially new classes and properties – even though it would be (scientifically) valuable to have this kind of information in a structured

---

[10]https://www.w3.org/2019/09/lexicog/

[11]Note that whenever we can assume that the ordering of senses is given in temporal order we can define precedence relations between them using, you guessed it, Allen relations.

form; this is purely for reasons of space but it is something we hope to address in further work. Instead we will use the temporal information included in the examples to enrich the description of the intervals associated with each sense.

In terms of the illustrative examples given in the entry we take those that allow us to give some kind of a (vague) temporal outline to the use of that sense. We therefore utilize the periods $C1300$, $a1475$ and 1996 for the main sense and the two periods/intervals[12] $a1827$ and 1996 for the second Irish English interval. Putting everything together we can define the two intervals in question as in Listing 11.

Listing 11: First girl sense intervals.

```
:sense_I1_interval a owl-time:Interval ;
    owl-time:hasEnd :present ;
    owl-time:intervalFinishedBy
        :sense_I1_irish_english_interval;
    owl-time:intervalContains
    :a1475 , :circa_1300 , :year_1996 .

:sense_I1_irish_english_interval a owl-time:Interval;
    owl-time:intervalFinishes :sense_I1_interval ;
    owl-time:intervalContains :a182 .
```

Another way of integrating this information into the entry is to view each of the illustrative examples as describing a very restricted sub-sense of the main sense (the main sense being in this case 'A child of either sex; a young person'): indeed **the** sub-sense of the main sense restricted to that particular use of the word. This allows us to create a new pSense for each example to which we can attach all the temporal information included in the illustrative example, and which can then be related to the main sense using the appropriate Allen relations. Finally it is important to note that a word or any lexical entry will always have some minimal temporal information associated with it thanks to the fact that it belongs to a language or a language stage to which we can usually associate a minimal of temporal information.

4.2. Modelling semantic shifts: the *sad* example.

The *sad* example given in Section 4.1.1. could be modelled explicitly using etymologies (and indeed the more extended history of the word presented in (Durkin, 2009) would be better modelled this way). However in cases where we want to track and describe a change in the sense of one word or the phonological changes in the pronunciation of a single form, it is often more convenient and efficient not to represent this via an etymology. Summarising the problem then our task is, given two lexical senses l_1, l_2 which have undergone a process of semantic shift of type s, to model the typed sense shift relationship *semanticShift* between them:

semanticShift (l_1, l_2, s)

We can also choose to make this a fluent, a diachronic relationship and add a temporal parameter, i.e., semanticShift (l_1, l_2, s, t). However in this case, as in the case of relationships such as parentOf, we believe that both modelling choices are natural, and we have decided therefore not to make it a fluent. We also introduce a new object property between senses senseShiftsTo which enables us

---

[12]Note that we have been modelling years as intervals throughout.

to model the fact that one sense 'gives birth to' another. We use the following property chain to relate this to the properties mentioned previously:

shiftSource o shiftTarget .

We define the *sad* entry as having three separate senses

Listing 12: The entry for sad

```
:sad a :pLexicalEntry ;
    :temporalExtent [a owl-time:Interval ;
        :intervalFinishes :EnglishInterval ];
    ontolex:sense
    :sad_sense_1 , :sad_sense_2 , :sad_sense_3 .
```

Moreover we also define two shift objects relating together the second and third senses of the words. (We have used rdfs:comment here to describe each shift however we are currently working on developing a taxonomy of semantic shifts which we will present in future work and to which we can link such shifts).

Listing 13: Two semantic shifts for the senses of sad

```
:sad_shift_1 a :SemanticShift ;
    :shiftSource :sad_sense_1 ;
    :shiftTarget :sad_sense_2 ;
    rdfs:comment "metaphorized and narrowed"@en .

:sad_shift_2 a :SemanticShift ;
    :shiftSource :sad_sense_2 ;
    :shiftTarget :sad_sense_3 ;
    rdfs:comment "broadened"@en .
```

The three senses of sad which we have singled out (and which are of course far from being exhaustive for the word can be defined as follows.

Listing 14: The senses of sad

```
:sad_sense_1 a :pLexicalSense ;
    :senseShiftsTo :sad_sense_2 .

:sad_sense_2 a :pLexicalSense ;
    :senseShiftsTo :sad_sense_3 .

:sad_sense_3 a :pLexicalSense;
    :temporalExtent [a owl-time:Interval ;
        :intervalDuring :a1300 ].
```

5. Conclusions and Further Work

In this article we have attempted to consolidate and build upon work which we have previously introduced, with the aim, this time, of making a detailed and convincing case for the expressive advantages of the perdurant approach to modelling diachronic lexical information. A secondary, though related aim has been to demonstrate how naturally certain, common, kinds of temporally-enriched dictionary data can be modelled in this way. In future work, as we have mentioned above, we aim to integrate bibliographic information more generally, making use of vocabularies such as CiTO as well as making use of the new Frequency Corpus and Attestations extension of ontolex lemon currently being developed by the W3C ontolex group. We also plan to investigate the efficiency of temporal reasoning using the perdurantist approach along with vocabularies like OWL-time and the rules developed by (Batsakis et al., 2017) and to test it on different sizes of dataset; something which we had previously begun to do in (Khan et al., 2018). We are also planning, with colleagues, to undertake a more detailed

21

study of the different kinds of temporal information that are common found in dictionaries and legacy lexical resources in order to test the robustness and expressivity of our model.

6. Bibliographical References

Allen, J. F. (1983). Maintaining knowledge about temporal intervals. *Communications of the ACM*, 26(11):832–843.

Batsakis, S., Petrakis, E. G., Tachmazidis, I., and Antoniou, G. (2017). Temporal representation and reasoning in owl 2. *Semantic Web*, 8(6):981–1000.

Bosque-Gil, J., Gracia, J., and Montiel-Ponsoda, E. (2017). Towards a module for lexicography in ontolex. In *LDK Workshops*, pages 74–84.

Caplan, B. and Matheson, C. (2006). Defending musical perdurantism. *The British Journal of Aesthetics*, 46(1):59–69.

De Melo, G. (2014). Etymological wordnet: Tracing the history of words. Citeseer.

Durkin, P. (2009). *The Oxford guide to etymology*. Oxford University Press.

Effingham, N. (2012). Endurantism and perdurantism. *The continuum companion to metaphysics*, pages 170–197.

Hansson Wahlberg, T. (2014). Institutional objects, reductionism and theories of persistence. *dialectica*, 68(4):525–562.

Khan, F. and Bowers, J. (2020). Towards a lexical standard for the representation of etymological data. In *Convegno annuale dell'Associazione per l'Informatica Umanistica e la Cultura Digitale*.

Khan, F., Boschetti, F., and Frontini, F. (2014). Using lemon to Model Lexical Semantic Shift in Diachronic Lexical Resources. Proceedings of the Workshop on Linked Data in Linguistics 2014 (LDL-2014).

Khan, F., Bellandi, A., and Monachini, M. (2016). Tools and instruments for building and querying diachronic computational lexica. In *Proceedings of the Workshop on Language Technology Resources and Tools for Digital Humanities (LT4DH)*, pages 164–171, Osaka, Japan, December. The COLING 2016 Organizing Committee.

Khan, F., Díaz-Vera, J., and Monachini, M. (2018). Representing meaning change in computational lexical resources: The case of shame and embarrassment terms in old english. *Formal Representation and the Digital Humanities*, page 59.

Khan, A. F. (2018). Towards the representation of etymological data on the semantic web. *Information*, 9(12):304, Nov.

Krek, S., Kosem, I., McCrae, J. P., Navigli, R., Pedersen, B. S., Tiberius, C., and Wissik, T. (2018). European lexicographic infrastructure (elexis). In *Proceedings of the XVIII EURALEX International Congress on Lexicography in Global Contexts*, pages 881–892.

Krieger, H.-U. (2014). A detailed comparison of seven approaches for the annotation of time-dependent factual knowledge in rdf and owl. In *Proceedings 10th Joint ISO-ACL SIGSEM Workshop on Interoperable Semantic Annotation*, page 1.

McCrae, J., Spohr, D., and Cimiano, P. (2011). Linking lexical resources and ontologies on the semantic web with lemon. In *Extended Semantic Web Conference*, pages 245–259. Springer.

McCrae, J. P., Bosque-Gil, J., Gracia, J., Buitelaar, P., and Cimiano, P. (2017). The OntoLex-Lemon Model: Development and Applications. pages 587–597, September.

Moran, S. and Bruemmer, M. (2013). Lemon-aid: using lemon to aid quantitative historical linguistic analysis. In *Proceedings of the 2nd Workshop on Linked Data in Linguistics (LDL-2013): Representing and linking lexicons, terminologies and other language data*, pages 28–33, Pisa, Italy, September. Association for Computational Linguistics.

OUP. (2008). *Oxford English Dictionary, Third Edition*. Oxford: Oxford University Press.

Passarotti, M. C., Cecchini, F. M., Franzini, G., Litta, E., Mambrini, F., and Ruffolo, P. (2019). The lila knowledge base of linguistic resources and nlp tools for latin. In *2nd Conference on Language, Data and Knowledge (LDK 2019)*, pages 6–11. CEUR-WS. org.

Sider, T. (1997). Four-dimensionalism. *The Philosophical Review*, 106(2):197–231.

Welty, C., Fikes, R., and Makarios, S. (2006). A reusable ontology for fluents in owl. In *FOIS*, volume 150, pages 226–236.

Proceedings of the 7th Workshop on Linked Data in Linguistics (LDL-2020), pages 23–27
Language Resources and Evaluation Conference (LREC 2020), Marseille, 11–16 May 2020
© European Language Resources Association (ELRA), licensed under CC-BY-NC

From Linguistic Descriptions to Language Profiles

Shafqat Mumtaz Virk[1], Harald Hammarström[2], Lars Borin[1], Markus Forsberg[1], Søren Wichmann[3]
[1]Språkbanken Text, Department of Swedish, University of Gothenburg
[2]Department of Linguistics and Philology, University of Uppsala
[3]Leiden University Centre for Linguistics, Leiden University
[3]Laboratory for Quantitative Linguistics, Kazan Federal University
[3]Beijing Advanced Innovation Center for Language Resources, Beijing Language University
[1]{shafqat.virk, lars.borin, markus.forsberg}@svenska.gu.se
[2]{harald.hammarstrom}@lingfil.uu.se
[3]{wichmannsoeren}@gmail.com

Abstract

Language catalogues and typological databases are two important types of resources containing different types of knowledge about the world's natural languages. The former provide metadata such as number of speakers, location (in prose descriptions and/or GPS coordinates), language code, literacy, etc., while the latter contain information about a set of structural and functional attributes of languages. Given that both types of resources are developed and later maintained manually, there are practical limits as to the number of languages and the number of features that can be surveyed. We introduce the concept of a *language profile*, which is intended to be a structured representation of various types of knowledge about a natural language extracted semi-automatically from descriptive documents and stored at a central location. It has three major parts: (1) an introductory; (2) an attributive; and (3) a reference part, each containing different types of knowledge about a given natural language. As a case study, we develop and present a language profile of an example language. At this stage, a language profile is an independent entity, but in the future it is envisioned to become part of a network of language profiles connected to each other via various types of relations. Such a representation is expected to be suitable both for humans and machines to read and process for further deeper linguistic analyses and/or comparisons.

Keywords: Typological information, linguistic descriptions, language networks

1. Introduction

Approximately 7,000 distinct languages constitute our record of linguistic diversity (Hammarström, 2015). Languages are equal witnesses – where e.g., English is but one – to the variation and constraints of the unique communication system of our species (Evans and Levinson, 2009). They harbour information on what happens to language given tens of thousands of millennia of diversification, under all imaginable circumstances of human interaction. As such they may be used to investigate theories that may otherwise not be testable with anything less than a laboratory the size of human history.

Two web-publications maintain catalogues of the languages of the world: Ethnologue (Eberhard et al., 2019) and Glottolog (Hammarström et al., 2019). Ethnologue provides metadata such as number of speakers, location (in prose words), literacy etc. Glottolog provides classification, location (in GPS coordinates), and bibliographical references. For in-depth information about a lesser-known language, specialists typically consult any available descriptive grammar. For example, for the language Ulwa (ISO 639-3 language code: yla) of Papua New Guinea, there exists

> Barlow, Russell. (2018) A grammar of Ulwa. University of Hawai'i at Mānoa doctoral dissertation. xiv+546 pp.

Around 4,000 languages have at least one published grammatical description but the breadth, depth, and quality of these vary (Hammarström et al., 2018).

For analysis of the languages themselves, there are a number of databases which keep a record of various characteristics (also known as linguistic features) of individual languages. For example, the World Atlas of Language Structures (WALS; Haspelmath et al. 2005), contains information on some 200 features spanning 2500 languages (but is sparsely filled in). A very extensive list of linguistic databases can be found at `http://languagegoldmine.com/` (accessed 2020-04-05).

These inventories and databases are highly useful resources but have clear limits on the number of features and/or languages they contain. As such they do not represent all the information available about the same language in descriptive publications. This situation is inevitable as (1) a fixed list of linguistic features is designed for a database, but languages differ from each other in a myriad of ways which cannot be known a priori; and (2) databases are curated manually by reading the descriptive documents, which is a time-consuming activity.

For these reasons we aim to go beyond the manual curation of linguistic databases in order to capture the valuable knowledge about many other languages and features remaining within descriptive publications. Thus, our aim is to extract all the information about a language described in a publication, and represent it in a structured manner. These structured representations can be successively normalized and thus form the basis for large-scale comparison of languages. If successful, it will widen the scope of investigations and comparisons across languages considerably. Toward this end, advancements in natural language processing and information extraction may be exploited.

A related concern is that various types of knowledge about languages are maintained separately. Consequently, one has to explore different resources to access knowledge about the same language. For example, some general and referential type of data (i.e. about language names, the number and names of dialects, the areas where they are spoken, the number of speakers, etc.) are often maintained in the form of digital inventories, the attributive type of data (i.e. various phonological, morphological, and grammatical features) are maintained as typological databases, and many other details are found in descriptive documents (grammars, dictionaries, etc.) and, since recently, increasingly in web-pages, blogs etc.

Further, several of the important resources on natural languages are not open-access. For example, Ethnologue has most of its information behind a paywall.[1] Since only a particular creative arrangement of words – but not facts in general – can be copyrighted, the prospects for free and open structured representations are much better, even when extracted from copyrighted source materials.

In this paper, we present the concept of a language profile in order to address the above-mentioned limitations and concerns. A language profile can be envisaged as a digital representation of a natural language containing various types of information about the language stored at a central location in a structured format and publicly available for further use. It aims to be a dynamic representation in the sense that it is not tied to a predefined set of features (like typological databases), but targets any traceable features. Included are also introductory and referential information about a target language extracted from the descriptions and other available resources. Various types of information about a language are grouped into various sections, and the resulting structure is called *a language profile*. In the present paper, we describe the concept of a language profile only. In future work, we plan to describe how language profiles can be linked in a full network (a LangNet) using different kinds of comparisons/relations (e.g., genetic, geographical, typological similarity). Conceptually, such a network of languages is similar to other networks in the area of NLP such as WordNet, VerbNet, FrameNet, etc., except that it is at the level of languages. We believe that such a rich representation model, and the network of languages will be a useful resource for linguistic studies.

The remainder of the paper is organized as follows: Section 2 describes in detail the structure and components of a language profile, while details on semi-automatic development of a language profile from linguistic descriptions are given in Section 3.

2. Language Profiles

As mentioned in the introduction section, a language profile is necessarily a structured digital representation of a natural language. In this section, we will present the structure and various proposed components of a language profile. In doing so, we will use a natural language called 'Ulwa', and build a minimal part of its profile. At this stage, this language profile will be built semi-automatically, but a long term objective is to automatize the process as much as possible. We will indicate which parts are built automatically

and which manually, and will provide suggestions, wherever possible, for automatizing the corresponding parts.

1. **Metadata Part:** The metadata part contains basic metadata such as official language name, number of speakers, areas where spoken, etc., and referential (e.g., ISO code and/or glottocode, language family, etc.) information. Table 1 shows this part of the 'Ulwa' language profile.

   In this case, most of the fields and their values in this part of the profile are available in the language catalogue Ethnologue (Eberhard et al., 2019) in the Yaul entry (`https://www.ethnologue.com/language/yla`). As such it resembles information already available in language inventory databases, but improves on these by being more dynamic, linkable and aggregateable. The list of possible fields of metadata is not bounded, and can be extended indefinitely. Each field in the profile and information within it will have a structured representation. For example, the location in the above given profile is not a simple string, but rather a geographical location with a name and co-ordinates. This can be linked to existing inventories of geographical locations such as GeoNames (`http://www.geonames.org`). The same applies to the dialect names, families and branches in the classification field, official and alternative language names, etc. Appropriate data structures will be proposed for various fields, with proper IDs to be used for various types of inter- and intra-profile connections. Further, each piece of information will have a recorded source which may be weighted according to usage needs whenever there are many different sources for the same field.

2. **Attributive Part:** This is the major part of a language profile and is intended to contain the typological and other structural information of a target language. Again, other databases exist with a similar type of information (e.g., WALS – see above). The key difference is as follows. The attributive part of a language profile does not contain answers to a predefined set of typological and other questions. Rather, it contains all attributive (i.e. phonological, morphological, and grammatical) information which can be extracted (semi)automatically from the available descriptive data about a given language. As an example, consider the attributive part of the 'Ulwa' language profile given in Table 2. The information in this part was automatically extracted from a language description (Barlow, 2018). (A description of the automatic extraction of the typological information is given in Section 3.)

   In this example, there is no categorization of the features. In the future, we intend to divide the attributive part into various subparts e.g. phonological, morphological, grammatical attributive information, and so on. The feature ID field is left blank intentionally at this stage, and a detailed set of feature IDs is to be worked out at a later stage.

---

[1]Except in third-world countries, where it continues to be freely available.

Field-ID	Field-Name	Number::Name::Value	Source
fet:p1:meta-name	Official Name(s)	1::-::Ulwa 2::	(Barlow, 2018)
fet:p1:classification	Classification	1::-::Ulmapo	(Barlow, 2018)
fet:p1:speakers	Speakers	1::Native::700 2::Second Language::	(Barlow, 2018)
fet:p1:dialects	Dialect(s)	1::-::Manu dialect 2::-::Maruat-Dimiri-Yaul	(Barlow, 2018) (Barlow, 2018)
fet:p1:location	Location(s)	1::-::Manu 2::-::Maruat 3::-::Dimiri 4::-::Yaul	(Barlow, 2018) (Barlow, 2018) (Barlow, 2018) (Barlow, 2018)

Table 1: The metadata part of the Ulwa language profile

FeatureID	Feature	Value	Source
—	Subject and NP order	NP–SubjectMarker	(Barlow, 2018)
—	Object and NP order	NP–ObjectMarker	(Barlow, 2018)
—	Constituent Order	SOV	(Barlow, 2018)
—	PostpositionalPhrase–Oblique-markedNP Order	Both	(Barlow, 2018)
—	ObliguePhrase–SubjectOFClause Order	SubjectOFClause-ObliguePhrase	(Barlow, 2018)
—	ObliguePhrase–Verb Order	ObliguePhrase–Verb	(Barlow, 2018)
—	Negator–Verb Order	Negator–Verb	(Barlow, 2018)
—	AdPosition–NP Order	NP–AdPosition	(Barlow, 2018)
—	Possessor–Possessum Order	Possessor–Possessum	(Barlow, 2018)
—	Adjective–Noun Order	Noun–Adjective	(Barlow, 2018)
—	Demonstrative–Noun Order	Noun–Demonstrative	(Barlow, 2018)
—	Numeral–Noun Order	Noun–Numeral	(Barlow, 2018)
—	RelativeClause–HeadNoun Order	RelativeClause–HeadNoun	(Barlow, 2018)
—	PossessivePronoun–Noun Order	PossessivePronoun–Noun	(Barlow, 2018)
—	ObliqueMarker–Noun Order	Noun–ObliqueMarker	(Barlow, 2018)
—	TraniativeVerb–ObjectMarker Order	TransativeVerb–ObjectMarker	(Barlow, 2018)
—	NominalizedVerb–SubjectMarker Order	SubjectMarker–NominalizedVerb	(Barlow, 2018)
—	Verb–DirectObject Order	DirectObject–Verb	(Barlow, 2018)
—	TransitiveVerb–ObjectMarker Order	ObjectMarker–TransitiveVerb	(Barlow, 2018)
—	Oblique–Verb Order	Oblique–Verb	(Barlow, 2018)
—	Oblique- Subject Order	Subject–Oblique	(Barlow, 2018)
—	Adverb–Subject Order	Subject–Adverb	(Barlow, 2018)
—	Adverb–Object Order	Adverb–Object	(Barlow, 2018)
—	Adverb–Oblique-markedNP Order	Adverb–Oblique-markedNPs	(Barlow, 2018)
—	NasalSegments–VoicelessStops Order	NasalSegments–VoicelessStops	(Barlow, 2018)
—	LabialNasal–PalatoAlveolar Order	LabialNasal–PalatoAlveolar	(Barlow, 2018)
—	HomorganicNasals–VoicelessStops Order	HomorganicNasals–VoicelessStops	(Barlow, 2018)
—	Liquids–LabialStops Order	LabialStops–Liquids	(Barlow, 2018)
—	Liquids–VelarStops Order	VelarStops–Liquids	(Barlow, 2018)

Table 2: The attributive part of the Ulwa language profile

3. **References Part:** The reference part contains a list of available resources about the language at hand. A Bib-TeX type of entry will be maintained for each descriptive document and other type of resource (e.g. word list, dictionary, etc.). One such entry for the 'Ulwa' language is as follows:

```
@phdthesis{g:Barlow:Ulwa,
author = {Barlow, Russell},
title = {A grammar of Ulwa},
school = {University of Hawai'i
          at Mānoa},
pages = {xiv+546},
year = {2018},
glottolog_ref_id = {554079},
hhtype = {grammar},
inlg = {English [eng]},
lgcode = {Manu Ulwa = Yaul [yla]},
macro_area = {Papua}
}
```

Every item of information in each section of the language profile has a source linked to an entry from the reference section. The maintenance of references within the profile ensures that the crucial source links can be kept in sync.

3. Building a Language Profile

Building a language profile is a complex process. It requires gathering information about a language from all available sources, i.e., manuals, digital inventories, linguistic descriptions, etc. This is a long-term process, and will require gradual efforts to incrementally develop a large set of rich language profiles.

At this stage, we have relied on manual collection of information for the introductory as well as the reference part, although parts of it can be automatized (information about language name and number of speakers can be extracted automatically using the frame based methodology explained below, which was used to build the attributive part automatically).

The automatic extraction of typological information from descriptive grammars is a novel task, and there exists only a few studies and systems reported previously (Virk et al., 2017; Virk et al., 2019). In Virk et al. (2019), a frame-semantic based approach is proposed for developing a parser to automatically extract typological linguistic information from plain-text grammatical descriptions of natural languages. As a case study, the authors have shown how the parser can be used to extract value of an example typological feature. However, the system has not been used for any actual typological work. We continue that work and use the parser to extract typological feature values (shown in Table 2) of a language profile. A brief description of the parser and how it has been used for our purposes follows.

The parser relies on a lexico-semantic resource, LingFN (Malm et al., 2018), and its frame-labeled data for training machine learning models to build a parser. The development of LingFN itself is based on the theory of frame-semantics (Fillmore, 1976; Fillmore, 1977; Fillmore, 1982), and is motivated by the development of Berke-ley FrameNet (Baker et al., 1998) and other, domain-specific framenets (e.g. a framenet to cover medical terminology (Borin et al., 2007), *Kicktionary*,[2] a soccer language framenet). Let us take an example to better understand what LingFN is, and how its frame-labeled data is used to build the frame-semantic parser which in turn is used for automatic extraction of typological features. Consider the following sentence which is taken from a descriptive grammar of the Ulwa language.

> In Ulwa, adjectives in NPs sometimes precede their head nouns.

The sentence contains information about the relative position (sequencing) of two syntactic categories i.e. 'adjectives' and 'head nouns'. Their position wrt one another is not always the mentioned one but could be the other way around, as conveyed by the adverb 'sometimes'. This is useful information that we are interested in extracting automatically. One of the possible approaches is to develop a frame-semantic based information extraction system. For that purpose, the first step is to design (or use from the Berkeley FrameNet) special structures to represent this type of phenomenon (i.e. sequencing). In frame-semantics such structures are called semantic frames, and in general, a semantic frame is a structured representation of a an entity, an object, and a scenario. In our case, a semantic frame represents a linguistic entity (e.g. nouns, verbs, etc.) or phenomenon (e.g. affixation, agreement, sequence, etc). Let us say for the sequencing phenomena, we have designed a semantic frame with the structure shown in Table 3. (For more details on development of the SEQUENCE and other linguistic domain semantic frames with annotated example sentences, we refer the reader to Malm et al. (2018)).

SEQUENCE
Entity_1
Entity_2
Entities_3
Order
Frequency
Language_Variety

Table 3: Sequence Semantic Frame

Entity_1, Entity_2, Entities, Order, Frequency, and Language_Variety are referred to as frame-elements, which constitute various semantic parts of the sequencing phenomena. With such structures (i.e. semantic frames) at hand, the next step is to annotate linguistic descriptions with developed semantic frames. The annotation of the above given sentence is as follows:

```
In [Ulwa]_Language Variety,
    [adjectives]_Entity_1 in NPs
    [sometimes]_Frequency
    [[precede]_LU]_Order
    their [head nouns]_Entity_2.
```

String segments labeled as one of the frame-elements are enclosed within a pair of brackets while the frame-element label (bold) follows an underscore sign. Note that in case of above given sentence, the word 'precede' is both a lexical unit (a word triggering a particular frame) and also a frame-element.

Now imagine, if we have enough sentences annotated with the SEQUENCE (and other frames from LingFN), one could train machine learning models for automatic labeling of these frames on un-annotated data. This is exactly what is proposed by the authors in (Virk et al., 2019), and they have a developed a parser for this purpose. What the parser does is to take un-annotated sentences containing typological linguistic information and annotate them with linguistic domain frames and their associated frame-elements. As suggested by the authors in the same paper, the annotations can be converted to typological information in any required format using a rule based module. This is exactly what we have done to extract feature values shown in Table 2 for the Ulwa language. Note, only the SEQUENCE frame was used to extract the whole information present in Table 2. In the future we plan to extend this work to other typological features and hence enhance the attributive part of a language profile.

4. Conclusions and Future Work

We have presented the idea of a language profile, which is envisaged as a digital structured representation of a natural language. It has two major objectives. The first objective is to overcome a major limitation of existing typological databases which contain information about a pre-defined set of linguistic features. We propose work towards automatically extracting information about all the features described in a descriptive document. The second objective is to collect various types of information available about a language stored in a structured way and at a common place together with information about the sources. The idea is at an embryonic stage and is to be further matured and extended in the future.

5. Acknowledgements

The work presented here was funded by (1) the *Dictionary/Grammar Reading Machine: Computational Tools for Accessing the World's Linguistic Heritage* (DReaM) Project awarded 2018–2020 by the Joint Programming Initiative in Cultural Heritage and Global Change, Digital Heritage and Riksantikvarieämbetet, Sweden; (2) the Swedish Research Council as part of the project *South Asia as a linguistic area? Exploring big-data methods in areal and genetic linguistics* (2015–2019, contract no. 421-2014-969); (3) *From Dust to Dawn: Multilingual Grammar Extraction from Grammars* project funded by Stiftelsen Marcus och Amalia Wallenbergs Minnesfond 2007.0105, Uppsala University; and (4) the University of Gothenburg, its Faculty of Humanities and its Department of Swedish, through their truly long-term support of the Språkbanken Text research infrastructure.

6. References

Baker, C. F., Fillmore, C. J., and Lowe, J. B. (1998). The Berkeley FrameNet project. In *Proceedings of ACL/COLING 1998*, pages 86–90, Montreal. ACL.

Barlow, R. (2018). *A grammar of Ulwa*. Ph.D. thesis, University of Hawai'i at Mānoa.

Borin, L., Toporowska Gronostaj, M., and Kokkinakis, D. (2007). Medical frames as target and tool. In *FRAME 2007: Building Frame Semantics Resources for Scandinavian and Baltic Languages. (Nodalida 2007 Workshop Proceedings)*, pages 11–18, Tartu. NEALT.

Eberhard, D. M., Simons, G. F., and Fennig, C. D. (2019). *Ethnologue: Languages of the World*. Dallas: SIL International, 22 edition.

Evans, N. and Levinson, S. (2009). The myth of language universals: Language diversity and its importance for cognitive science. *Behavioral and Brain Sciences*, 32(5):429–492.

Fillmore, C. J. (1976). Frame semantics and the nature of language. *Annals of the New York Academy of Sciences*, 280(1):20–32.

Fillmore, C. J. (1977). Scenes-and-frames semantics. In Antonio Zampolli, editor, *Linguistic Structures Processing*, pages 55–81. North Holland, Amsterdam.

Fillmore, C. J. (1982). Frame semantics. In Linguistic Society of Korea, editor, *Linguistics in the Morning Calm*, pages 111–137. Hanshin Publishing Co., Seoul.

Hammarström, H., Castermans, T., Forkel, R., Verbeek, K., Westenberg, M. A., and Speckmann, B. (2018). Simultaneous visualization of language endangerment and language description. *Language Documentation & Conservation*, 12:359–392.

Hammarström, H., Forkel, R., and Haspelmath, M. (2019). Glottolog 4.0. Jena: Max Planck Institute for the Science of Human History. Available at http://glottolog.org. Accessed on 2019-09-12.

Hammarström, H. (2015). Ethnologue 16/17/18th editions: A comprehensive review. *Language*, 91(3):723–737. Plus 188pp online appendix.

Martin Haspelmath, et al., editors. (2005). *World Atlas of Language Structures*. Oxford: Oxford University Press.

Malm, P., Virk, S. M., Borin, L., and Saxena, A. (2018). Lingfn: Towards a domain-specific linguistic framenet. In Tiago Timponi Torrent, et al., editors, *Proceedings of the Eleventh International Conference on Language Resources and Evaluation (LREC 2018)*, Paris, France, may. European Language Resources Association (ELRA).

Virk, S., Borin, L., Saxena, A., and Hammarström, H. (2017). Automatic extraction of typological linguistic features from descriptive grammars. In *Proceedings of TSD 2017*, pages 111–119, Cham. Springer.

Virk, S. M., Muhammad, A. S., Borin, L., Aslam, M. I., Iqbal, S., and Khurram, N. (2019). Exploiting frame-semantics and frame-semantic parsing for automatic extraction of typological information from descriptive grammars of natural languages. In *RANLP-Proceedings*, sep.

Proceedings of the 7th Workshop on Linked Data in Linguistics (LDL-2020), pages 28–35
Language Resources and Evaluation Conference (LREC 2020), Marseille, 11–16 May 2020
© European Language Resources Association (ELRA), licensed under CC-BY-NC

Terme-à-LLOD: Simplifying the Conversion and Hosting of Terminological Resources as Linked Data

Maria Pia Di Buono[1], Philipp Cimiano[2], Mohammad Fazleh Elahi[2], Frank Grimm[2]
[1]UNIOR NLP Research Group, University of Naples L'Orientale
[2]Semantic Computing Group, Bielefeld University
mpdibuono@unior.it
{cimiano, melahi, grimm}@cit-ec.uni-bielefeld.de

Abstract

In recent years, there has been increasing interest in publishing lexicographic and terminological resources as linked data. The benefit of using linked data technologies to publish terminologies is that terminologies can be linked to each other, thus creating a cloud of linked terminologies that cross domains, languages and that support advanced applications that do not work with single terminologies but can exploit multiple terminologies seamlessly. We present Terme-à-LLOD (TAL), a new paradigm for transforming and publishing terminologies as linked data which relies on a virtualization approach. The approach rests on a preconfigured virtual image of a server that can be downloaded and installed. We describe our approach to simplifying the transformation and hosting of terminological resources in the remainder of this paper. We provide a proof-of-concept for this paradigm showing how to apply it to the conversion of the well-known IATE terminology as well as to various smaller terminologies. Further, we discuss how the implementation of our paradigm can be integrated into existing NLP service infrastructures that rely on virtualization technology. While we apply this paradigm to the transformation and hosting of terminologies as linked data, the paradigm can be applied to any other resource format as well.

Keywords: Linguistic Linked Open Data, Terminological Resources, NLP services

1. Introduction

Terminological resources, mainly termbases, represent a core source of data for translation and localization (Stanković et al., 2014). Further, they have important applications in text mining as they provide concepts with which elements of text can be tagged for semantic normalization as well as semantic indexing (Witschel, 2005). Therefore, many intermediate representations of terminological information and tools for termbase management have been developed so far with the main goal of improving the portability and interoperability of those resources. Among the representations of terminological information, the TermBase eXchange (TBX) format has become a standard for terminology information exchange. Such an exchange plays an important role in ensuring consistency and contributes to terminology production and quality through interactive validation processes (joh,).

In recent years, there has been interest in publishing terminological resources as linked data in order to improve interoperability and reuse and a number of approaches proposing to use linked data principles to publish terminologies have been proposed (Cimiano et al., 2015; Rodriguez-Doncel et al., 2015; Montiel-Ponsoda et al., 2015).

The general benefits of publishing language resources as linked data have been described by Chiarcos et al. (2013). In short, the benefit of using linked data technologies to publish terminologies is that terminologies can be linked to each other, in order to create a cloud of linked terminologies that cross domains, languages and that support advanced applications that do not work with single terminologies but can exploit multiple terminologies seamlessly (see the work of Montiel et al. (2015) on integrating two terminologies, TERMACT and Terminesp, using Linked Data). Along these lines, a number of projects have published specific guidelines on how to publish terminological resources using linked data and Semantic Web technologies. For example, as a result of the EC-funded LIDER project[1] and as part of the work of the W3C community group on Best Practices for Multilingual Linked Open Data (BPMLOD)[2], guidelines have been released describing how to publish terminologies in TBX format as linked data using the ontolex-lemon model (McCrae et al., 2011; McCrae et al., 2015). More recently, the Linked Heritage Project[3] has released recommendations for how to manage terminologies in the framework of the Semantic Web.

Yet, a fundamental problem remains, that is that implementing all these guidelines and recommendations is challenging as one needs a detailed understanding of the corresponding vocabularies in addition to technical understanding of data models (e.g., RDF) as well as how to host linked data at a server level. We present a new approach that we call Terme-à-LLOD (TAL), aiming to fill this gap and simplifying the task of converting a terminological resource in TBX format into a linked data resource and ease the task of hosting the linked data resource in such a way that i) URIs resolve, ii) the resource can be browsed, and iii) a SPARQL endpoint is offered. This new paradigm for transforming and publishing standardized terminological resources as linked data relies on a virtualization approach. The approach rests on a pre-configured virtual image of a server that can be downloaded and installed. In our approach we rely on Docker[4], but any other virtualization environment can be used instead.

The remainder of the paper is organized as follows: Section

---

[1]http://www.lider-project.eu/
lider-project.eu/index.html
[2]https://www.w3.org/2015/09/
bpmlod-reports/multilingual-terminologies/
[3]http://linkedheritage.eu/
[4]https://www.docker.com

2. describes our new approach and its virtualization process to simplify the transformation and hosting of terminological resources. Following this, Section 3. presents two case studies comprising the transformation of the Inter-Agency Terminology Exchange (IATE)[5] terminology as well as a sample of termbases provided by the Centrum Voor Terminologie (CvT)[6] at Ghent University into Linked Data. Finally, Section 4. shows how our approach can be integrated into existing NLP service infrastructures that rely on virtualization technology such as European Language Grid (ELG)[7] and Teanga[8]. Section 5. discusses related work and how our approach can be integrated into other NLP service frameworks. The paper ends with the conclusion and future work.

2. Terme-à-LLOD Approach

Terme-à-LLOD is a new virtualization paradigm for easing the process of transforming terminological resources into RDF and hosting them as linked data. The virtualization paradigm relies on three main components (Figure 2): a converter (A), a Virtuoso Server[9] (B) (Erling and Mikhailov, 2010; Erling, 2012), and a container (C).

The converter element managing the automatic format transformation is based on the TBX2RDF service[10] (Cimiano et al., 2015) developed by the LIDER project. TBX2RDF maps TBX inputs, including TBX public dialects, i.e., TBX-Core, TBX-Min and TBX-Basic, into RDF format, reusing a set of classes and properties from existing linked open data vocabularies (e.g., OntoLex-Lemon[11]). An example of converting TBX to RDF is can be seen in Figure 2.

The converter produces an RDF output which serves as input to a Virtuoso server, the second component of the TAL virtualization technology. Once the RDF output has been uploaded, the pre-installed server, which hosts the service, exposes the converted data through an endpoint which allows to access them. The server also provides a SPARQL endpoint to other services.

The third element of the virtualization technology is a Docker container that can be easily installed on any Docker environment. The Docker container allows to bundle components, libraries and configuration files of the TAL service and to run the service on different computing environments. Once the container is installed and instantiated, the terminological resource can be pushed via HTTP/Advanced Message Queuing Protocol (AMQP) request to the TBX2RDF converter. Subsequently, the TAL service invokes the transformation to Linked Data using the converter and hosts the resulting RDF as linked data together with a SPARQL endpoint.

The benefit of such a virtualization approach is that the owner of a terminology can easily publish the terminology

---

```
<termEntry id="IATE-84">
  <descripGrp>
     <descrip type="subjectField">1011</descrip>
  </descripGrp>
  <langSet xml:lang="en">
     <tig>
        <term>competence of the Member States</term>
        <termNote type="termType">fullForm</termNote>
        <descrip type="reliabilityCode">3</descrip>
     </tig>
  </langSet>
  <langSet xml:lang="da">
     <tig>
        <term>medlemsstatskompetence</term>
        <termNote type="termType">fullForm</termNote>
        <descrip type="reliabilityCode">3</descrip>
     </tig>
  </langSet>
  <langSet xml:lang="nl">
     .....
  </langSet>
  <langSet xml:lang="es">
     .....
  </langSet>
  .....
</termEntry>
```

```
<http://webtentacle1.techfak.uni-bielefeld.de/tbx2rdf_iate/
competence+of+the+Member+States-en>
      a ontolex:LexicalEntry ;
      dct:language <http://www.lexvo.org/id/iso639-3/eng> ;
      tbx:reliabilityCode 3 ;
      <http://www.lexinfo.net/ontology/2.0/lexinfo#termType>
            <http://www.lexinfo.net/ontology/2.0/lexinfo#fullForm> ;
      <http://www.w3.org/ns/lemon/lime#language>
            "en" ;
      ontolex:canonicalForm <http://webtentacle1.techfak.uni-bielefeld.de/
      tbx2rdf_iate/data/iate/competence+of+the+Member+States-en#CanonicalForm> ;
      ontolex:sense <http://webtentacle1.techfak.uni-bielefeld.de/
      tbx2rdf_iate/data/iate/competence+of+the+Member+States-en#Sense> .

<http://webtentacle1.techfak.uni-bielefeld.de/tbx2rdf_iate/
data/iate/dal%C4%ABbvalstu+kompetence-lv#Sense>
      a ontolex:LexicalSense ;
      ontolex:isLexicalizedSenseOf :IATE-84 .

<http://webtentacle1.techfak.uni-bielefeld.de/tbx2rdf_iate/
data/iate/competence+of+the+Member+States-en#CanonicalForm>
      ontolex:writtenRep "competence of the Member States"@en .

<http://webtentacle1.techfak.uni-bielefeld.de/tbx2rdf_iate/
data/iate/medlemsstatskompetence-da#CanonicalForm>
      ontolex:writtenRep "medlemsstatskompetence"@da .
.......
```

Figure 1: TBX (top) to RDF (bottom) conversion

as linked data without the need to understand the underlying vocabularies in detail nor of the RDF data model or about how to set up a linked data server. Yet, the data remains under full control and can be published under a namespace to represent ownership and provenance.

2.1. Virtualization Process

The virtualization technology is contained into a pre-configured virtual image that can be hosted in a corresponding environment consisting of virtual machines communicating with each other over standard protocols. All capabilities of a TAL service are advertised in an OpenAPI descriptor file. This lets consumers discover how to communicate with the service and what result values to expect.

The TAL service automatically gathers the latest version of the TBX2RDF service from GitHub and installs it in a multi-stage container build that makes knowledge of the underlying Java development stack transparent to the end user. TAL adds a Node.js application behind a nginx reverse proxy for HTTP communication with the service. This application is used to orchestrate the different internals of the container and monitor the status or health of the container.

The service is initially provided with term glossaries as standardized TBX files, as defined by ISO standard

---

[5] https://iate.europa.eu
[6] http://www.cvt.ugent.be
[7] https://www.european-language-grid.eu/
[8] https://teanga.techfak.uni-bielefeld.de/
[9] https://virtuoso.openlinksw.com/
[10] http://tbx2rdf.lider-project.eu/
converter/
[11] https://www.w3.org/2016/05/ontolex/

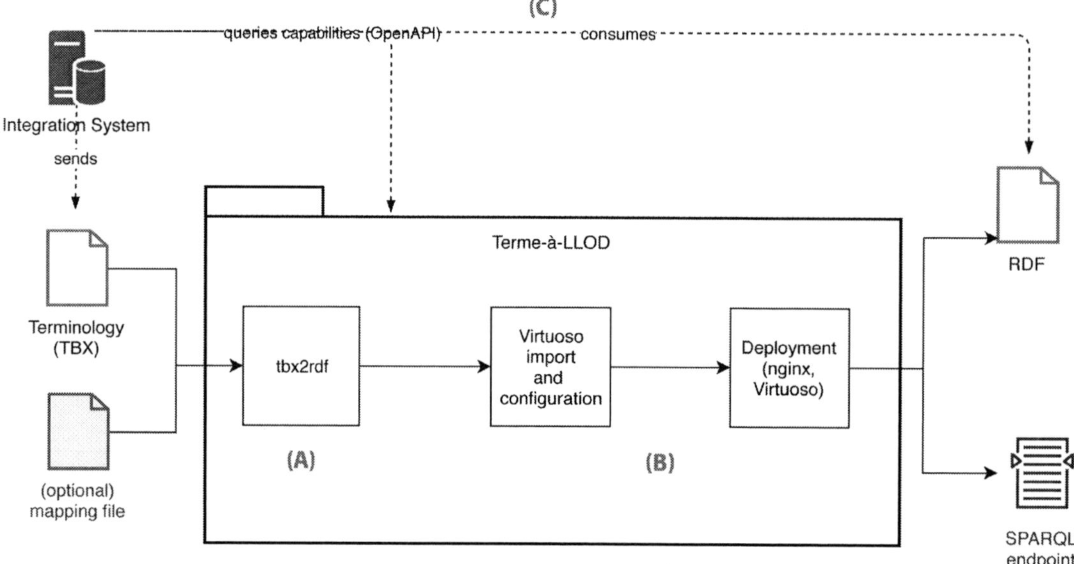

Figure 2: TAL virtualization paradigm

30042:2008, as well as an optional file containing mapping information between TBX and the desired target RDF namespace. A stack of open source software is then used to convert and deploy the glossary data in queryable linked open data formats, namely as a resource description framework (RDF) download and a SPARQL endpoint to query this data.

The container bundles the TBX2RDF converter, implemented as a Java program that reads in the document and builds the DOM tree. The DOM tree is traversed and elements are mapped to appropriate object-oriented datastructures. These datastructures are then serialized as RDF.

The resulting RDF is exposed to a web server for further downstream tasks that require the full dataset and automatically populates an instance of the Virtuoso open source database engine[12].

Since terminology databases can be of considerable size, the container additionally exposes a status application that allows an end user to monitor the conversion progress and status of each service instance. During regular use, the ecosystem issues a new instance of the TAL Docker container that is available on GitHub[13]. It is either initialized as an empty instance or provided with the state or database content of a previously created instance.

The only knowledge required to setup a service instance is minimal and generally regards the specific ecosystem used to work with the service. Specialized knowledge of TBX, LLOD or NLP technologies is not necessary and abstracted away in order to make these resources more approachable. In fact, a Docker container is a lightweight, standalone, executable package ("container image") of software that can be seen as a template to bootstrap everything required to run an application: code, runtime, a lean operating system, sys-

tem libraries and settings. The Docker engine (e.g., pure Docker, Kubernetes or a platform-as-a-service cloud offering) enables containerized applications to run anywhere consistently on essentially any infrastructure. A Docker volume is used to retain the results of costly conversion processes across updates and reboots. During bootup the TAL container starts a Node.js application and nginx web server. The service is immediately discoverable through the OpenAPI descriptor. The conversion process itself has to only be run once, e.g., by the party maintaining a particular terminology. Subsequent users can consume from the initialized service instance by either post-processing the generated RDF artifact that is exposed via HTTP or querying the SPARQL endpoint that hosts the resulting linked data structures.

3. Use Cases: IATE and GENTERM

In order to provide a proof-of-concept of this approach to simplify the process of transforming terminological resources into RDF and hosting the RDF as linked data, we used a sample of data from two sources. The data source is the Inter-Agency Terminology Exchange (IATE) repository and the second are a number of termbases hosted by the Centrum Voor Terminologie (CvT) at Ghent University.

3.1. IATE

IATE, a central terminology database for all the institutions, agencies and other bodies of the European Union, provides a single access point to the existing European terminological resources, besides an infrastructure for the constitution, shared management and dissemination of these resources (joh,). With a current total number of 935K entries, 7.1 MM terms and 26 languages[14], this database represents the reference in the terminology field, and is considered to be

---

[12]http://vos.openlinksw.com/owiki/wiki/VOS

[13]https://github.com/ag-sc/terme-a-llod and https://hub.docker.com/r/agsc/terme-a-llod

[14]https://iate.europa.eu/download-iate

TBX field	RDF element
TBX resource	`void:Dataset`
Term	`skos:Concept`
Langset	`ontolex:Lexicon`
TIG/NTIG	`ontolex:LexicalEntry`
TermGrp	`ontolex:canonicalForm`
TermCompList	`ontolex:decomp`
TermCompGrp	`decomp:correspondsTo`
DescrGrp	properties of the lexical entry
TransGrp/Transaction	`tbx:Transaction`

Table 1: Conceptual mapping of TBX fields and RDF elements.

TBX input	Runtime	# Terms	# Triples	# Lang
IATE	25.2m	5851035	52603182	25
Pharmaceutical*	5.2s	4629	71347	2
Diseases*	3.0s	799	12650	2
Waste management*	2.5s	396	6109	2
Solar energy*	2.9s	205	3758	2
Printmaking*	2.5s	223	3426	2

Table 2: Information about IATE and GENTERM conversion process (Entries marked with * are courtesy of GENTERM).

the largest multilingual terminology database in the world. Data, provided in TBX format and made available without a copyright protection, can be freely downloaded and reproduced, for personal use or for further non-commercial or commercial dissemination[15].

3.2. GENTERM

The second sample of data has been extracted from the termbases developed by the Centrum Voor Terminologie (CvT) - GENTERM[16]. The center, active within the Department of Translation, Interpreting and Communication of Ghent University, co-ordinates the Department's activities on terminology and terminography and makes available a small set of termbases, which are the result of several students' projects. GENTERM termbases belong to different domains (e.g., pharmaceutica, waste management, solar energy, diseases, printmaking). We provide a proof-of-concept of the workins conversion with all these six term bases.

3.3. Transformation to linked data

We converted the IATE and CvT TBX terminologies using our Terme-à-LLOD service and expose test instances on a central demonstration server[17] that can be used in combination with other workflows.

As already mentioned, the conversion process is mainly based on the use of the TBX2RDF converter. Several vocabularies, mainly W3C recommendations, have been used during the conversion process, namely OntoLex-lemon, SKOS, RDF-schema, DCAT, VOID, PROV-O, LIDER

TBX Ontology. The TBX fields we consider during the conversion process and the mapping elements selected from aforementioned vocabularies are shown in Table 1. The TBX Resource field is not explicitly represented, as the whole dataset represents the TBX resource. A TBX resource is thus represented as a void:Dataset to which provenance and licensing information can be attached. Furthermore, a langset is not represented as such in the data. Instead, one ontolex:Lexicon is created for each language for which a LangSet is defined. The collection of all the terms for a given language will belong to the corresponding language-specific ontolex:Lexicon. The DescrGrp field contains descriptions of the term or context that are mapped to appropriate properties of the lexical entry or the context. A general overview of the conversion process is available in Table 2. For each termbasis used in the conversion process, we present the runtime needed, the number of terms stored in the termbasis, the number of triples resulting in the output files, and the number of languages we converted. Figure 3 shows an example of TAL final output, namely the exposure of an RDF terminological resource which can be browsed to access more specific information about each term.

3.4. Linking IATE and GENTERM

After the conversion process, we established links among the different termbases tested in the use case by means of Simple Knowledge Organization System (SKOS)[18] concepts. The linking across GENTERM and IATE terminologies has been accomplished matching the corresponding lexical entries in different languages by means of a

---

[15]https://iate.europa.eu/legal-notice

[16]http://www.cvt.ugent.be/downloads.htm

[17]http://scdemo.techfak.uni-bielefeld.de/termeallod/

[18]SKOS is a vocabulary for representing knowledge organization systems (KOS), such as thesauri, classification schemes, subject heading and taxonomies in RDF.

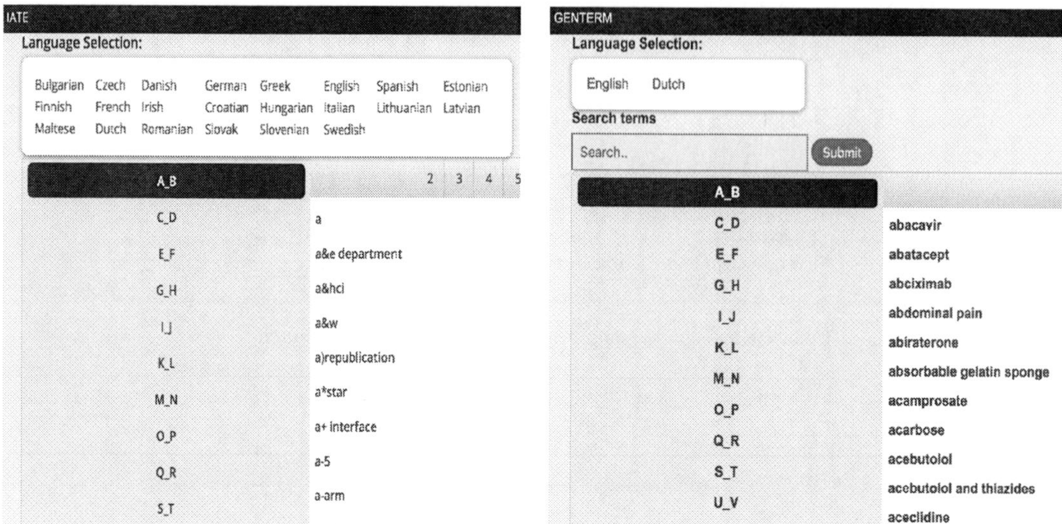

Figure 3: Example of converted terminological resources exposed in TAL service.

string comparison based on `skos:exactMatch`. This match allows linking, for instance, the term *nefopam*, from the Pharmaceutical termbasis in GENTERM, to the corresponding term in IATE, which has an alpha-numeric identifier, i.e., IATE-3545983. Once links among the terminologies have been established, users can explore a term across all the converted and exposed termbases.

Table 3 shows the number of links between GENTERM and IATE. Even though the GENTERM terminology covers different domains in two languages (English and Dutch), the termbases available are very small in comparison to IATE. This explains the low number of links for some of the proposed domains, e.g., GENTERM Solar energy-IATE in Table 3.

4. Integration into language infrastructures

Language infrastructures represent one of the leading areas for the digital economic growth[19], as well as a key element to enable an inclusive Digital Single Market[20]. Several initiatives and projects aim at providing tools supporting interoperability and sharing of existing language technologies and data sets. In order to contribute to the development of common language technologies and support these sharing initiatives, as a proof-of-concept we have developed an approach to integrate our Terme-à-LLOD approach into two language infrastructures, namely Teanga and ELG. Furthermore, such an integration proves the interoperability of our approach which relies on virtualization services.

Teanga is a linked data based platform for natural language processing (NLP) which enables the use of many NLP services from a single interface (Ziad et al., 2018). Many platforms have been developed to improve the interoperability among different NLP services and, consequently, reduce the manual effort required to process data. One of the main issues in these proposals is the need of following specific standards to develop NLP services which interoperate smoothly on the platform. To address this issue, Teanga uses linked data and open, semantic technologies to describe the boundaries between different services in terms of application programming interface (API) descriptors. Given an API endpoint, these descriptors can be used to automatically discover the capabilities of a particular service and specify data types of possible inputs and outputs to the particular NLP service.

ELG is an initiative to establish the primary platform for language technologies (LT) in Europe (Rehm et al., Forthcoming). Its main goal is involving several stakeholders from the language technology sector to create a community which shares technologies and data sets through the platforms, deploys them through the grid and connects them with other resources. ELG addresses some of the recommendations identified in the European Parliament resolution of 11 September 2018 on language equality in the digital age, namely creating a European LT platform for sharing of services and enabling and empowering European SMEs to use LTs.

The grid platform has been built with robust, scalable, reliable, widely used technologies that are constantly developed further. It presents the ability to scale with the growing demand and supply of resources through an interactive modern web interface, providing the base technology for a catalogue or directory of functional services, data sets, tools, technologies, models and LT companies, research organisations, research projects, service and application types, languages. ELG deals with several types of content, that is, services, language resources, data sets, tools and directory content. The TAL service presented in this paper belongs to the type functional content, comprising of containerized services that can be uploaded and integrated into other systems. To support this integration, the

---

[19]https://www.tractica.com/research/natural-language-processing/

[20]https://ec.europa.eu/commission/priorities/digital-single-market_en

Termbases	Lang	Number of Links
GENTERM Pharmaceutical-IATE	English	1380
	Dutch	1084
GENTERM Diseases-IATE	English	22
	Dutch	27
GENTERM Waste management-IATE	English	114
	Dutch	109
GENTERM Solar energy-IATE	English	12
	Dutch	20
GENTERM Printmaking-IATE	English	35
	Dutch	21

Table 3: Results from the linking process.

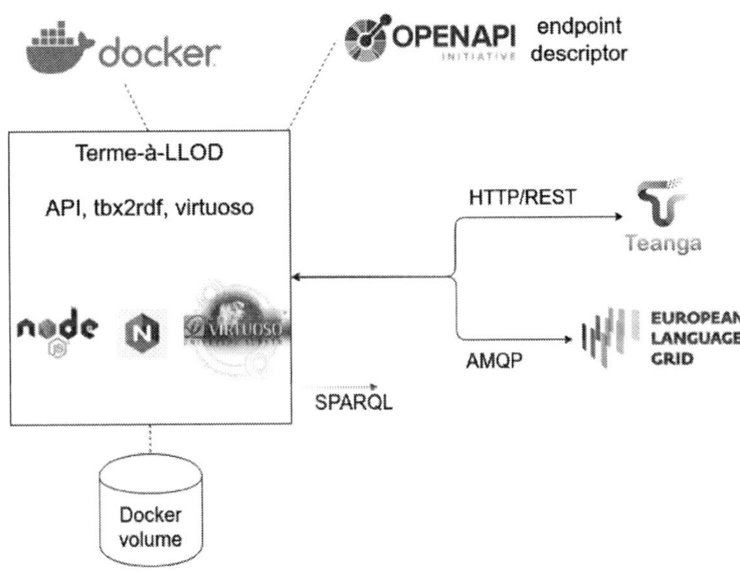

Figure 4: Integration of TAL service into language infrastructures

ELG platform provides an easy and efficient way for LT providers to create and upload containers (Rehm, 2019).

The integration of our TAL service into Teanga and ELG (Figure 4) enables the ecosystem to incorporate data from external terminology glossaries as linked data. Such an integration, based on the development of a docker container, increases the usability of our service, providing a principled way for integrating our service into other applications consuming the terminological data. The ELG cluster and the workflow of Teanga application, namely the integration servers, can query the OpenAPI descriptor in TAL service. When used as a service endpoint, the service automatically connects to a message queue via the AMQP that acts as a service bus for inter-service communication and lets other software consume data.

In recent years, containerization replaced many use cases where the only previous option was full virtualization of a system. Especially in modern, service-based, architectures virtualization often implied many of the same hardships as maintaining a system on bare metal machines, includ-ing operating system maintenance and the ability to scale such a system still being costly and subject to the underlying virtualization infrastructure. By introducing containers, most of these aspects of software deployments are abstracted into purely operational questions and become practically transparent to the developer. The containerization of the TAL service ensures portability across systems by abstracting the underlying hardware following a virtualization approach while at the same time supporting efficient deployment of the application.

5. Related Work

The TermBase eXchange (TBX) format has become an international standard (ISO 30042:2019)[21] for exchange of terminological information. It allows the representation of structured concept-oriented terminological data providing

---

[21]For this documentation we refer to the official documentation available at `https://www.gala-global.org/sites/default/files/uploads/pdfs/tbx_oscar_0.pdf`

an XML-based framework to manage terminology, knowledge and content by means of several processes, such as analysis, descriptive representation, dissemination, and interchange (exchange). OntoLex-Lemon has been proposed early on as a Linked Data format for representing terminological resources (Cimiano et al., 2015). Ontolex-lemon has been applied to the conversion of Terminesp into Linked Data (Bosque-Gil et al., 2015) as well as to the transformation of a set of freely available terminology databases from the Catalan Terminological Centre, TERM-CAT (Montiel-Ponsoda et al., 2015).

Guidelines for converting TBX data to Linked Data have been developed as part of the LIDER project[22]. These guidelines explain how the TBX data model can be mapped to the Ontolex-lemon model and provides a step-by-step example how TBX data can be transformed into RDF following this mapping.

An alternative set of recommendations and guidelines have been developed by the Linked Heritage and Athena projects (Leroi et al., 2011). The document proposes a three-step methodology to digitalize terminologies for publication in the Semantic Web consisting of three three steps: i) conceive your terminology, ii) make your terminology interoperable, iii) link your terminology to a network. As datamodel, the document proposes to use the SKOS model rather than the Ontolex-lemon model.

The approach proposed in this paper has focused on the transformation of terminological resources; yet, the principled approach of simplifying the work of transforming resources into RDF would apply to other data formats as well. There has been some work on transforming lexicographic resources as well as WordNets into Linked Data using lemon-Ontolex (McCrae et al., 2012; Eckle-Kohler et al., 2015; Ehrmann et al., 2014; McCrae et al., 2014). There has been work on transforming corpora into RDF (Chiarcos and Fäth, 2017). The approach described here could be applied to those data formats as well.

We have integrated our transformation component into the Teanga (Ziad et al., 2018) and ELG (Rehm et al., Forthcoming) infrastructrues. There are other NLP architecures into which TAL container could be integtated.

WebLicht[23] is an environment for building, executing, and visualizing the results of NLP pipelines, which is integrated into the CLARIN infrastructure (Hinrichs and Krauwer, 2014). NLP tools are implemented as web services that consume and produce the Text Corpus Format (TCF)[24], an XML format designed for use as an internal data exchange format for WebLicht processing tools. It ensures semantic interoperability among all WebLicht tools and resources by defining a common vocabulary for linguistic concepts in TCF schema. The services and resources are developed as web services in the CLARIN framework. The services are exposed using metadata descriptions Component Metadata

Infrastructure (CMDI) [25]. CMDI describes functionalities offered by a service, pre and postconditions, and specifications of data that is consumed and produced by service.

The Language Application (LAPPS)[26] (Ide et al., 2014) Grid is a framework that provides access to NLP processing tools and resources and enables pipelining these tools to create custom NLP applications, as well as access to language resources such as mono- and multilingual corpora and lexicons that support NLP. The semantic interoperability of language services is achieved by the Web Services Exchange Vocabulary (Ide et al., 2016), which specifies terminology for a core of linguistic objects and features exchanged by services. Recently, the services are deployed in the cloud using Docker images. While we have integrated our TAL service into ELG and Teanga as a proof-of-concept, it could also be integrated into the WebLicht enviroment as well as LAPPS Grid following the same principles.

6. Conclusion

We have proposed a virtualization approach to support the conversion and hosting of terminologies as linked data. The approach can in principle be applied to any language and lexical resource beyond terminologies using the same principles.

We have demonstrated the applicability of our approach via the conversion into RDF and hosting as linked data of six terminologies in total: the well-known IATE termbase and five smaller termbases hosted by Ghent University. A public Docker container has been implemented and is free available for everyone wanting to convert and host their terminologies. We have described the integration of our approach into state-of-art language infrastructures, namely Teanga and ELG.

Within the European project Prêt-à-LLOD[27], which focuses on making linguistic data ready to use by the use of state-of-the-art technologies, in particular linked data, a further integration of this service is currently planned. Prêt-à-LLOD aims at creating a new methodology for building data value chains applicable to a wide-range of sectors and applications and based around language resources and language technologies that can be integrated by means of semantic technologies. The Terme-à-LLOD approach proposed here follows the aims of the EC-funded Prêt-à-LLOD project of providing *Linked-data based NLP services as data* so that they are sustainable and can be readily used and deployed by third parties. In future work we will enhance the architecture and implementation of the TAL service towards supporting linking any other linked data compliant terminology to the one hosted by TAL.

7. Acknowledgements

This work has been funded by project Prêt-à-LLOD which is funded under European Union's Horizon 2020 research and innovation programme under grant agreement No. 825182.

---

[22]https://www.w3.org/2015/09/
bpmlod-reports/multilingual-terminologies/

[23]https://weblicht.sfs.uni-tuebingen.de/
weblichtwiki/index.php/Main_Page

[24]https://weblicht.sfs.uni-tuebingen.de/
weblichtwiki/index.php/The_TCF_Format

[25]https://www.clarin.eu/content/
component-metadata

[26]http://www.lappsgrid.org/

[27]https://www.pret-a-llod.eu

8. Bibliographical References

Bosque-Gil, J., Gracia, J., Aguado-de Cea, G., and Montiel-Ponsoda, E. (2015). Applying the ontolex model to a multilingual terminological resource. In Fabien Gandon, et al., editors, *The Semantic Web: ESWC 2015 Satellite Events*, pages 283–294, Cham. Springer International Publishing.

Chiarcos, C. and Fäth, C. (2017). CoNLL-RDF: Linked corpora done in an nlp-friendly way. In *Language, Data, and Knowledge - First International Conference, LDK 2017, Galway, Ireland, June 19-20, 2017, Proceedings*, pages 74–88.

Chiarcos, C., McCrae, J., Cimiano, P., and Fellbaum, C. (2013). Towards open data for linguistics: Linguistic linked data. In *New Trends of Research in Ontologies and Lexical Resources*, pages 7–25. Springer.

Cimiano, P., McCrae, J. P., Rodríguez-Doncel, V., Gornostay, T., Gómez-Pérez, A., Siemoneit, B., and Lagzdins, A. (2015). Linked terminologies: applying linked data principles to terminological resources. In *Proceedings of the eLex 2015 Conference*, pages 504–517.

Eckle-Kohler, J., McCrae, J. P., and Chiarcos, C. (2015). lemonuby - A large, interlinked, syntactically-rich lexical resource for ontologies. *Semantic Web*, 6(4):371–378.

Ehrmann, M., Cecconi, F., Vannella, D., McCrae, J. P., Cimiano, P., and Navigli, R. (2014). Representing multilingual data as linked data: the case of babelnet 2.0. In *Proceedings of the Ninth International Conference on Language Resources and Evaluation (LREC)*, pages 401–408.

Erling, O. and Mikhailov, I. (2010). Virtuoso: RDF support in a native RDBMS. In *Semantic Web Information Management*, pages 501–519. Springer.

Erling, O. (2012). Virtuoso, a hybrid rdbms/graph column store. *IEEE Data Eng. Bull.*, 35(1):3–8.

Hinrichs, E. and Krauwer, S. (2014). The CLARIN research infrastructure: Resources and tools for ehumanities scholars. In *Proceedings of the Ninth International Conference on Language Resources and Evaluation (LREC 2014)*, Reykjavik, Iceland, may. European Language Resources Association (ELRA).

Ide, N., Pustejovsky, J., Cieri, C., Nyberg, E., Wang, D., Suderman, K., Verhagen, M., and Wright, J. (2014). The language applications grid. In *Proceedings of the Ninth International Conference on Language Resources and Evaluation (LREC 2014)*, Reykjavik, Iceland, may. European Language Resources Association (ELRA).

Ide, N., Suderman, K., Verhagen, M., and Pustejovsky, J. (2016). The language applications grid web service exchange vocabulary. In *Revised Selected Papers of the Second International Workshop on Worldwide Language Service Infrastructure WLSI (2015)*, pages 18–32, Kyoto, Japan. Springer-Verlag New York, Inc.

). iate.

Leroi, M.-V., Holland, J., and Cagnot, S. (2011). *Your terminology as a part of the semantic web recommendations for design and management*. Repro Stampa Ind. Grafica, Villa Adriana Tivoli.

McCrae, J., Spohr, D., and Cimiano, P. (2011). Linking lexical resources and ontologies on the semantic web with lemon. In *Extended Semantic Web Conference*, pages 245–259. Springer.

McCrae, J., Montiel-Ponsoda, E., and Cimiano, P. (2012). Integrating wordnet and wiktionary with lemon. In *Linked Data in Linguistics*, pages 25–34. Springer.

McCrae, J., Fellbaum, C., and Cimiano, P. (2014). Publishing and linking wordnet using lemon and RDF. In *Proceedings of the 3rd Workshop on Linked Data in Linguistics*.

McCrae, J. P., Cimiano, P., and Doncel, V. R. (2015). Guidelines for linguistic linked data generation: Multilingual terminologies (tbx). *https://www.w3.org/2015/09/bpmlod-reports/multilingual-terminologies/*.

Montiel-Ponsoda, E., Bosque-Gil, J., Gracia, J., de Cea, G. A., and Vila-Suero, D. (2015). Towards the integration of multilingual terminologies: an example of a linked data prototype. In *Proceedings of the conference Terminology and Artificial Intelligence (TAI)*, pages 205–206.

Rehm, G., Berger, M., Elsholz, E., Hegele, S., Kintzel, F., Marheinecke, K., Piperidis, S., Deligiannis, M., Galanis, D., Gkirtzou, K., Labropoulou, P., Bontcheva, K., Jones, D., Roberts, I., Hajic, J., Hamrlova, J., Kacena, L., Choukri, K., Arranz, V., Mapelli, V., Vasiļjevs, A., Anvari, O., Lagzdiņš, A., Meļņika, J., Backfried, G., Dikici, E., Janosik, M., Prinz, K., Prinz, C., Stampler, S., Thomas-Aniola, D., Gomez Perez, J. M., Silva, A. G., Berrio, C., Germann, U., Renals, S., and Klejch, O. (Forthcoming). European language grid: An overview. In *Submitted to LREC 2020*.

Rehm, G. (2019). European language grid: An overview. In *META FORUM, Brussels, Belgium* `https://www.european-language-grid.eu/wp-content/uploads/2019/10/00-03-ELG-Overview-Georg-Rehm.pdf`.

Rodriguez-Doncel, V., Santos, C., Casanovas, P., Gómez-Pérez, A., and Gracia, J. (2015). A linked data terminology for copyright based on ontolex-lemon. In *AI Approaches to the Complexity of Legal Systems*, pages 410–423. Springer.

Stanković, R., Obradović, I., and Utvić, M. (2014). Developing termbases for expert terminology under the tbx standard. *Editors Gordana Pavlović Lažetić Duško Vitas Cvetana Krstev*.

Witschel, H. F. (2005). Terminology extraction and automatic indexing. *Terminology and Content Development*, page 363.

Ziad, H., McCrae, J. P., and Buitelaar, P. (2018). Teanga: A linked data based platform for natural language processing. In *Proceedings of the Eleventh International Conference on Language Resources and Evaluation (LREC 2018)*.

Proceedings of the 7th Workshop on Linked Data in Linguistics (LDL-2020), pages 36–44
Language Resources and Evaluation Conference (LREC 2020), Marseille, 11–16 May 2020

Annohub – Annotation Metadata for Linked Data Applications

Frank Abromeit, Christian Fäth, Luis Glaser

Applied Computational Linguistics Lab, Goethe University Frankfurt, Germany
{abromeit,faeth}@em.uni-frankfurt.de, lglaser@informatik.uni-frankfurt.de

Abstract

We introduce a new dataset for the Linguistic Linked Open Data (LLOD) cloud that will provide metadata about annotation and language information harvested from annotated language resources like corpora freely available on the internet. To our knowledge annotation metadata is not provided by any metadata provider, e.g. linghub, datahub or CLARIN so far. On the other hand, language metadata that is found on such portals is rarely provided in machine-readable form, especially as Linked Data. In this paper, we describe the harvesting process, content and structure of the new dataset and its application in the Lin|gu|is|tik portal, a research platform for linguists. Aside from that, we introduce tools for the conversion of XML encoded language resources to the CoNLL format. The generated RDF data as well as the XML-converter application are made public under an open license.

Keywords: LLOD, OLiA, CoNLL, Tiger-XML

1. Motivation

Over the past decade, an ever growing amount of linguistic resources has become available on the web under an open license. The Linguistic Linked Open Data (LLOD) cloud[1] currently encompasses not only annotated corpora and dictionaries, but also terminological repositories, ontologies and knowledge bases. However, despite the efforts of improving interoperability and interconnection of resources by using semantic web vocabularies and technologies, many resources are still heterogeneously annotated and intransparently labeled with regard to their compatibility. This problem is by no means limited to LLOD but applies to machine readable language resources in general. Metadata repositories like META-SHARE[2], CLARIN centers[3] or DataHub[4] lack information about applicable annotation schemes. As for language metadata, language encoding standards vary across different metadata providers[5], and in addition metadata is not always provided as linked data.

With *Annohub* (annotation hub) we tackle this deficit by creating a collection of languages and annotation schemes used in existing language resources, and thus aim to augment existing metadata repositories. Annohub therefore utilizes classification schemes supported by and linked to the thesaurus of the Bibliography of Linguistic Literature (BLL).[6] This encompasses the Ontologies of Linguistic Annotation (OLiA) (Chiarcos and Sukhreva, 2015) and its respective Linking Models for compatibility with a large amount of linguistic annotation schemes (Dimitrova et al., 2016), and also Glottolog (Nordhoff and Hammarström, 2011) and lexvo (de Melo, 2015) as supported language identifiers (Dimitrova et al., 2018).

In previous work (Abromeit and Chiarcos, 2019) we focused on the analysis of language resources available in tab-separated column formats, a de-facto standard for annotated corpora as popularized as part of the CoNLL Shared Tasks. In the paper we describe the extension of our analysis to text resources encoded in RDF and XML formats thereby introducing tools that can be used for transforming XML language resources into the CoNLL format.

Finally, we discuss how the harvested metadata is integrated into the Lin|gu|is|tik portal (Chiarcos et al., 2016), a research platform for linguists funded by the DFG project *Fachinformationsdienst Linguistik* (FID) and hosted at the University Library Frankfurt. A special focus is put on our continued efforts on mapping BLL language identifiers to Glottolog and lexvo. Both, the Annohub RDF dump and the BLL linking models are available at `https://www.linguistik.de/de/lod/`. The XML-CoNLL converter application can be found at `https://github.com/acoli-repo/xml2conll`.

2. Finding annotated language resources

Our premier source of metadata for existing language resources is the linghub RDF dump[7] that contains over 200,000 linguistic resources. Additionally we query various CLARIN centers[8] via the OAI protocol[9], but also manually collect metadata from providers such as `http://opus.nlpl.eu/` and others. All harvested resource metadata is stored in a database which is used to keep track of already processed resources. Of course, duplicate entries are a problem especially when a resource is available at different locations. We did not tackle this problem in detail yet. It is planned, however, to subsequently integrate new metadata entries, that we discovered, into the linghub portal.

2.1. Document classification

On the basis of the collected metadata, we identify language resources which could contain annotated text, such as corpora, lexica and also linguistic metadata as found in

---

[1]The LLOD cloud (`http://linguistic-lod.org`) is an integral part of the general Linked Open Data cloud under `https://www.lod-cloud.net`

[2]`http://www.meta-share.eu` and `http://www.meta-net.eu`

[3]`https://www.clarin.eu/`

[4]`https://datahub.io`

[5]e.g. different ISO639 encodings, lexvo URLs or even plain text language descriptors

[6]`https://data.linguistik.de/bll/index.html`

[7]`http://linghub.org/download`

[8]`https://centres.clarin.eu/restxml/`

[9]`https://www.openarchives.org/OAI/openarchivesprotocol.html`

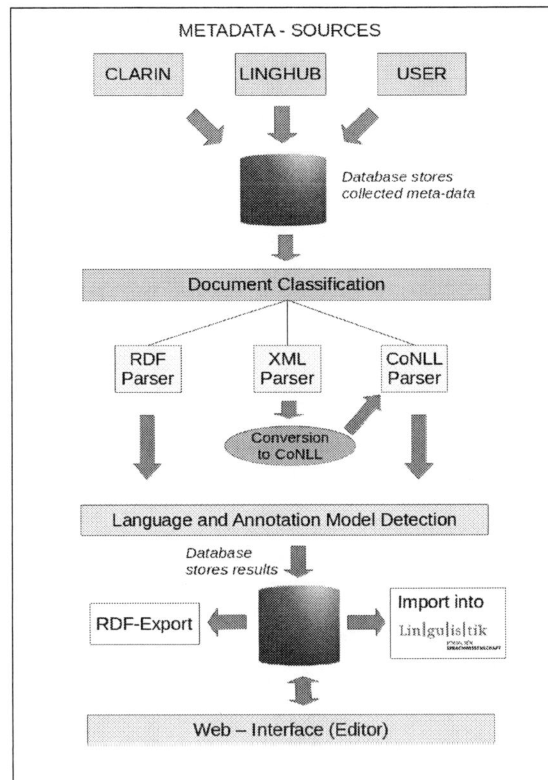

Figure 1: Annohub architecture

ontologies. For the identification of relevant files we rely on standard techniques for content type detection like (html/mime) type, file extensions and also employ the Apache Tika content analysis toolkit[10]. A considerable amount of linguistic resources is provided in archive formats[11]. Archives can include large numbers of files and we observed archives with up to 100,000 files. Since processing all files in such cases would take too long, we sample at maximum 100 files (depending on the file type) for the subsequent analysis. Currently, we support RDF, CoNLL[12] [13], CoNLL-RDF (Chiarcos and Fäth, 2017) and XML type documents with certain limitations (see chapter 6.1.)

2.2. Document processing

Linghub resources are automatically processed by first querying the linghub RDF dump via SPARQL and then feeding RDF, CONLL, XML and archive resource types into the Annohub NLP pipeline (see fig. 1). Since the automatic processing of language resources listed in CLARIN centers is not implemented yet, we currently only use the CLARIN resource metadata (e.g. author, title, etc.), that we harvest via the OAI protocol to augment manually found language resources. These can be processed by means of

the Annohub web application with the respective *download URL* or by csv file import. Additionally, processing can be triggered from the command-line interface.

3. Extraction of annotation information

We are mainly dealing with annotations from the field of syntax and morphology. Word annotations (e.g. part-of-speech tags) usually take the form of string tokens, which have been assigned to a word either automatically by a tool, or manually by a researcher. Alternatively, ontology classes (e.g. `http://www.lexinfo.net/ontology/2.0/lexinfo#adverb`) typically found in RDF corpora are used to annotate words. Feature annotations (e.g. *number*), as found in CoNLL data [14], involve a feature name and a feature value (e.g. Number=Plur). Finally, dependency information about the syntactic relation between words[15] in a sentence is relevant to us. In order to extract annotations from texts, specific parsers for CoNLL, XML and RDF data have been developed.

3.1. CoNLL annotation extraction

A CoNLL file has dedicated columns for e.g. part-of-speech, morphological features and dependency information. However, since CoNLL is a format family with distinct dialects mostly originating from specific CoNLL shared tasks, the number of columns and also the ordering of columns in a CoNLL file is not standardized. Therefore, first the columns storing POS-tag, feature and dependency information have to be determined. For each such column the set of occurring tags is fed into our model detection component (see fig. 1).

3.2. XML annotation extraction

In a preprocessing step we convert XML files to the CoNLL format (see chapter 6.). Thus, the extraction process is the same as for CoNLL files.

3.3. RDF annotation extraction

Extracting linguistic annotations from RDF language resources is a more complex task since such resources often contain multiple types of annotations at the same time, for example for syntax, semantics and pragmatics. Another problem is that, although RDF vocabularies like Lexinfo[16], NIF[17] or OntoLex-Lemon[18] exist which have been specifically designed to model syntax and morphology, researchers sometimes use their own proprietary RDF vocabularies.

One way to implement the extraction process would be to get the object values for selected RDF predicates typically

---

[10]`https://tika.apache.org/`

[11]gzip,zip,tar,rar to name a few

[12]`https://universaldependencies.org/format.html`

[13]CoNLL-U, CoNLL-X and other TSV formats

[14]`https://universaldependencies.org/u/feat/index.html`

[15]`https://universaldependencies.org/u/dep/index.html`

[16]`https://www.lexinfo.net/ontology/2.0/lexinfo.owl`

[17]`https://persistence.uni-leipzig.org/nlp2rdf/ontologies/nif-core/nif-core.html`

[18]`https://www.w3.org/2016/05/ontolex`

used for annotating (e.g. `http://www.lexinfo.net/ontology/2.0/lexinfo#partOfSpeech`) via SPARQL queries[19] from an RDF file. However, in this approach the list of RDF predicates known to the algorithm would limit the results. To avoid this limitation we approach the extraction problem in a more generic way by sampling object values from the set of *all* RDF predicates that occur in an RDF file, (see algorithm 1) and comparing them with the list of annotations defined in the OLiA[20] ontologies (Chiarcos and Sukhreva, 2015). The OLiA ontologies provide a formalized, machine-readable view on linguistic annotations for more than 75 different language varieties. They cover morphology, morphosyntax, phrase structure syntax, dependency syntax, aspects of semantics, and recent extensions to discourse, information structure and anaphora, all of these are linked with an overarching reference terminology module. Furthermore OLiA includes several multi-lingual or cross-linguistically applicable annotation models such as the Universal Dependencies (77 languages), EAGLES (11 European languages) and Multext-East (16 Eastern European and Near Eastern languages).

Algorithm 1 *RDF annotation detection*

1: **Input** : The set of all different RDF predicates in a file
2: **For** each RDF predicate *p* :
3:     Take a sample of *n* object values *o* from triples
    (s p o)
4:     **If** *o* is of type *literal* :
5:         Try to match *o* against the set of known
        annotation tags (in OLiA linking models)
6:     **Else** :
7:         Try to match *o* against the set of known
        annotation classes (in OLiA annotation models)
8: **Repeat** the algorithm with the set of predicates with values that could be matched to tags or classes in OLiA as *input* and omit in the second pass step 3 in order to retrieve all annotation matchings.

---

4. Annohub dataset

The RDF data model for Annohub is depicted in fig. 2. For modeling language resources, we utilize commonly used RDF vocabularies including DCAT[21], Dublin Core [22], DCMI Metadata Terms[23] and PROV[24]. Each language resource is modeled as a DCAT dataset. It includes general resource information like title, author, etc. that we harvest automatically from the metadata providers linghub[25] and CLARIN[26]. The metadata for language resources that were collected manually was taken from the websites of the resource providers. Each annotated text file that comes with

a resource is represented as a separate dataset. It contains general information like file type, file size, etc. The analysis results of each file comprise the detected languages and identified annotations from the field of syntax and morphology. By application of the Ontologies of Linguistic Annotations (OLiA) it is also possible to detect the annotation schemes (tag sets) that were used.

4.1. Annotation model analysis

The annotation model analysis is similar for all processed document types. It is exemplarily described here for CoNLL files.

Annotation model analysis for CoNLL files A CoNLL file has dedicated columns for part-of-speech, morphological features and dependency information. Generally, for each of these, a specific annotation model is used. By definition, a CoNLL column can contain annotations only from a single annotation model. A CoNLL file dataset therefore may link to several *annohub:AnnotationScheme* instances, but only to one for each column.

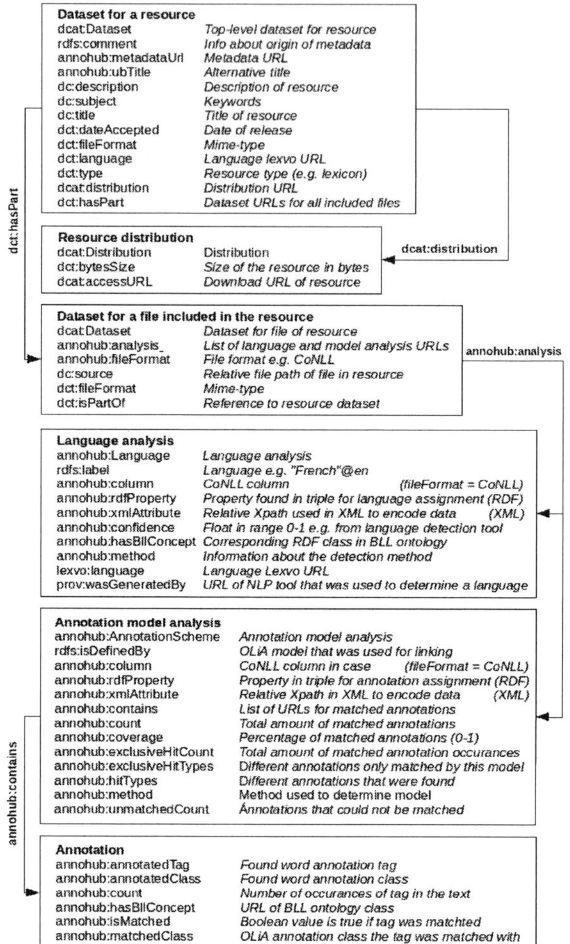

Figure 2: Annohub RDF data model

---

[19] `https://www.w3.org/TR/sparql11-overview/`
[20] `http://purl.org/olia`
[21] `https://www.w3.org/TR/vocab-dcat/`
[22] `http://purl.org/dc/elements/1.1/`
[23] `http://purl.org/dc/terms/`
[24] `http://www.w3.org/ns/prov#`
[25] `http://linghub.org/`
[26] `https://centres.clarin.eu/restxml/`

CoNLL model analysis results In the property *annohub:column* the considered column of a file is marked. The information of what annotation scheme (e.g. Universal-Dependencies-part-of-speech[27]) has been detected in a column is included with the *annohub:isDefinedBy* property. Its value is a URL that points to an OLiA linking model[28] (e.g. `http://purl.org/olia/ud-pos-link.rdf`). This provides a mapping of all identified tags to annotation classes in the OLiA ontology. Part-of-speech annotations are highly ambiguous across different annotation models. For example *DT* is equally used in 6 different annotation models[29] to declare a word as *Determiner*. The algorithm used to determine a best fitting annotation scheme is fully described in (Abromeit and Chiarcos, 2019) chapter 3 (*Automated detection of annotation models*). It is also used for RDF document types. The results of this algorithm comprise several statistical parameters that can be used to assess the quality of the model analysis results which are provided in the *annohub:annotationScheme* class, and are described as follows. This statistical data is also available in the Annohub editor application and is helpful for the verification of the detected annotation schemes. A detailed description of the editor application is also presented in the above mentioned publication.

- *annohub:exclusiveHitTypes* is the number of different tags that could be matched only by that model

- *annohub:hitTypes* is the number of different tags that could be matched

- *annohub:unmatchedTags* is the number of unmatched tags

- *annohub:coverage* is the value of matched/unmatched tags which is a float value (0-1)

- *annohub:count* is the total number of occurrences of matched tags

- *annohub:exclusiveHitCount* is the number of occurrences of matched tags (but only for *exclusiveHitTypes*)

Furthermore the property *annohub:method* stores information on how the model assignment was achieved. It is *AN-NOMODEL* by default and *SELECTION* if it was changed manually by means of the Annohub editor.

All properties but *annohub:column* also apply to the model analysis for **RDF** and **XML** files. For these file types instead *annohub:rdfProperty* and *annohub:xmlAttribute* are used to specify the location where an annotation was found. Detailed information about each matched tag (or annotation URL, as found in RDF files) and its counterpart in OLiA is stored in instances of *annohub:Annotation* by using *annohub:annotatedTag*, *annohub:annotatedClass* or *annohub:matchedClass*. Finally *annohub:hasBllConcept* provides a link to a class in the BLL ontology that is related to a word's annotation (see chapter 5.).

4.2. Language analysis

The language analysis is different for each of the examined data formats.

4.2.1. Language analysis for RDF files

In RDF files there are several sources for language information. First language tagged literals can provide an ISO-639-1 (2-letter) code. Secondly language information can be encoded with specific RDF predicates where the language info is a URL (e.g. `http://lexvo.org/id/iso639-3/nld`) or a literal value that contains a ISO language code. We employ standard RDF predicates that are widely used to encode language information taken from the Dublin Core, OntoLex-Lemon and lexvo ontologies[30] and discard cases where the language info is encoded as plain text (e.g. *English, Old (ca. 450-1100)*). The extracted language information is finally normalized to a ISO639-3 representation.

RDF language analysis results All detected languages are encoded as lexvo-URL[31] with the property *lexvo:language*. Additionally the full (english) language name taken from the ISO639-3 code table [32] is provided in *rdfs:label*. In the property *annohub:confidence* a probability for a detected language is stored. Because the language info in RDF files is explicitly given as URL or ISO code its value is 1.0. The property *annohub:method* stores where the language info originates from. It's a string constant which is *LANGTAG* for tagged literals and *LANGPROP* for languages that were encoded with a RDF property. The value of *annohub:rdfProperty* is simply *p* in the RDF triple (s p o) where o stores language information. That property can also be used to determine the type of a resource (e.g. `http://www.w3.org/ns/lemon/lime#language`) indicates a document of type lexicon. Finally *annohub:hasBllConcept* links to a class in the BLL ontology[33] that relates to a language (see also chapter 5.).

4.2.2. Language analysis for CoNLL files

In previous work (Abromeit and Chiarcos, 2019) we performed a quantitative analysis of the language detection procedure for the CoNLL format. For the language detection we use the *Optimaize*[34] n-gram based language classification tool. As input we choose a fixed number of k[35]

---

[27]`https://universaldependencies.org/u/pos/index.html`

[28]as documented at `http://purl.org/olia`

[29]e.g. `http://purl.org/olia/brown.owl#DT` as well as for the GENIA, QTag, Mamba and Penn Treebank annotation schemes

[30]11 properties taken from the Dublin Core, OntoLex-Lemon and lexvo ontologies, e.g. `http://purl.org/dc/terms/language`, `http://www.w3.org/ns/lemon/lime#language`, `http://lexvo.org/ontology#iso639P3PCode`)

[31]`http://lexvo.org/ontology`

[32]`https://iso639-3.sil.org/code_tables/download_tables`

[33]`https://data.linguistik.de`

[34]`https://github.com/optimaize/language-detector`

[35]We choose k=15 for scalability reasons. Increasing k might improve results but has not been tested

sample sentences from the WORD (LEMMA) column in a CoNLL file. Then we run the language classification on each sentence and select the language as winner Lw which was detected for the majority of sentences. The probability Lp for a language is then

$$\frac{\#sample\ sentences\ where\ Lw\ was\ detected}{\#sample\ sentences}$$

In situations where no majority winner was found one of the best languages is randomly selected. For a discussion on misclassification errors we refer to the mentioned evaluation paper above.

CoNLL language analysis results The detected WORD (LEMMA) columns of a CoNLL file are stored with the *annhub:column* property. Languages are encoded in the same manner as for RDF files where the language probability Lp is saved in *annohub:confidence* as a float value in the range [0-1] and *annohub:method* describes how the language was determined. Its value is either *LANGPROFILE* in case the *Optimaize* tool provided the result or *SELECTION* if it was assigned manually by means of the Annohub editor. In order to allow other language detection tools the detection tool info is provided with *prov:wasGeneratedBy* which is in this case the URL of the *Optimaize* language-detector library. Finally *annohub:hasBllConcept* stores a URL which is a class from the BLL ontology[36] that is related to a language (see chapter 5. for more details).

4.2.3. Language analysis for XML files

Since XML files are converted to CoNLL files before processing the only difference to the CoNLL language analysis is in the *annohub:xmlAttribute* property. It stores a relative XPath that describes the location of the word/lemma information in an XML document.

5. Integration of Annohub and the Lin|gu|is|tik portal

After harvesting linguistic resources of heterogeneous sources and formats and extracting their annotations and language information, an additional linking step is performed to make them not only available through Annohub but also searchable and browsable within the Lin|gu|is|tik portal. This process is relying on ontological links between BLL index terms and other repositories for linguistic classifications, i.e. OLiA (Chiarcos and Sukhreva, 2015), Glottolog (Nordhoff and Hammarström, 2011) and lexvo (de Melo, 2015). In this chapter we give a brief overview on how these links are established.

5.1. Linking of linguistic annotations

In earlier efforts of the DFG-funded series of projects (Chiarcos et al., 2016) we had created a linking of the BLL-Thesaurus with OLiA for linguistic terminology, mostly on the field of syntax and morphosyntax. For this purpose the BLL thesaurus had been transformed to RDF in a two-step

process. While the original thesaurus hierarchy is automatically exported in SKOS format on a regular basis, the BLL ontology is manually assessed and updated in order to improve usability and interoperability in the context of LLOD. Within the ontology, BLL index terms are rendered as OWL classes and then linked to OLiA classes through subclass relations.

5.2. Linking of language identifiers

Recently, the scope of BLL ontology has been extended to include the index terms for language identifiers and a linking to both Glottolog and lexvo. Our last release only included the language identifiers subsumed under the ontological class `Indo-European language identifiers` of which approximately 60% could be linked to at least one LLOD repository (Dimitrova et al., 2018). For the current version we also include terminology from non-Indo-European languages.

Family	both	lexvo	Glottolog	none	Total
Indo-Eur.	236	104	7	298	645
Other	1329	416	32	187	1964
Total	1565	520	39	485	2609

Table 1: Linking of Language Identifiers

Table 1 shows the current status of the linking which is, however, an ongoing effort and thus subject to change. While the status of the language identifiers in the Indo-European family is consistent with the last release, the non-Indo-European branch adds almost 2000 new classes of which approximately 90% are linked to at least Glottolog or lexvo. The higher coverage of links within this branch of the thesaurus stems from the BLL's focus on European languages. While the terminology on the Indo-European branch is more granularly organized and comprises a comprehensive set of dialects, language families and historical terms, the non-Indo-European branch mostly contains well-established identifiers for actual languages which have a one-to-one correspondence in other repositories.

Both the revised version of the BLL ontology and the language linking are available under `https://www.linguistik.de/de/lod/`.

6. Support for XML language resources

The XML formalism has been widely used for the representation of linguistic resources. This is partly due to the fact that NLP tools use this format for input and output. Also, popular formats like TEI[37] are built on it. Today, a substantial part of available corpora data is still only available in XML formats[38] although new Linked Open Data formats have been introduced. We have built tools that can be used to convert corpus data from XML to the CoNLL[39] format that is widely used in the community. Furthermore, for the

---

[36]`https://data.linguistik.de`

[37]`https://github.com/TEIC/TEI`

[38]Examples are `http://opus.nlpl.eu/` and `https://spraakbanken.gu.se/`

[39]`https://universaldependencies.org/format.html`

CoNLL format, tools for the conversion into the RDF format are available[40].

6.1. Supported XML formats for CoNLL conversion

Stand-off annotation XML formats have annotations stored in separate files from the text data (e.g. ATLAS (Bird and Liberman, 2001), PAULA XML (Dipper, 2005) or GrAF (Ide and Suderman, 2007). We do not support these formats at the moment because this would involve a reconstruction of the data. Moreover we focus on XML resources that include annotations and the raw text data together within a single file like Tiger-XML (W. Lezius and Gerstenberger, 2002) does. In Tiger XML[41] a graph element contains a list of terminal nodes that represent the words of a sentence. Each terminal element has word information like reference_id, part-of-speech, morphological features, word and lemma. However, there is no defined standard with respect to the naming of XML elements and attributes. In practice, a class of XML documents can be identified that shares the encoding formalism of Tiger-XML. For parsing the XML several issues have to taken into account :

1. XML documents can include optional elements that store text structure information like chapter, paragraph, chunk

2. All names of XML elements and attributes are user-defined

3. All attributes of a terminal element (e.g. lemma, POS, etc.) are optional

Instead of writing a specific XML parser for each document class we developed a template-based method that uses a description of a documents XML structure. This description (*template*) is then used by our XML parser application to extract the annotated content.

6.2. Template based XML-CoNLL conversion

With the template-based conversion we are able to perform a lossless transformation from the XML to the CoNLL format. It can be applied, if the following requirements are met:

1. The XML represents the concept of a sentence

2. The XML represents the concept of a word/token

3. All word level annotations are represented as descendants of the word node

4. The name of the annotations are given as attribute names / the annotations are not reified.

Intuitively, one writes a set of rules (template) in a JSON file that is used as input together with an XML file to generate CoNLL from it. A template provides a mapping from the data found at a (relative) XPath in the XML

---

[40]https://github.com/acoli-repo/conll-rdf
[41]http://www.coli.uni-saarland.de/
projects/salsa/salto/doc/html/node55.html


```
<?xml version="1.0" encoding="utf-8"?>
<document>

<CHAPTER ID="1"><P id="1">
<s id="1">
 <w tree="NC" lem="aprobación" id="w1.1">Aprobación</w>
 <w tree="PDEL" lem="del" id="w1.2">del</w>
 <w tree="NC" lem="acta" id="w1.3">Acta</w>
 <w tree="PREP" lem="de" id="w1.4">de</w>
 <w tree="ART" lem="el" id="w1.5">la</w>
 <w tree="NC" lem="sesión" id="w1.6">sesión</w>
 <w tree="ADJ" lem="anterior" id="w1.7">anterior</w>
</s></P><SPEAKER ID="1" NAME="La Presidenta"><P id="2">
<s id="2">
 <w tree="ART" lem="el" id="w2.1">El</w>
 <w tree="NC" lem="acta" id="w2.2">Acta</w>
 <w tree="PREP" lem="de" id="w2.3">de</w>
...
```

Figure 3: Example XML file

---

document to a CoNLL column where this data should be placed. In addition to this column mapping, a template specifies the word nodes and the sentence boundaries in the XML format. This has two consequences: firstly, the resulting CoNLL will have a valid separation of sentences with a newline. Secondly, the sentence boundaries allow the XML to be streamed sequentially. Thus arbitrary XML file sizes can be read, because a XML-DOM tree is only created for each sentence and not the entire document.

Specification of a template A template definition contains the following information:

1. `id`: An arbitrary identifier for the template. It is used for the template matching algorithm

2. `sentencePath`: The name of the XML nodes that contain a single sentence as their subtree

3. `wordPath`: XPath expression that will return a list of nodes. Each column row will represent data relative to a single node in that list

4. `columnPaths`: XPath expressions relative to a single node contained in the list specified in 3. Each of these XPath expressions is assigned to a specific column in the resulting CoNLL

5. `description`: Provide a description of this template, e.g. what corpus family this template was tailored to. Useful for debugging. (optional)

6. `featurePaths`: Identical to 4 in structure. Resulting values will be conflated into a single column with the `key1=value1|key2=value2` style CoNLL-U uses for morphosyntactic features. (optional)

Template matching algorithm In our processing workflow (fig.1) documents which have been classified as XML documents are fed into our processing pipeline. However at this point it is not clear if an XML document contains any useful linguistic content. In order to rule out useless content we check the document's XML structure against a set of given XML-conversion template definitions. Algorithm 2 computes a score that is then used to decide which XML

```
0        w1.1       aprobación          Aprobación
1        w1.2       del          del
2        w1.3       acta          Acta
3        w1.4       de          de
4        w1.5       el          la
5        w1.6       sesión          sesión
6        w1.7       anterior          anterior

0        w2.1       el          El
1        w2.2       acta          Acta
2        w2.3       de          de
...
```

Figure 4: Resulting CoNLL for XML depicted in fig. 3

```
{
  "id" : "8",
  "sentencePath" : "s",
  "wordPath" : "//w",
  "columnPaths" : {
    "id" : "@id",
      "lem" : "@lem",
        "token" : "text()"
  }
}
```

Figure 5: Template for XML in fig. 3 to produce CoNLL in fig. 4

documents will be passed to the next processing stage (Language and Annotation Model detection). We define the *best fitting template* for a given XML file as the template with the highest recall score.

Algorithm 2 *Template XML-CoNLL conversion*

1: **For** each sample sentence **s**:
2:     Create the DOM tree **d** for **s**
3:     **For** each conversion template **t**:
4:         Compare all attribute names found in **d** with the attribute names specified in the `columnPaths` field of **t**
5:         Calculate recall, precision and accuracy for **t**
6: Sort all templates **t** in descending order by recall, precision, accuracy
7: Output the top-most template as best matching template

Limitations   The rule-based approach requires human input and is limited to the set of available templates. So it cannot identify documents with an unknown XML structure. It is highly accurate and the best solution if a language resource needs to be converted that has many XML documents that all share the same structure. It also can produce acceptable results if the best matching template is not a perfect match. Finally, we only support XML dialects that do not reify their annotations: E.g. encoding the first lemma in fig. 3 as <w annotation="lem" value="aprobación"> would break the algorithm.

6.3.   Generic XML-CoNLL conversion

In the following, we describe a algorithm that solves some of the problems of the template approach. It is well suited to a scenario were a stream of XML documents enters our analysis pipeline where

- the structure of XML documents is unknown

- it can be assumed that many XML documents do not contain useful content

- the amount of documents is much larger than for the template-based approach

Generic matching algorithm   The primary goal of algorithm 3 is to find the element in a XML document that contains the most annotation information. As a first step a list of all available XML nodes which are unique up to a list index is computed [42]. In the following a example computation of the algorithm is described for the XML source in fig.3. The results are depicted in table 2. A row in table 2 stores all relative XPath of one unique XML node. In the first column the relative XPath, in the second column the value (attribute or text value) and in the third column the score (matching annotations) are depicted. From the table it can be seen that only the values of `document/CHAPTER/P/s/w//@tree` could be matched with known annotations. Although only the attribute `document/CHAPTER/P/s/w//@tree` from elements `document/CHAPTER/P/s//w` could be matched we conclude that also the other attributes like `document/CHAPTER/P/s/w//@lemma` contain *word*, *lemma* or *dependency* information.[43]   Hence we extract all attribute and text values from XML elements `document/CHAPTER/P/s//w`. These are then used to build a CoNLL file from it. Since we only use a small portion of the XML document for the detection process the method can be used to quickly rule out XML documents that do not contain any annotation information at all. We have found that taking 10 sample values (see algorithm 3 step 2) is sufficient for this purpose.

Algorithm 3 *Generic XML-CoNLL conversion*

1: Generate the list of unique XML nodes
2: Take **n** sample values[44] for each of the nodes in 1.
3: Filter nodes that have only numeric values
4: Compute a *score* which is simply the sum of all different values of one XML node that could be matched against the set of known annotations
5: The XML node with the highest score provides the most annotation information. Extract all attribute and text values from XML elements that are represented by a relative XPath for that node

---

---

[42] A list of XML child nodes that have the same parent node is represented by a relative XPath

[43] In general, attribute names don't have to be meaningful (like here : *lemma*)

[44] XML attribute or text value

Relative XPath for xml nodes	Found values	Score
document		0
document/CHAPTER//@id	1,2	0
document/CHAPTER/P//@id	1,2	0
document/CHAPTER/P/s//@id	1,2	0
document/CHAPTER/P/s/w//@tree	**ART, NC**	2
document/CHAPTER/P/s/w//@lem	el,sesión	0
document/CHAPTER/P/s/w//@id	1,2	0
document/CHAPTER/P/s/w//text()	la,sesión	0
document/CHAPTER/SPEAKER//@id	1	0
document/CHAPTER/SPEAKER//@name	La Presidenta	0

Table 2: Example computation for alg. 3

7. Results

So far 2317 files from 1508 resources have been processed. Of these were 1572 RDF, 263 CoNLL and 482 XML files. Table 3 below shows in how many files at least one language or annotation model could be detected.

File type	Processed	Model found	Language found
RDF	1572	393 (25%)	503 (32%)
CoNLL	263	263 (100%)	254 (97%)
XML	482	350 (73%)	375 (78%)
Total	2317	1006 (43%)	1132 (49%)

Table 3: Results by file type

Obviously, for the CoNLL format the percentage of files that yielded results is nearly 100%. This can be explained by the fact that CoNLL files include usable data by default. For the few cases were no language could be detected a parse error might be the cause for the error, or the language info was missing in the CoNLL data. A large portion of the processed XML files (~75%) could be converted to the CoNLL format. Because most XML files were manually selected from language resource providers like `http://opus.nlpl.eu/` and `https://spraakbanken.gu.se`, this result is not unexpected and the error rate (~25%) can be explained with other XML files that were included in archive resources (e.g. zip, tar) together with the real data. On the other hand RDF resources were automatically collected and did not reveal as much usable data as we expected. In fact the RDF format is commonly used for semantic web data, perhaps even more than for LLOD data. In total, 22 different annotation models and 3855 different languages could be identified. In addition to that, we detected RDF namespaces for vocabularies of linguistic interest such as OLiA[45], GOLD[46], NIF[47], OntoLex-Lemon[48], UBY[49] and LexInfo[50]. However, these are not included in the Annohub RDF dump for now.

The results for files listed in table 3 are finally reviewed by a linguist with the Annohub editor application. It is used to correct wrong results and to select the resources that are published in the Annohub RDF dataset. Currently the dataset contains 609 different language resources that include 915 files. In table 4 the distribution for different resource types is shown.

	Corpus	Lexicon	Ontology	Total
Resources	391	214	4	609

Table 4: Language resource classification

For future releases we are planning to extend this classification to other resource types like wordnets, etc.

	linghub.org	CLARIN	USER	Total
Resources	128	77	404	609

Table 5: Overview of metadata providers

Table 5 shows the metadata providers for resources included in Annohub. At the date of writing, the *linghub* [51] portal is updated with new resources that have been collected by members of the Prêt-à-LLOD [52] working group. We are planning to include the results for these as well as more results for language resources listed on CLARIN in future releases.

8. Summary

We introduced a new LLOD dataset which provides annotation model and language information for publicly available language resources. By means of SPARQL queries this data can be linked with other existing LLOD resources, as we have shown by the use case of the Lin|gu|is|tik portal. Certainly, the availability of annotation metadata will enable other new Linked Data applications. Finally, the provided tools for the conversion of XML data to the CoNLL format also contribute to the LLOD cloud since other converters[53] for a later conversion to the CoNLL-RDF (Chiarcos and Fäth, 2017) format exist.

9. Acknowledgements

The research described in this paper was conducted in the context of the Specialized Information Service Linguistics (FID), funded by German Research Foundation (DFG/LIS, 2017-2019). The contributions of the second author were conducted with additional support from the Horizon 2020 Research and Innovation Action 'Prêt-à-LLOD', Grant Agreement number 825182. The authors would like to thank Christian Chiarcos for providing expert advice throughout the project. We would also like to thank Thorsten Fritze and Yunus Söyleyici for technical support and Vanya Dimitrova for helpful comments.

10. Bibliographical References

Abromeit, F. and Chiarcos, C. (2019). Automatic Detection of Language and Annotation Model Information in CoNLL Corpora. In Maria Eskevich, et al., editors, *2nd Conference on Language, Data and Knowledge (LDK*

---

[45] `http://purl.org/olia/olia.owl`

[46] `http://purl.org/linguistics/gold`

[47] `http://persistence.uni-leipzig.org/nlp2rdf/ontologies/nif-core#`

[48] `http://www.w3.org/ns/lemon/ontolex#`

[49] `http://purl.org/olia/ubyCat.owl`

[50] `http://www.lexinfo.net/ontology/2.0/lexinfo`

[51] `http://linghub.org`

[52] `https://www.pret-a-llod.eu/`

[53] `https://github.com/acoli-repo/conll-rdf`

2019), volume 70 of *OpenAccess Series in Informatics (OASIcs)*, pages 23:1–23:9, Dagstuhl, Germany. Schloss Dagstuhl–Leibniz-Zentrum fuer Informatik.

Bird, S. and Liberman, M. (2001). A formal framework for linguistic annotation. *Speech Communication 33(1-2)*, pages 23–60.

Chiarcos, C. and Fäth, C. (2017). CoNLL-RDF: Linked Corpora Done in an NLP-Friendly Way. In *Language, Data, and Knowledge - First International Conference, LDK 2017, Galway, Ireland, June 19-20, 2017, Proceedings*, pages 74–88.

Chiarcos, C. and Sukhreva, M. (2015). OLIA - Ontologies of Linguistic Annotation. *Semantic Web Journal*, 518:379–386.

Chiarcos, C., Fäth, C., Renner-Westermann, H., Abromeit, F., and Dimitrova, V. (2016). Lin|gu|is|tik: Building the Linguist's Pathway to Bibliographies, Libraries, Language Resources and Linked Open Data. In Nicoletta Calzolari (Conference Chair), et al., editors, *Proceedings of the Tenth International Conference on Language Resources and Evaluation (LREC 2016)*, pages 4463–4471, Portorož, Slovenia, May. European Language Resources Association (ELRA).

de Melo, G. (2015). Lexvo.org: Language-Related Information for the Linguistic Linked Data Cloud. *Semantic Web Journal*, 6:393–400.

Dimitrova, V., Fäth, C., Chiarcos, C., Renner-Westermann, H., and Abromeit, F. (2016). Building an Ontological Model of the BLL Thesaurus: First Steps Towards and Interface with the LLOD Cloud. In John P. McCrae, et al., editors, *Proceedings of the 5th Workshop on Linked Data in Linguistics: Managing, Building and Using Linked Language Resources (LDL-2016)*, pages 50–58, Portorož, Slovenia, May. European Language Resources Association (ELRA).

Dimitrova, V., Fäth, C., Chiarcos, C., Renner-Westermann, H., and Abromeit, F. (2018). Interoperability of Language-related Information: Mapping the BLL Thesaurus to Lexvo and Glottolog. In Nicoletta Calzolari (Conference chair), et al., editors, *Proceedings of the Eleventh International Conference on Language Resources and Evaluation (LREC 2018)*, Miyazaki, Japan, May 7-12, 2018. European Language Resources Association (ELRA).

Dipper, S. (2005). Xml-based stand-off representation and exploitation of multi-level linguistic annotation. In *Berliner XML Tage 2005, Humboldt-Universität zu Berlin, 12. bis 14. September 2005*, pages 39–50.

Ide, N. and Suderman, K. (2007). GrAF: A graph-based format for linguistic annotations. In *Proceedings of the Linguistic Annotation Workshop*, pages 1–8, Prague, Czech Republic, June. Association for Computational Linguistics.

Nordhoff, S. and Hammarström, H. (2011). Glottolog/Langdoc: Defining dialects, languages, and language families as collections of resources. In Tomi Kauppinen, et al., editors, *Proceedings of the First International Workshop on Linked Science 2011*, pages 53–58, Bonn, Germany.

W. Lezius, H. B. and Gerstenberger, C. (2002). *Tiger-xml quick reference guide*. Technical report, IMS,University of Stuttgart.

Proceedings of the 7th Workshop on Linked Data in Linguistics (LDL-2020), pages 45–51
Language Resources and Evaluation Conference (LREC 2020), Marseille, 11–16 May 2020
© European Language Resources Association (ELRA), licensed under CC-BY-NC

Challenges of Word Sense Alignment: Portuguese Language Resources

Ana Salgado[1,2], Sina Ahmadi[3], Alberto Simões[4], John McCrae[3], Rute Costa[2]

[1]Academia das Ciências de Lisboa, Instituto de Lexicologia e Lexicografia da Língua Portuguesa, Lisbon, Portugal
[2]NOVA CLUNL, Universidade NOVA de Lisboa, Lisbon, Portugal
[3]Data Science Institute, National University of Ireland Galway
[4]2Ai – School of Technology, IPCA, Barcelos, Portugal

anasalgado@campus.fcsh.unl.pt; {sina.ahmadi,john.mccrae}@insight-centre.org; rute.costa@fcsh.unl.pt; asimoes@ipca.pt

Abstract

This paper reports on an ongoing task of monolingual word sense alignment in which a comparative study between the Portuguese Academy of Sciences Dictionary and the *Dicionário Aberto* is carried out in the context of the ELEXIS (European Lexicographic Infrastructure) project. Word sense alignment involves searching for matching senses within dictionary entries of different lexical resources and linking them, which poses significant challenges. The lexicographic criteria are not always entirely consistent within individual dictionaries and even less so across different projects where different options may have been assumed in terms of structure and especially wording techniques of lexicographic glosses. This hinders the task of matching senses. We aim to present our annotation workflow in Portuguese using the Semantic Web standards. The results obtained are useful for the discussion within the community.

Keywords: lexicography, sense alignment, linguistic linked data, Portuguese

1. Introduction

The concept of the dictionary has changed with the advent of the world wide web (WWW) and the digital age. The interoperability of linked data technologies has played an essential role in the evolution of lexicography (Shadbolt et al., 2006; Heath and Bizer, 2011; Gracia et al., 2017). It has been shown how lexicographic content can be represented and connected dynamically, thus allowing us to abandon once and for all the editorial perspective that still pervades most digital resources which continue to mirror the structure used in the paper versions.

The use of semantic standards enables the organization of vast amounts of lexical data in ontologies, Wordnets and other machine-readable lexical resources resorting to novel tools for the transformation and linking of multilingual datasets (McCrae and Declerck, 2019; Chiarcos et al., 2012). Linked Open Data (LLOD) promotes the use of the RDF data model to publish lexical data on the web for a global information system and interoperability issues.

There have been many efforts underway on behalf of numerous researchers to align different lexical resources (e.g. (Navigli, 2006; Knight and Luk, 1994) dealing with the word sense alignment (WSA) task. We define this task as linking a list of pairs of senses from two or more lexical resources using semantic relationships. To mention a few previous projects, Meyer and Gurevych (2011) align the Princeton WordNet with the English Wiktionary[1], and Henrich et al. (2012) link the GermaNet–the German Wordnet with the German Wikipedia[2].

WSA involves searching for matching senses within dictionary entries of different lexical resources and linking them, which poses significant challenges. The lexicographic criteria are not always entirely consistent within individual dictionaries and even less so across different projects where different options may have been assumed in terms of structure and especially wording techniques of lexicographic glosses. It has been demonstrated that the task of WSA is beneficial in many natural language processing (NLP) applications, particularly word sense disambiguation (Navigli and Ponzetto, 2012) and information extraction (Moro et al., 2013).

In this paper, we are focused on the monolingual word sense alignment (MWSA) task, which involves in sense alignment within two different resources in the same language. As an observer in the European Lexicographic Infrastructure–ELEXIS[3] (Krek et al., 2019; Declerck et al., 2018), the Academia das Ciências de Lisboa (ACL) contributed to the task of MWSA in which the Portuguese Academy of Sciences Dictionary is compared to and aligned with the senses in the *Dicionário Aberto*. We will report our experiences in annotating the senses with four semantic relationships, namely, narrower, broader, exact and related. Representing the final data in the Ontolex-Lemon model (McCrae et al., 2017), we believe that the outcomes of this project will pave the way for further research on automatic WSA for the Portuguese language and enhance the accessibility of the data on the Semantic Web and Linked Data.

The rest of the paper is organized as follows. In Section 2, we introduce our Portuguese lexicographic resources and provide a description of their content and structure. Section 3 summarises the methodology for annotation workflow. In Section 4, we point out the major challenges of the MWSA task for the Portuguese resources. We describe the conversion of the data into Ontolex-Lemon model in Section 5. Finally, we conclude in Section 6 with a summary of our contributions.

2. Lexicographic data

In the scope of ELEXIS, one of the main purposes is to extract, structure and link multilingual lexicographic resources. One of the tasks to achieve this goal consists

---

[1]https://en.wiktionary.org
[2]https://de.wikipedia.org

[3]This project aims to create a European network of lexical resources (http://www.elex.is).

of word sense alignment manual task in several languages (Ahmadi et al., 2020).The datasets are publicly freely available[4].The first established task is to provide semantic relations, as we will demonstrate in Section 3.

2.1. DLPC and DA

For the completion of this task, we align the following two Portuguese dictionaries:

- the *Dicionário da Língua Portuguesa Contemporânea* (DLPC) (Academia das Ciências de Lisboa, 2001), with the seal of ACL, coordinated by Malaca Casteleiro and published in 2001, with the financial support of the Calouste Gulbenkian Foundation, under the commercial responsibility of Editorial Verbo. This dictionary also represents the first complete edition of a Portuguese Academy dictionary, from A to Z (previous attempts in 1793 and 1976 did not go further than the letter A). The DLPC contains around 70,000 entries. In 2015, some preparatory work for an online Portuguese Academy of Science Dictionary (DACL) was performed through the Instituto de Lexicologia e Lexicografia da Língua Portuguesa (ILLLP) and a database was developed by a team working in Natural Language Processing at the University of Minho, which now draws on the participation of IPCA and NOVA CLUNL[5]. The present work, therefore, had the retro-digitised version of DLPC as a starting point.

- the *Dicionário Aberto* (DA) (Simões and Farinha, 2010), a Portuguese language dictionary obtained by the full transcription of *Nôvo Diccionário da Língua Portuguêsa*, authored by Cândido de Figueiredo, and published in 1913 by Livraria Clássica. Having the 1913 edition entered the public domain, it was digitised and text-converted by a team of distributed proof-readers volunteers between 2007 and 2010 and was made publicly available on the Gutenberg Project website on 8 March 2010. During the transcription process, and as entries got reviewed, and therefore, considered final, they were made freely available on the web. For three years, the dictionary has expanded by including more transcribed entries. After the complete transcription, the dictionary was subject to automatic orthography update and was used for different experiments regarding NLP tasks, as the automatic extraction of information for the creation of Wordnets or ontologies (Gonçalo Oliveira, 2018; Oliveira and Gomes, 2014). The updated version of the dictionary is available under license CC-BY-SA 2.5 PT. The DA contains 128,521 entries. Although the number of entries seems high, it is necessary to bear in mind that this resource registers orthographic variants of the same entry as we will mention later.

2.2. Formats

Concerning formats, both Portuguese language resources are available in printed editions and XML versions.

The DLPC was published in a two-volume paper version, the first volume from A to F and the second from G to Z, in a total of 3880 pages. This dictionary, available in print and as a PDF document, was converted into XML using a slightly customized version of the P5 schema of the Text Encoding Initiative (TEI) (Simões et al., 2016). The XML was generated based on the dictionary PDF file, from which most of the information on the microstructure was recovered automatically. The new ongoing digital edition, DACL, is only privately available and has been edited with LeXmart (Simões et al., 2019). At the same time, the dictionary is being converted to the TEI Lex-0 format (Salgado et al., 2019b), a streamlined version of the TEI Dictionary Chapter. The present work, therefore, had this digital version as a starting point.

Regarding the DA, the paper version comprises 2133 pages. Currently, the dictionary is available online. Unlike DLPC, DA was transcribed manually by volunteers. This task required that the annotation format would be easy to learn, but also, that it would be similar to the format used in the transcription of other books for the Project Gutenberg[6]. Therefore, entries were only annotated with changes of font types, i.e., italics and bold, and not semantic tags. Although the dictionary is also available in XML, following the general guidelines of the Dictionary Chapter of TEI, the annotation granularity is bigger than DLPC. Specific portions of the microstructure were easy to annotate. Consider, for example, the grammatical information, geographic variant, or the knowledge domain. These entities are from a controlled list of vocabulary, and after creating the list it was straightforward to annotate them. For the construction of these lists we used the tables from the front-matter of the dictionary. Nevertheless, as these lists were manually generated, they were completed by performing dummy runs of the tagging algorithm, and finding out parts of the entries that were not detected. For other situations, like the annotation of usage examples, or to distinguish between two different senses, there are no clear marks to allow an algorithm to perform that automatically. While some hints could help, a good annotation would require manual validation. Under DA every line in the definition element tag can be a different sense, but can also be a usage example or even the continuation of the previous sense definition (Simões et al., 2012). To correctly detect other parts of the microstructure would require further manual revision that was not possible at that time. Further developments on both dictionaries are programmed as soon as funding is available.

2.3. Micro-structure analysis

The DLPC's micro-structure is more complex than the DA's, with more structured and hierarchical information. Both dictionaries follow lexicographic conventions such as bold type in headwords. Nevertheless, comparing the sample of entries, we may observe certain typographic differences: ACL features initial lowercase entries while the DA

---

[4]https://github.com/elexis-eu/MWSA

[5]The team works with Alberto Simões (IPCA) and José João Almeida (Natural Language Processing of the Computer Science Department), and the consultancy of Álvaro Iriarte Sanromán. The participation of NOVA CLUNL is related to the DACL's transition into the TEI Lex-0 format.

[6]https://www.gutenberg.org/ebooks/31552

Headword (POS)	DLPC sense	Semantic relation	Sense match	DA sense
banco (s. m.)				
	Assento estreito e comprido, de material variável, com ou sem encosto, para várias pessoas.	related	Assento, geralmente tosco, de ferro, madeira ou pedra, e de formas variadas.	Assento, geralmente tosco, de ferro, madeira ou pedra, e de formas variadas.
	banco dos réus. 1. Lugar destinado aos réus, no tribunal. 2. Situação em que se é objeto de acusação em tribunal.	none		Escabelo.
	Assento para uma pessoa, sem encosto, de tampo redondo ou quadrado, sustentado por três ou quatro pés. ≈ mocho.	related	Assento, geralmente tosco, de ferro, madeira ou pedra, e de formas variadas.	Mesa estreita e oblonga, sobre que trabalham certos artífices.
	Assento comprido e largo, com encosto alto, de tampo amovível, que pode servir também de tampa de uma arca. ≈ arquibanco, escabelo, escano.	exact	Escabelo.	Balcão de comércio.

Figure 1: An example spreadsheet used for the annotation task.

has capitalized entries. Furthermore, only the DLPC provides full pronunciation information. The DLPC etymological information figures after the grammatical properties of the lexical item while, in the DA, such information appears at the end of the entry. While the DLPC indicates the part-of-speech and gender, the DA displays the gender in the case of nouns[7]. One of the main features of the DLPC is the split of entries. Not only etymological homonyms are treated as independent entries, but also homonyms of the same etymological family belonging to different part-of-speech are differentiated by numeric superscripts to the right of the lemma in order to distinguish the respective entries (e.g. *perfurador* can function as an adjective, or a noun so is split into two entries).

Regarding the structure, the senses are numbered in the DLPC, providing better organised and more fine-grained information, while in the DA only a paragraph distinguishes the different senses. This was the result of the lack of metadata added to the dictionary during the transcription process. Nevertheless, the dictionary has the basic microstructure annotated, including grammatical information, definitions, quotations, usage examples and etymological information. The DLPC has, in general, more structured information such as synonyms (preceded by ≈), examples (shown in italics), cross-reference to lexical units that preferentially co-occur are represented by the symbol +, usage labelling, among other relevant features.

In the next section, we will explain in more detail how the workflow annotation took place. The data was delivered in XLM files and in an Excel format where the data was converted into spreadsheets.

3. Methodology

In the previous two sections, we have presented the resources we decided to analyze and pointed out that they have very different features. Before we move to the annotation workflow, we would like to define some of the terms used in this particular task:

- The lemma is a "lexical unit chosen according to lexicographical conventions to represent the different forms of an inflection paradigm" (ISO, 2007).

- A sense is one of the possible meanings or interpretations in a specific context.

- A gloss is a textual description of a sense's meaning meant for human interpretation.

3.1. Entries selection

The selection of entries took into account some points previously defined by the ELEXIS team (Ahmadi et al., 2020), namely: all open class words should be represented; monosemous and polysemous lemmas should appear; and, finally, the lemmas of both resources must had the same part-of-speech. Taking these points into account, we decided to select isolated lemmas randomly and also select data sets followed alphabetically. As a sample of entries, we chose:

A. random entries as long as they appeared in both dictionaries: *banco* [bank], *bandarilha* [banderilla], *café* [coffee], *computador* [computer], *coração* [heart], *dicionário* [dictionary], *futebol* [football], *lexicografia* [lexicography], *mililitro* [milliliter], *praia* [beach], *sorridente* [smiling] and *tripeiro* [tripe seller and native of Porto].

B. all the lexical items that came up between *especial* [special] and *esperanto* [Esperanto], *perfume* [perfume] and *perlimpimpim* [a lexical unit used in a fixed combination *pós de perlimpimpim* [magical powder], a sequence of units sorted alphabetically from letters E and P.

The total number of entries collected is 146 containing 786 distinct senses (8301 tokens).

After selecting the sample entries, we created dynamic spreadsheets as the means of the annotation task (Figure 1). This sheet contains the following information:

---

[7]This a common lexicographic practice: when it is marked as *m.* (masculine), it is understood that the lemma is a noun.

headwords (DLPC and DA lemmas identification); part-of-speech (DLPC POS); senses in DLPC (DLPC senses); semantic relation; sense match (DA equivalent sense); part-of-speech (DA POS); and, finally, senses in DA (DA senses).

3.2. Annotation workflow

The annotation task was carried out fully manually. Given a lemma, corresponding senses in both dictionaries, the DA and DLPC, were brought together in the spreadsheets. This way, all the possible combinations of the senses across the two resources were provided to the annotator. Unlike regular dictionaries, where a limited number of semantic relationships are defined, such as synonymy and antonymy, we considered a broader range of semantic relationships, namely the followings:

- `exact`: the two senses are semantically equivalent;

- `narrower`: the sense in DLPC describes a narrower concept than that in the DA;

- `broader`: the sense in DLPC describes a broader concept than that in the DA;

- `related`: there is a possible alignment, detecting a possible related relationship.

In the case where no semantic relationship is found for a sense, none is selected. Note that not all the semantic relationships are symmetric; therefore, the order of the columns determines the relationship. We matched the senses of the two dictionaries, using the label corresponding to the properties cited above. The result is a mapping between senses. In overall, 463 and 323 senses are aligned in the DLPC and DA, respectively. Among the whole number of 275 aligned senses, 207 exact, 38 narrower, 28 related and 2 broader are provided.

4. Challenges of MWSA

We now move on to the challenges of WSA. When we first chose these two lexicographic resources, we knew that we would be dealing with a significant time lag: the DLPC was published in 2001, and the DA in 1913. In 88 years, the Portuguese lexicon and language undergone many transformations: a Portuguese spelling reform, semantic changes of the lexical items (*computador* [computer], for example, in the DA, is not defined as an electronic device, new words have appeared, such as *futebol* [football], which is not included in the DA). All these factors are obstacles to the successful performance of this task.

The Portuguese spelling has also changed. In the DA, their development team decided to maintain old spelling variants, e.g. *periphrástico* and *perifrástico* (Figure 2), thus enabling the search of all the orthographic variants.

For this task, we have ignored the old orthographic variant forms of a given lexical unit, as they are present in duplicate in DA (with an updated version of the form). Since the DLPC is a contemporary dictionary, these orthographic

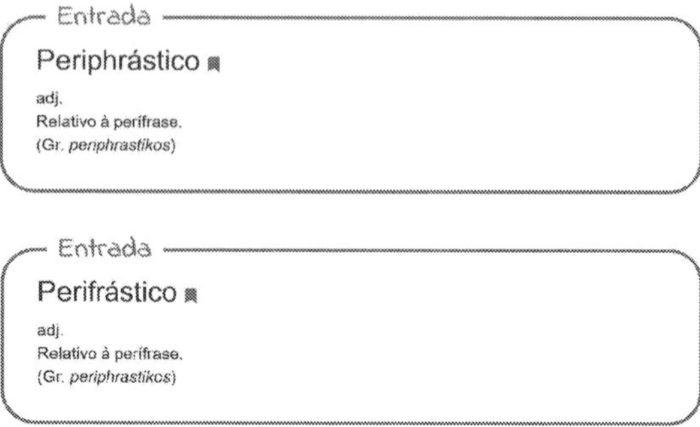

Figure 2: *periphrástico* [periphrastic] and *perifrástico* [periphrastic] in DA

mililitro [mililítru]. *s. m.* (De *mili-¹* + *litro*). Unidade de medida de capacidade (símb. *ml*) equivalente à milésima parte do litro.

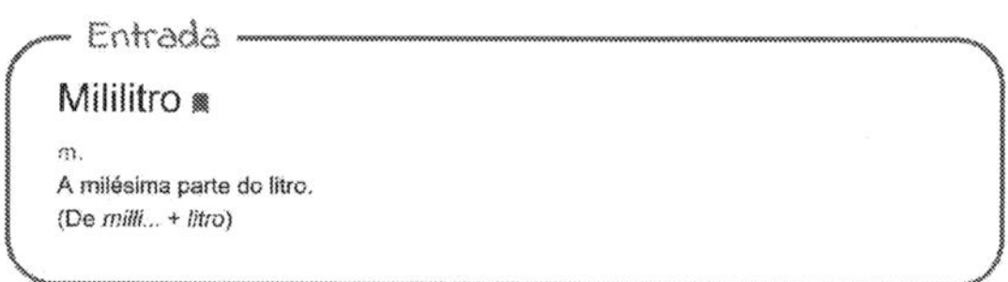

Figure 3: *mililitro* [milliliter] in DLPC (above) and DA (below)

forms would never appear in the DA and were not useful for the ongoing task[8].

Since we do not intend to discuss the wording techniques of the gloss, we can say that between certain lexical items senses, there is an exact correspondence of sense. There are cases where we can establish an exact relation between the senses even in structural terms (see, *mililitro* [millilitre] that has only one sense in both dictionaries, i.e., one-thousandth of a litre). However, these easily solvable cases are not what we mostly encounter when dealing with different dictionaries (Figure 3).

There are several other cases where there are exact relations, but there are other senses that appear in only one of the dictionaries. In Figure 4, DLPC sense 1 related to the bullfighting domain [banderilla] corresponds to the only sense of the DA. Sense 2 related to the bookbinding domain only appears in the DLPC.

Nevertheless, and although the first sense is identical in both resources, the disallowance is not identical in textual terms, since the meaning is described differently. The

---

[8]From the DA XML file, we ignored the following entries: *perhydrol, perianthado, periântheo, periânthio, periantho, periappendicite, perichécio, perichôndrio, perichondrite, perichondrio, pericoróllia, pericyclo, pericystite, perididymite, peridídymo, perídyo, perígrapho, perigynândrio, perigynadro, perigynia, perígyno, perimísio, perimorphose, perinephrite, periophthalmia, periorthógono, periosteóphyto, peripheria, periphérico, periphorantho, períphoro, períphrase, periphrástico, peripyema, peristáchio, perisféthio, peristýlico, perissýstole, perithécio, perityphlite.*

DLPC also uses a domain label, "*Taurom.*" while in the DA, there is no label.

> **bandarilha** [bɐ̃dɐɾíʎɐ]. *s. f.* (Do cast. *banderilla*). **1.** *Taurom.* Haste munida de ponta de metal penetrante, enfeitada com uma bandeira ou com fitas de papel de cores e que se espeta no cachaço dos touros, durante a corrida. ≃ FARPA, FERRO. *A elegância com que espetou o par de bandarilhas no touro pôs a praça de pé.* «*Abrem-se então as portas e a manada entra, esta que será toureada hoje consoante os preceitos inteiros da arte, passada à capa, espetada de bandarilhas, castigada de varas*» (SARAMAGO, *Levantado do Chão*, p. 165). *Cravar, espetar as +s; um par de +s; térçio de +s.* **bandarilhas a quarteio,** variedade de farpas em que o toureiro faz um quarto de volta ao espetá-la no touro. **bandarilhas a recorte,** movimento que consiste em colocar os ferros no touro no momento em que o toureiro evita a marrada. **2.** *Encad.* Tira de papel que se cola na margem de um original ou prova, quando as emendas não cabem nas margens.

Bandarilha

f.
Farpa, enfeitada com bandeiras ou fitas, e destinada a cravar-se no cachaço dos toiros, quando se correm.
(Por *bandeirilha*, cast. *banderilla*)

Figure 4: *bandarilha* [banderilla] in DLPC (above) and DA (below)

In other cases, the correspondence of senses is evident, but the lexicographic criteria adopted differ as shown in Figure 5. The structure of these lexicographic articles is different. The DLPC has two entries for *tripeiro* (*tripeiro*[1] and *tripeiro*[2]) as an adjective and a noun, part-of-speech homonyms. The first entry is an adjective, and the second is a noun; the DA has only one entry and only gender information. Between *tripeiro*[2] (DLPC) and *tripeiro* (DA), there is an exact match in the first sense, an obsolete sense, as a tripe seller although the technique of writing the gloss differs ("Pessoa que vende tripas" [Person who sells tripes] in DLPC and "Vendedor de tripas" [Tripe seller]) in DA. These two glosses point to the same concept. However, although the DA did not record sense numbers, the first two senses could be divided. We can established a match between sense two that start with "pop." [popular] in DLPC and "Deprec." [depreciative] in DA, another tricky topic is usage information. This topic is related to the various types of inconsistencies regarding usage labelling (Salgado et al., 2019a). Anyway, the only difference is that DLPC uses a cross-reference, and the DA provides the gloss.

Other times, the senses are exact correspondences, but the editorial perspective is different as shown in the example of Figure 6: for *pergamináceo* [pergameneous] (DLPC), the DA presents a gloss and the DLPC a cross-reference. On the other hand, *pergiminháceo* (DA) has a cross-reference *pergamináceo*.

The DA, as mentioned above, does not use numbers for senses. Thus, we have considered each paragraph as an independent sense. However, a DLPC sense may correspond to more than one DA sense. See *praia* [beach] entry in the sense of "Beira-mar" [seaside] (Figure 7).

> **tripeiro**[1] [tripɐ́jru]. *adj. m. e f.* (De *tripa* + suf. *-eiro*). *Pop.* O m. que *portuense*[1].
> **tripeiro**[2] [tripɐ́jru]. *s. m. e f.* (De *tripa* + suf. *-eiro*). **1.** Pessoa que vende tripas. **2.** *Pop.* O m. que *portuense*[2].

Tripeiro

m.
Vendedor de tripas.
Aquele que se sustenta de tripas.
Deprec.
Habitante do Porto.
(De *tripa*)

Figure 5: *tripeiro* [tripe seller and native of Porto] in DLPC (above) and DA (below)

> **pergamináceo, a** [pirgɐminásju, -ɐ]. *adj.* (Do b. lat. *pergamīnum* 'pergaminho' + suf. *-áceo*). **1.** Que se assemelha ao pergaminho; que, pelo seu aspecto, faz lembrar essa pele. ≃ PERGAMINHÁCEO. **2.** Que é feito de pergaminho.
>
> **pergaminháceo, a** [pirgɐmiɲásju, -ɐ]. *adj.* (De *pergaminho* + suf. *-áceo*). O m. que *pergamináceo*.

Pergamináceo

adj.
O mesmo ou melhor que *pergaminháceo.* Cf. Arn. Gama, *Ult. Dona*, 55.

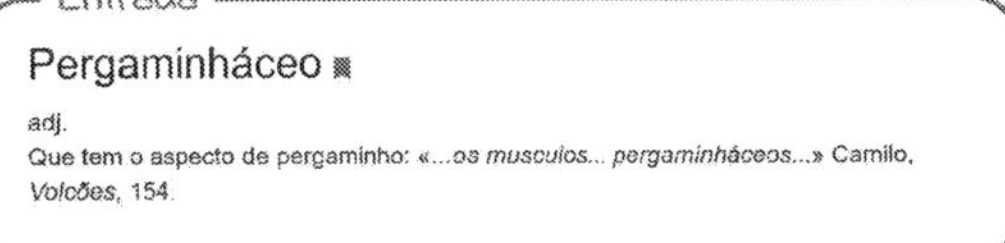

Pergaminháceo

adj.
Que tem o aspecto de pergaminho: «...os musculos... pergaminháceos...» Camilo, *Volcões*, 154.

Figure 6: *pergamináceo/pergaminháceo* [pergameneous] in DLPC (above) and DA (below)

In the DA (Figure 7), the senses "Beira-mar" [seaside] and "Região, banhada pelo mar; litoral; margem" [Region, bathed by the sea; coast] correspond to sense 2 of the DLPC: "Zona banhada pelo mar; zona balnear" [Zone bathed by the sea; bathing area].

The same can be said, for example, of *especial* [special], whose DLPC gloss, "Que tem, dadas as características, uma finalidade ou um uso particular. ≈ adequado, específico, próprio. ≠ geral." [Which has, given the characteristics, a purpose or a particular use. ≈ suitable, specific, own], may correspond to three paragraphs of the DA: "Próprio. / Peculiar. / Particular." [Own. / Peculiar. / Particular.].

Looking at the three glosses of banco [stool/bench] as "assento" [seat] in the DLPC:

- "Assento estreito e comprido, de material variável, com ou sem encosto, para várias pessoas." [Narrow and long seat, of variable material, with or without backrest, for several people.]

- "Assento para uma pessoa, sem encosto, de tampo re-

praia [prájɐ]. *s. f.* (Do lat. tardio *plagia*, talvez do gr. πλάγιος 'oblíquo'). **1.** Faixa arenosa do litoral marítimo, de fraca inclinação, muito utilizada por banhistas nas zonas de veraneio ou em estâncias de turismo. *«e a débil pegada que o meu obscuro pé imprimiu nas praias do Mindelo há-de ficar gravada na história»* (GARRETT, *Discursos*, p. 121). **casa⁺ de praia. colchão⁺ de praia. voleibol⁺ de praia. 2.** Zona banhada pelo mar; zona balnear. ≃ BEIRA-MAR, COSTA, LITORAL. *Passaram as férias na praia.*

— Entrada —

Praia ▥

f.

Orla de terra, geralmente coberta de areia, confinando com o mar.

Beiramar.

Região, banhada pelo mar; litoral; margem.

Pl. *Marn.*

Depósito geral das águas que alimentam a salina, e que também se chama loiças, (cp. *loiça*).

(Do lat. *plaga*)

Figure 7: *praia* [beach] in DLPC (above) and DA (below)

dondo ou quadrado, sustentado por três ou quatro pés. ≈ mocho." [One person seat, without backrest, with round or square top, supported by three or four feet; stool]

- "Assento comprido e largo, com encosto alto, de tampo amovível, que pode servir também de tampa de uma arca. ≈ arquibanco, escabelo, escano.)" [Long and wide seat, with high back, removable top, which can also serve as a chest lid. ≈ bench cabinet; bench.]

It is tough to ascertain whether it is possible to make a correspondence with the first sense of the DA, also this one related to a seat: "Assento, geralmente tosco, de ferro, madeira ou pedra, e de formas variadas." [Seat, usually rough, of iron, wood or stone, and of different shapes.]
The last sense of the DLPC is a synonym of "escabelo" (also in the DA, so this is an "exact" correspondence), but it may also be associated with the first sense of the DLPC. Let us now turn to the *lexicografia* [lexicography] entry in the DLPC:

- "Ling. Ramo da linguística que se ocupa dos aspectos teóricos e práticos que têm em vista a elaboração de dicionários, vocabulários, glossários." [Branch of linguistics that deals with the theoretical and practical aspects that aim to develop dictionaries, vocabularies, glossaries.]

The same entry in DA, it is described as:

- "Ciência ou estudo, que tem por objecto as palavras que devem constituir um léxico." [Science or study, whose object is the words that must constitute a lexicon.]

Although the gloss differs (we intend to explore the issue of definition in more detail in future work), in these cases, we always attribute an exact relationship since both refer to the same concept.

5. Data Conversion

In order to increase the interoperability of the annotated data with other language resources, we convert the final datasets into the Ontolex-Lemon model (McCrae et al., 2017). This model provides rich linguistic groundings for ontologies which enables various representations such as morphology and syntax. Our final output provides the headword, the part-of-speech tag along with the senses for each entry. Therefore, the following properties are respectively used: `ontolex:writtenRep`, `lexinfo:partOfSpeech` and `skos:definition`. Linking between the senses is made with the SKOS matching properties. An example of this data in Turtle is given below:

```
<#banco_noun> a ontolex:LexicalEntry ;
  rdfs:label "banco"@pt ;
  ontolex:sense <#sense0>, <#sense12>,
    <#sense13> .

<#sense0> skos:definiton
  "Assento estreito e comprido, de
  material variável, com ou sem encosto,
  para várias pessoas. "@pt .

<#sense12> skos:definition
  "banco dos réus. 1. Lugar destinado
  aos réus, no tribunal. 2. Situação
  em que se é objecto de acusação
  em tribunal."@pt .

<#sense0> skos:relatedMatch <#sense1> .
<#sense95> skos:exactMatch <#sense96> .
<#sense97> skos:narrowMatch <#sense96> .
```

The data is publicly available as part of the MWSA benchmark at `https://github.com/elexis-eu/MWSA`.

6. Conclusion

This paper focuses on the task of monolingual word sense alignment for the Portuguese language. Focusing on two lexicographic resources in Portuguese, namely, *Dicionário da Língua Portuguesa Contemporânea* and *Dicionário Aberto*, we presented the challenges and difficulties to manually align senses and annotate their semantic relationships. In addition, we also describe the conversion of our aligned data into the Ontolex-Lemon model which improves interoperability and accessibility within the Linked Data and Semantic Web technologies. We believe that our dataset is beneficial to create tools and techniques to automatically align senses within Portuguese lexicographic resources. Moreover,

7. Acknowledgements

The authors would like to thank the anonymous reviewers for their thoughtful comments towards improving our manuscript. Research financed by Portuguese National Funding through the FCT – Fundação para a Ciência e Tecnologia as part of the project Centro de Linguística da Universidade NOVA de Lisboa – UID/LIN/03213/2020, by the European Union's Horizon 2020 research and innovation program under Grant Agreement No. 731015 (ELEXIS), and through the FCT/MCTES as part of the project 2Ai – School of Technology, IPCA – UIDB/05549/2020.

8. Bibliographical References

Ahmadi, S., McCrae, J. P., Nimb, S., Khan, F., Monachini, M., Pedersen, B. S., Declerck, T., Wissik, T., Bellandi, A., Pisani, I., Troelsgård, T., Olsen, S., Krek, S., Lipp, V., Váradi, T., Simon, L., Győrffy, A., Tiberius, C., Schoonheim, T., Ben Moshe, Y., Rudich, M., Abu Ahmad, R., Lonke, D., Kovalenko, K., Langemets, M., Kallas, J., Dereza, O., Fransen, T., Cillessen, D., Lindemann, D., Alonso, M., Salgado, A., Sancho, J. L., Ureña-Ruiz, R.-J., Simov, K., Osenova, P., Kancheva, Z., Radev, I., Stanković, R., Perdih, A., and Gabrovšek, D. (2020). A Multilingual Evaluation Dataset for Monolingual Word Sense Alignment. In *Proceedings of the 12th Language Resource and Evaluation Conference (LREC 2020)*, Marseille, France.

Chiarcos, C., Nordhoff, S., and Hellmann, S. (2012). *Linked Data in Linguistics: Representing and Connecting Language Data and Language Metadata*. Springer.

Declerck, T., McCrae, J., Navigli, R., Zaytseva, K., and Wissik, T. (2018). Elexis-european lexicographic infrastructure: Contributions to and from the linguistic linked open data. In *I. Kernerman & S. Krek (Arg.), Proceedings of the LREC 2018 Workshop Globalex*, pages 17–22.

Gonçalo Oliveira, H. (2018). A survey on portuguese lexical knowledge bases: Contents, comparison and combination. *Information*, 9(2):34.

Gracia, J., Kernerman, I., and Bosque-Gil, J. (2017). Toward linked data-native dictionaries. In *Electronic Lexicography in the 21st Century: Lexicography from Scratch. Proceedings of the eLex 2017 conference*, pages 19–21.

Heath, T. and Bizer, C. (2011). Linked data: Evolving the web into a global data space. *Synthesis lectures on the semantic web: theory and technology*, 1(1):1–136.

Henrich, V., Hinrichs, E. W., and Suttner, K. (2012). Automatically linking germanet to wikipedia for harvesting corpus examples for germanet senses. *JLCL*, 27(1):1–19.

ISO. (2007). Presentation/representation of entries in dictionaries — Requirements, recommendations and information. Standard, International Organization for Standardization, Geneva, CH, February.

Knight, K. and Luk, S. K. (1994). Building a large-scale knowledge base for machine translation. In *AAAI*, volume 94, pages 773–778.

Krek, S., Declerck, T., McCrae, J. P., and Wissik, T. (2019). Towards a Global Lexicographic Infrastructure. In *Proceedings of the Language Technology 4 All Conference*.

McCrae, J. P. and Declerck, T. (2019). Linguistic Linked Open Data for All. In *Proceedings of the Language Technology 4 All Conference*.

McCrae, J. P., Bosque-Gil, J., Gracia, J., Buitelaar, P., and Cimiano, P. (2017). The ontolex-lemon model: development and applications. In *Proceedings of eLex 2017 conference*, pages 19–21.

Meyer, C. M. and Gurevych, I. (2011). What psycholinguists know about chemistry: Aligning wiktionary and wordnet for increased domain coverage. In *Proceedings of 5th International Joint Conference on Natural Language Processing*, pages 883–892.

Moro, A., Li, H., Krause, S., Xu, F., Navigli, R., and Uszkoreit, H. (2013). Semantic rule filtering for web-scale relation extraction. In *International Semantic Web Conference*, pages 347–362. Springer.

Navigli, R. and Ponzetto, S. P. (2012). Babelnet: The automatic construction, evaluation and application of a wide-coverage multilingual semantic network. *Artificial Intelligence*, 193:217–250.

Navigli, R. (2006). Meaningful clustering of senses helps boost word sense disambiguation performance. In *Proceedings of the 21st International Conference on Computational Linguistics and the 44th annual meeting of the Association for Computational Linguistics*, pages 105–112. Association for Computational Linguistics.

Oliveira, H. G. and Gomes, P. (2014). Eco and onto. pt: a flexible approach for creating a portuguese wordnet automatically. *Language resources and evaluation*, 48(2):373–393.

Salgado, A., Costa, R., and Tasovac, T. (2019a). Improving the consistency of usage labelling in dictionaries with tei lex-0. *Lexicography*, 6(2):133–156.

Salgado, A., Costa, R., Tasovac, T., and Simões, A. (2019b). Tei lex-0 in action: Improving the encoding of the dictionary of the academia das ciências de lisboa. *Electronic lexicography in the 21st century (eLex 2019): Smart lexicography*, page 93.

Shadbolt, N., Berners-Lee, T., and Hall, W. (2006). The semantic web revisited. *IEEE intelligent systems*, 21(3):96–101.

Simões, A., Sanromán, Á. I., and Almeida, J. J. (2012). Dicionário-aberto: A source of resources for the portuguese language processing. In *International Conference on Computational Processing of the Portuguese Language*, pages 121–127. Springer. `http://www.dicionario-aberto.net/`.

Simões, A., Almeida, J. J., and Salgado, A. (2016). Building a dictionary using xml technology. In *5th Symposium on Languages, Applications and Technologies (SLATE'16)*. Schloss Dagstuhl-Leibniz-Zentrum fuer Informatik.

Simões, A., Salgado, A., Costa, R., and Almeida, J. J. (2019). LeXmart: A smart tool for lexicographers. In I. Kosem, et al., editors, *Electronic lexicography in the 21st century. Proceedings of the eLex 2019 conference*, pages 453–466.

9. Language Resource References

Academia das Ciências de Lisboa. (2001). *Dicionário da Língua Portuguesa Contemporânea*. João Malaca Casteleiro (ed.). Lisboa. Academia das Ciências de Lisboa e Editorial Verbo.

Simões, A. and Farinha, R. (2010). Dicionário aberto: um recurso para processamento de linguagem natural. *Viceversa: revista galega de traducción*, 16:159–171.

Proceedings of the 7th Workshop on Linked Data in Linguistics (LDL-2020), pages 52–60
Language Resources and Evaluation Conference (LREC 2020), Marseille, 11–16 May 2020
© European Language Resources Association (ELRA), licensed under CC-BY-NC

A Lime-Flavored REST API for Alignment Services

Manuel Fiorelli, Armando Stellato

University of Rome "Tor Vergata", Department of Enterprise Engineering, via del Politecnico 1, 00133 Roma, Italy
fiorelli@info.uniroma2.it, stellato@uniroma2.it

Abstract

A practical alignment service should be flexible enough to handle the varied alignment scenarios that arise in the real world, while minimizing the need for manual configuration. MAPLE, an orchestration framework for ontology alignment, supports this goal by coordinating a few loosely coupled actors, which communicate and cooperate to solve a matching task using explicit metadata about the input ontologies, other available resources and the task itself. The alignment task is thus summarized by a report listing its characteristics and suggesting alignment strategies. The schema of the report is based on several metadata vocabularies, among which the Lime module of the OntoLex-Lemon model is particularly important, summarizing the lexical content of the input ontologies and describing external language resources that may be exploited for performing the alignment. In this paper, we propose a REST API that enables the participation of downstream alignment services in the process orchestrated by MAPLE, helping them self-adapt in order to handle heterogeneous alignment tasks and scenarios. The realization of this alignment orchestration effort has been performed through two main phases: we first described its API as an OpenAPI specification (a la API-first), which we then exploited to generate server stubs and compliant client libraries. Finally, we switched our focus to the integration of existing alignment systems, with one fully integrated system and an additional one being worked on, in the effort to propose the API as a valuable addendum to any system being developed.

Keywords: Lime, OntoLex, VocBench, MAPLE, Ontology Matching

1. Introduction

Ontology matching (Euzenat & Shvaiko, 2013) is the task of computing an alignment between two (or more) ontologies that consists of correspondences between semantically related concepts. We consider a broader definition of the task, to cover thesauri and datasets, in general. We argued (Fiorelli et al., 2019) that a practical matching system should be flexible enough to recognize different matching scenarios and handle each of them with a suitable strategy possibly benefiting from additional support resources. Our framework MAPLE[1] achieves that goal by exploiting explicit metadata about the input ontologies and other available resources. MAPLE uses a combination of metadata vocabularies, including DCMI Metadata Terms[2], FOAF[3], VoID[4], DCAT[5] and Lime (Fiorelli et al., 2015). The latter is the metadata module of the OntoLex-Lemon model[6] (McCrae et al., 2017; Cimiano, McCrae, & Buitelaar, 2016), which is becoming a cornerstone of the growing Linguistic Linked Open Data cloud (Chiarcos, Nordhoff, & Hellmann, 2012), moving beyond its original focus on ontology lexicons. MAPLE uses Lime metadata to determine how lexical information is represented (i.e. the so-called *lexicalization model*), the degree of linguistic compatibility of the input ontologies (e.g. supported natural languages, relative coverage, relative expressiveness, etc.), as well to find suitable language resources (e.g. a wordnet) in some natural language to support synonym expansion. MAPLE compiles a *task report* that summarizes the characteristics of the given matching scenario and hints at possible matching strategies. This task report is intended to help a downstream matching system configure itself in order to manage the given matching scenario as best as possible. In this paper, we will refer to such a matching system as an *alignment service*, meaning a web service for the computation of alignments between datasets (in general). The contribution of this paper is precisely a REST API (Fielding, 2000) that an alignment service shall implement in order to comply with MAPLE. We used the OpenAPI[7] format to describe this API explicitly, ensuring that the produced specifications are both machine-readable and human friendly. These specifications establish a contract that make it possible for a user to invoke any alignment system for which a compliant server has been developed. We validated our work through the implementation of a sever for one alignment system, while planning an analogous one for an additional system.

2. Background

2.1 LIME: Linguistic Metadata

LIME is the module of OntoLex-Lemon dedicated to the description of lexicalized datasets and language resources such as wordnets. LIME extends VoID, by defining subclasses of *void:Dataset* based on the different roles that these datasets play form the view point of the ontology-lexicon interface.

A *lime:LexicalizationSet* is a dataset consisting of *lexicalizations* for a given *reference dataset* in some natural *language*, optionally using a *lexicon*, and expressed using a specific *lexicalization model*. A *lexicalization set* can describe the fact that an ontology (the *reference dataset*) contains RDFS labels (hence, RDFS is the *lexicalization model*) in English. If the ontology also contains labels in Italian, it would be necessary to introduce a second *lexicalization set*. Only if the *lexicalization model* is OntoLex-Lemon, then the *lexicalization set* shall reference a *lexicon*, providing the (reified) *lexical entries*. A *lexicalization set* may include metadata such as the number

---

[1] http://art.uniroma2.it/maple/
[2]   https://www.dublincore.org/specifications/dublin-core/dcmi-terms/
[3] http://xmlns.com/foaf/spec/
[4] https://www.w3.org/TR/void/
[5] https://www.w3.org/TR/vocab-dcat-2/
[6] https://www.w3.org/2016/05/ontolex/
[7] https://www.openapis.org/

of lexicalizations, the percentage of the reference dataset being covered and the average number of lexicalizations for the entities in the reference dataset.

Wordnets are represented in OntoLex-Lemon by mapping: i) each synset to an *ontolex:LexicalConcept*, ii) each word to an *ontolex:LexicalEntry, iii)* each sense to an *ontolex:LexicalSense*. While similar to the one of lexicalized datasets, the structure of wordnets is characterized by the use of lexical concepts and specific properties to bind these to lexical entries thorough lexical senses. Therefore, their metadata deserved a dedicated class, called *lime:ConceptualizationSet*, which relates a *lime:Lexicon* (describing the collection of lexical entries) to an *ontolex:ConceptSet* (describing the collection of lexical concepts). The description of a conceptualization set may include the number of lexical concepts, the number of lexical entries, the average ambiguity and average synonymy.

A *conceptualization set* (and the associated datasets) can be used for synonym expansion; given a word: i) find matching lexical entries (usually one per POS tag), ii) for each matched lexical entry, find the associated lexical concepts, and iii) retrieve other lexical entries associated to any of these lexical concepts.

2.2 MAPLE: MAPping architecture based on Linguistic Evidences

MAPLE is a framework facilitating the orchestration of different, loosely coupled actors with the aim to support a *robust matching system*. A user defines a *matching task* as a pair of datasets, say D_{left} and D_{right}. The purpose of MAPLE is to facilitate the configuration of a downstream alignment system to solve this task. To this end, MAPLE provides an *orchestrator* that analyzes the input datasets, in order to infer the characteristics of the task and hint at promising alignment strategies.

The *orchestrator* looks up the two datasets in a *metadata registry* to retrieve metadata about them: indeed, the descriptions of the two datasets jointly characterize (perhaps indirectly) the matching task.

MAPLE specifies a *metadata application profile* that a compliant registry must obey to, while the actual implementation of the registry is part of the integration with other systems. In this manner, it is possible to adopt and switch different strategies to acquire and store the metadata (e.g. automatic profiling, manual addition or retrieval of metadata published alongside the datasets). The *orchestrator* and other downstream components in the processing chain are completely unaware of the chosen strategy.

The *orchestrator* uses the metadata about the input datasets, to determine which information is available, how it is represented, and the extent of overlap between the two datasets.

The *orchestrator* first determines the nature of the input datasets (i.e. their metamodel), identifying whether they are ontologies, thesauri and other RDF datasets. This knowledge is important to set the goal of the alignment (e.g.

matching OWL classes vs matching SKOS concepts), while different combinations of dataset types may require different matching algorithms or dedicated configurations (e.g. taxonomy is encoded by the property *rdfs:subClassOf* in OWL ontologies and by the properties *skos:broader* and *skos:narrower* in SKOS thesauri).

MAPLE doesn't commit on any alignment technique, nonetheless it makes some assumptions:

- the seeding role of natural language lexicalizations
- the possibility to use wordnets for synonym expansion (and, in the future, for translation)

The *orchestrator* finds the *lexicalization sets* for the input datasets (see Section 2.1) and produces a ranked list of pairs of *lexicalization sets*. The *orchestrator* also tries to construct a *synonymizer* using a suitable wordnet included in the metadata registry. The order of the aforementioned list is determined by a complex scoring formula taking into account metrics about the lexicalization sets and, if available, about the *synonymizer*.

The *orchestrator* will compile a *task report* with the output of its analysis, which can be communicated to the *alignment system*.

3. Use Case and Requirements

As a software framework, MAPLE needs to be integrated into other systems, which in turn must implement or consume interfaces defined by MAPLE. Figure 1 illustrates a concrete use case applying MAPLE to VocBench 3[8] (Stellato et al., 2017; Stellato et al., in press), an open-source web application supporting collaborative editing of ontologies, thesauri and lexicons, complying with Semantic Web representation standards.

In this use case, the *matching task* comprises two datasets that are managed as two projects in VocBench.

VocBench provides an implementation of the *metadata registry* that covers locally managed datasets and remote ones (which are not associated with a VocBench project).

The *task report* produced by the orchestrator provided by MAPLE is returned to the *user* for explanation and refinement. The (possibly refined) task report is sent to the *alignment service* for the actual execution of the alignment task. The need for accepting the *task report* as an input instead of obtaining it from the orchestrator is motivated by the necessity to include the user in the loop.

In addition to the *task report*, the alignment service may accept some configuration parameters. The configuration is split in two: a *system configuration* that does not depend on the (explicit) choice of a *matcher*, and a *matcher configuration* that is bound to a specific matcher. *Matchers* and *configuration schemas* are clearly dependent on the alignment service, whose interface must include operations for retrieving them.

The computation of an alignment can be a slow task; therefore, it should be handled asynchronously without blocking the application (and thus the user) who submitted

---

[8] http://vocbench.uniroma2.it/

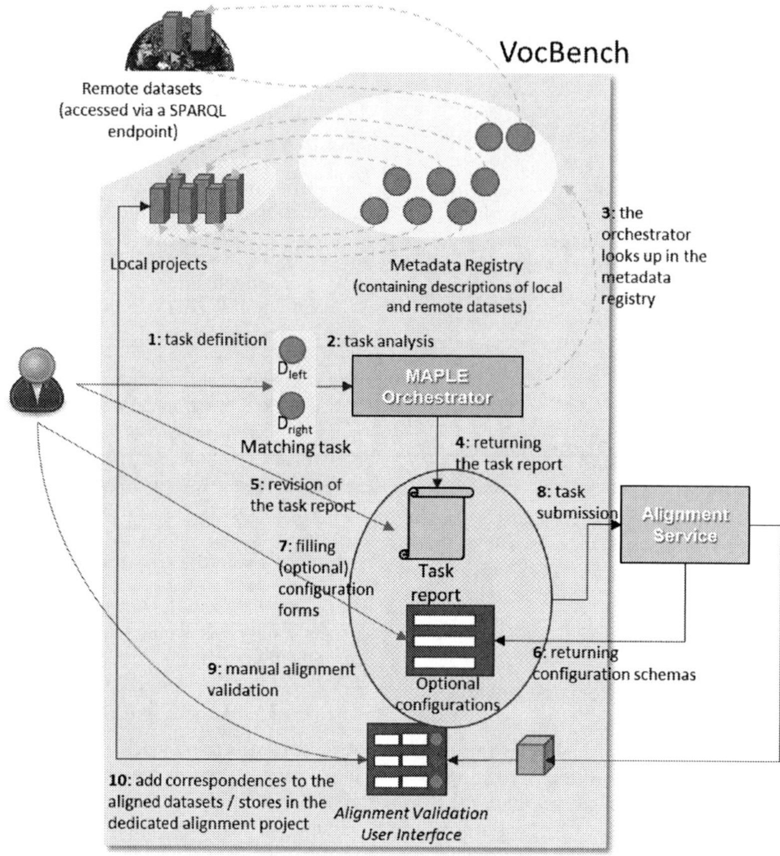

Figure 1: Use case integrating MAPLE, VocBench 3 and an external alignment service

it. Additionally, the alignment service shall support the submission of multiple tasks.

When an alignment task is completed, the user should be able to *download the alignment* into an alignment validation user interface. Validated alignments can then be integrated into either the left or right dataset. Moreover, the user can store that alignment into an *EDOAL project* dedicated to the alignment between these two datasets.

4. API Design Methodology

We designed a resource-centric API without using hypermedia (see Section 5.2), which is required by a strict compliance to the REST architectural style (Fielding, 2008). This kind of API, often called "pragmatic REST", comprises a collection of resources associated with endpoints (i.e. URLs) that can be operated on through standard HTTP verbs (e.g. GET to retrieve the representation of a resource, POST to create a new resource in a collection, etc.).

We analyzed the use case described in Section 3 to identify the resources, their representation and the verbs supported by each of them.

For the development of our API, we adopted the *API-first* approach: i.e. we started from the specifications of the API

itself using the OpenAPI format rather than from the implementation of a reference server. These API specifications are a first-class artifact of the development process and, as such, they can be version controlled, verified, validated and published. Interoperability between clients and servers is guaranteed by the compliance to the same specifications. In fact, compliance to a given API is facilitated by tools that generate *client libraries* (to consume the API) and *server stubs* (to ease the implementation of the API) from the API definition. One such tool is Swagger Codegen[9], which supports tens of different programming languages. Moreover, a lot of API tools can be configured for a certain API by simply loading its definition in OpenAPI format.

5. API Definition

The design of a REST API is focused on the identification of the *resources* in the domain of interest, their *representations* and the *HTTP verbs* that they support. Each kind of resource is often associated with two paths (or endpoints): i) the collection of resources of that kind (e.g. */matchers*), ii) each specific resource of that kind (e.g. */matchers/1*). We represented the resources and the request bodies using JSON, which is currently the de facto standard for web APIs. In our API, some resources are read-only, because they reflect the capabilities of a specific alignment

---

[9] https://swagger.io/tools/swagger-codegen/

```json
{
  "service": "Genoma REST API",
  "version": 1,
  "status": "active",
  "documentation": "https://../Home",
  "specs": [
    "http://../alignment-services-1.0.0.yaml"
  ],
  "configuration" : {
    ...
  }
}
```

Listing 1: Representation of the root resource

service or the result of a computation, while others can be manipulated. This distinction manifests in the support for verbs other then *GET*.

5.1 Resources

5.1.1 API root

The path / is the root of the API namespace. Performing a GET on this path returns a JSON object like the one in Listing 1.

The object contains metadata about the *implementation of the alignment service* such as its name (*service*), *version*, compliance to different *specs* and an optional system *configuration* schema (see Section 5.1.2). The *specs* property is an array of URLs for locating API definitions in the OpenAPI format. This array must contain at least the URL of the description of our REST API. Humans (e.g. developers) interfacing with this service may benefit from a reference to the *documentation* of the service.

When a sever has been just launched, it is not obvious when it is ready to accept requests. An approach to answer this question is to first attempt to retrieve the representation of the root: it can be assumed that a sever is not ready as long the service doesn't respond at all. Once the representation of the root path is returned, the property *status* tells whether the service is *starting*, *active*, *busy* (i.e. no longer accepting task submissions), *shutting down* or *failed*.

5.1.2 Matchers

The design goal of MAPLE is to disburden the user from manual configuration of the matching process to the maximum extent possible. However, an *alignment service* may support an option for manually choosing between different *matchers* (i.e. often associated with different combinations of matching techniques).

The path */matchers* is the collection of all available matchers, whereas the path */matchers/{id}* represents an individual matcher.

Listing 2 illustrates the JSON object describing a matcher, which contains its identifier (*id*), a textual *description* and an optional *configuration* schema.

The configuration schema defines the "shape" of the JSON object that represents the actual *matcher configuration* in a task submission (see Section 5.1.3). Moreover, the configuration schema can be used to produce a suitable user

---

¹⁰ https://json-schema.org/

```json
{
  "id": "example-matcher",
  "description": "example matcher",
  "configuration": {
    "type": "object",
    "properties": {
      "structuralFeatures": {
        "description": "whether to use structural features or not",
        "type": "boolean",
        "default": true
      },
      "synonymExpansion": {
        "description": "whether to do synonym expansion or not",
        "type": "boolean",
        "default": true
      }
    }
  }
}
```

Listing 2: Representation of a matcher

interface to edit the configuration. Instead of reinventing the wheel, we adopted a subset of JSON Schema[10].

If the alignment service does not support manual selection and configuration of the matcher, this collection should be empty.

5.1.3 Tasks

The computation of an alignment is managed as an asynchronous *task*, which needs to be modeled explicitly.

The path */tasks* is the collection of all tasks ever submitted to the alignment service. The description of individual tasks can be obtained from the endpoint */tasks/{id}*. Listing 3 contains a JSON object that exemplifies the representation of a task.

The *id* identifies this task and it can also be found inside the path associated with the task. The properties *leftDataset* and *rightDataset* reference the two datasets to align. The service may differentiate between the *submission time*, when the task was first queued into the system, and the *start time*, when the computation started (pragmatically, when the service allocated computing resources for the task). An *end time* is also included when the execution ends. In fact, the task *status* makes it possible to differentiate between a task that is just *submitted*, *running*, *failed* or *completed*. When a task is *running*, its *start time* is non null and the service is computing the alignment. The task will

```json
{
  "id": "c27d77380cf4[…]020871d5f95c2",
  "leftDataset": "http://example.org/void.ttl#EuroVoc",
  "rightDataset": "http://example.org/void.ttl#TESEO",
  "submissionTime": "202-02-10T18:00:00+01:00",
  "startTime": "202-02-10T18:00:30+01:00",
  "status": "running",
  "progress": 60
}
```

Listing 3: Representation of a task

```json
{
  "taskReport": {
    "leftDataset": { "@id": "http://example.org/void.ttl#TESEO",
      "conformsTo": "http://www.w3.org/2004/02/skos/core#",
      "uriSpace": "http://www.senato.it/teseo/tes/",
      "sparqlEndpoint": "http://localhost:7200/repositories/TESEO_core"
    },
    "rightDataset": { "@id": "http://example.org/void.ttl#EuroVoc",
      "conformsTo": "http://www.w3.org/2004/02/skos/core#",
      "uriSpace": "http://eurovoc.europa.eu/",
      "sparqlEndpoint": "http://localhost:7200/repositories/EuroVoc_core"
    },
    "supportDatasets": [{
        "@id": " http://example.org/void.ttl#TESEO_it_lexset",
        "@type": "http://www.w3.org/ns/lemon/lime#LexicalizationSet"
        "sparqlEndpoint": "http://localhost:7200/repositories/TESEO_core",
        "referenceDataset": "http://example.org/void.ttl#TESEO",
        "lexiconDataset": null,
        "lexicalizationModel": "http://www.w3.org/2008/05/skos-xl",
        "lexicalizations": 3378, "references": 3378,
        "avgNumOfLexicalizations": 1, "percentage": 1,
        "languageTag": "it",
      }, {
        "@id": "http://example.org/void.ttl#EuroVoc_it_lexset",
        "@type": "http://www.w3.org/ns/lemon/lime#LexicalizationSet"
        "sparqlEndpoint": "http://localhost:7200/repositories/EuroVoc_core",
        "referenceDataset": " http://localhost:7200/repositories/EuroVoc_core",
        "lexiconDataset": null,
        "lexicalizationModel": "http://www.w3.org/2008/05/skos-xl",
        "lexicalizations": 18545, "references": 7282,
        "avgNumOfLexicalizations": 2.546, "percentage": 1,
        "languageTag": "it",
      }, {
        "@id": "http://.../omw/MultiWordNet-it-lexicon",
        "@type": "http://www.w3.org/ns/lemon/lime#Lexicon",
        "sparqlEndpoint": "http://localhost:7200/repositories/OMW_core",
        "languageTag": "it", "lexicalEntries": 43011
      }, {
        "@id": "http://.../omw/pwn30-conceptset",
        "@type": "http://www.w3.org/ns/lemon/ontolex#ConceptSet",
        "sparqlEndpoint": "http://localhost:7200/repositories/OMW_core",
        "concepts": 117659
      }, {
        "@id": "http://.../void.ttl#MultiWordNet_ConceptualizationSet",
        "@type": "http://www.w3.org/ns/lemon/lime#ConceptualizationSet",
        "sparqlEndpoint": "http://localhost:7200/repositories/OMW_core",
        "lexiconDataset": "http://.../omw/MultiWordNet-it-lexicon",
        "conceptualDataset": "http://.../omw/pwn30-conceptset",
        "conceptualizations": 63133, "concepts": 35001, "lexicalEntries": 43011,
        "avgSynonymy": 0.537, "avgAmbiguity": 1.468
      }],
    "pairings": [{
        "score": 0.7836831074710862,
        "source": {"lexicalizationSet": "http://example.org/void.ttl#EuroVoc_it_lexset" },
        "target": {"lexicalizationSet": "http://example.org/void.ttl#TESEO_it_lexset" },
        "synonymizer": {
          "lexicon": "http://example.org/void.ttl#OMW_Lexicon",
          "conceptualizationSet": "http://.../void.ttl#MultiWordNet_ConceptualizationSet"
        }
      }]
  }
}
```

Listing 4: Representation of a task submission (this example doesn't include neither a matcher nor configurations)

eventually end either by completing the computation of the alignment or by *failing* for some *reason*. The reason is expressed as a JSON object with at least the property *message*, which shall contain a textual description of the failure. For a running task, the property *progress* contains the percentage (expressed as an integer between 0 and 100) of the task that has been carried on. A *completed* task is associated with an alignment that can be retrieved by means of a GET on the path *tasks/{id}/alignment*. The response is formatted according the format[11] of the Alignment API (David et al., 2011).

The submission of a *task* to the system can be made as a POST to the collection path */tasks*. The body of the request (see Listing 4) represents the submission in terms of a *task report* and, optionally, a *system configuration*, a *matcher* and (only if a *matcher* is provided) a *matcher configuration*.

Let us describe the content of a submission in reverse order, starting from the optional parts. If the alignment service allows that, the parameter *matcher* can be used to manually specify the matching algorithm (see Section 5.1.2). In this case, it is also possible to specify a *matcher configuration* as a JSON object, which shall conform to the configuration schema included in the representation of the matcher. Independently from the choice of a matcher, the user can also provide a *system configuration* as another JSON object, which shall conform to the configuration schema included in the representation of the root resource (see Section 5.1.1).

The *task report* is the only mandatory part of a task submission.

At the beginning of the report, the properties *leftDataset* and *rightDataset* contain the descriptions of the two datasets to match. The descriptions use properties that are in most cases eponym for properties defined by widely adopted metadata vocabularies. The description of a dataset includes its identifier (*"@id"*) (in the metadata registry), which is used in the rest of the task report to mention that dataset. The property *uriSpace* contains the namespace of the dataset (corresponding to *void:uriSpace*), while the property *sparqlEndpoint* contains the address of a SPARQL endpoint that provides access to the actual content of the dataset (corresponding to *void:sparqlEndpoint*). The property *conformsTo* (corresponding to *dcterms:conformsTo*) contains the URI of a modeling vocabulary that defines the type of the dataset (in the example, both datasets are SKOS thesauri).

The property *supportDatasets* is an array of JSON objects describing other potentially useful datasets. Like the ones above, these descriptions also include further properties that are bound to specific dataset types (*@type*).

In the example in Listing 4, the first two support datasets are *lime:LexicalizationSet*s that provide SKOS-XL labels in Italian for each of the input datasets. Indeed, Italian is the only natural language shared by these datasets, and consequently it is suggested as the basis for a monolingual matching scenario. The description of these lexicalization sets includes several properties borrowed from Lime to represent metrics.

The other three datasets define a subset of Open Multilingual Wordnet[12] (Bond & Paik, 2012) for Italian: i) the *ontolex:ConceptSet* describes the set of lexical concepts (i.e. synsets), ii) the *lime:Lexicon* describes the set of words in Italian, iii) the *lime:ConceptualizationSet* describes the

bindings between these words and these concepts (i.e. word senses).

At the end of the report, the property *pairings* contains a ranked list of pairs of lexicalizations for each of the input datasets. Each pairing suggests a different strategy to compare the input datasets from a lexical viewpoint. If available (as in the example), the pairing also includes a *synonymizer* describing a strategy for synonym expansion (see Section 2.1).

The response of this HTTP request is the description of the task just created: using the identifier contained in this description, it is possible to poll the alignment service for updates on the status of the task.

5.2   Linking

Hypermedia is one of the defining characteristics of the REST architectural style, which is neglected by "pragmatic" realizations like ours. The principle is that the representations of the resources should include links to other resources and, in general, make it explicit to the clients the available affordances. The design constraint HATEOAS (Hypermedia as the Engine of Application State) requires that any state transition of the applications should be guided by these links. Without hypermedia, the usage protocol of the API should be encoded in the clients, and possibly communicated through an out-of-band mechanism.

OpenAPI 3 (the version we used to define our API) introduced the notion of links: these are not implemented using hypermedia in the API responses, but are expressed in the API definitions at the operation level. Simplifying, a link tells how part of the response of one operation can be used as argument for another operation. In other words, these links allow for describing (part of) the usage protocol of the API.

Within our API definitions, for example, we used links to tell that the ID contained in the response of creation operations can be used as an argument of operations for retrieving the details of a resource or for deleting it.

6.   Implementation Report

The OpenAPI definition of the *alignment services* API is available online[13].

In Section 3, we gave the overall picture of our use case, integrating VocBench, MAPLE and remote alignment services. Our REST API meets all functional requirements elicited in that section; however, the VocBench user interface is not complete yet:

- users can't choose a matcher and specify its configuration nor can they specify a system configuration
- the task report generated by MAPLE can't be inspected or refined by users

The limitations above are clearly deficiencies of the components using the proposed alignment services API rather than a problem of the API itself: in fact, the

---

[11] http://alignapi.gforge.inria.fr/format.html
[12] http://compling.hss.ntu.edu.sg/omw/
[13]   http://art.uniroma2.it/maple/specs/alignment-services-1.0.0.yaml

capabilities of the API (currently) exceed the ability of other systems to consume them.

We have already implemented a compliant server for the ontology matching tool GENOMA (Enea, Pazienza, & Turbati, 2015) using Swagger Codegen. Additionally, we planned the integration of another matching system called Naisc[14] (McCrae & Buitelaar, 2018).

7.   Evaluation

The focus of our research effort is to provide concrete reusable support to alignment systems, separating the vertical discovery and exploration of efficient alignment techniques from the assessment of the alignment scenario and consequent fine tuning of these techniques to the situation. While the former is clearly not our goal – and thus requires no evaluation, as it mostly depends on the specific considered systems complying with our framework – we conducted an evaluation of the consistency of our approach and implementation in terms of specifications and API validation. Additionally, we provide a qualitative analysis based on our experiences in applying the API-first approach to the development of API-compliant components.

7.1   Verification of the Specifications

We used an online validator[15] to verify that our API definition conformed to the OpenAPI format. A non-conforming API definition might still be quite useful as a documentation for humans; nonetheless, this verification step is necessary to ensure that tooling[16] based on the OpenAPI format (e.g. code generators, testing frameworks, etc.) correctly process our API definition.

The validator confirmed that our API was valid, but it warned of not better specified circular references. We analyzed the API definition and, by revalidating a carefully edited definition, we ascertained that these circular references arose in the data model: in particular, in the data type *Schema*, which represents a JSON Schema that describes a *system configuration* (see Section 5.1.1) or a *matcher configuration* (see Section 5.1.2). Indeed, *Schema* is defined recursively: i.e. this data type occurs in its own definition. Let us consider Listing 2, in which the property *configuration* holds a *Schema* object. This schema models a JSON object that has the properties *structuralFeatures* and *synonymExpansion*. The value of each property is described recursively through a "nested" JSON Schema. In the example, the recursion terminates immediately, because both properties expect a primitive boolean value. However, a more complex configuration property might require several levels of nested JSON objects. Another source of recursion is the definition of *array* properties, whose *items* are modeled recursively with *Schema* objects.

Currently, we are aware of these negative consequences of circular references:

- The documentation generated by Swagger UI[17] doesn't display recursive data types correctly

- We were reported of problems with the OpenAPI Generator[18]. For GENOMA, we used Swagger Codegen without any issue: since GENOMA does not support custom configurations yet, there might be latent problems that we did not discover.

Unfortunately, removing recursion from the definition of *Schema* requires some redundancy in its definition and moreover, sacrificing the support for arbitrary nesting levels. We need to collect several more examples of configuration objects (see Section 9) to make an informed choice about whether the limitations introduced by a non-recursive definition are acceptable.

7.2   Validation of the API

The verification process described in the previous section is about whether we "built it right". However, it does not tell anything about whether we "built the right thing". With this regard, we should point out that we implemented (see Section 6) the use case described in Section 3, allowing the users of VocBench to actually interact with external alignment services using MAPLE. This has increased our confidence that the API we have defined is appropriate for its purpose. As pointed out in Section 9, we believe that onboarding of additional alignment systems should not affect the overall structure of the API, but mainly allow us to better understand the representation of configuration objects.

7.3   Qualitative Evaluation of the API-first approach

Swagger Codegen supports over 20 different languages for the generation of server stubs and over 40 different languages for the generation of client libraries.

The variety of server stubs simplifies the integration of matching systems implemented using different programming languages. In case of GENOMA (see Section 6), which is written in Java, we eventually decided to generate a sever stub utilizing the Spring framework. In fact, the generated stub provided the complete scaffolding of the server, leaving us just to provide the implementation of the operations of the API inside pre-generated methods. The generated code dealt with mapping of URL paths and parameters, clearly facilitating conformance to the API. With this regard, we should mention the automatic generation of a domain model from the JSON schemas (in the API definition) that model parameters and response bodies. This domain model uses standard Java types (e.g. Strings) instead of more specific types (e.g. RDF4J's IRI). This is advantageous since the alignment systems may use different libraries for the same purpose (e.g. RDF4J [19], Apache Jena[20] or OWLAPI[21] as RDF middleware). Initially, we were concerned about losing our customizations when regenerating the server because of changes of the API. However, we discovered that the generator produces a Java interface (which should not be edited at all) and a class implementing that interface (where the developer shall place its code). It is possible to regenerate the sole interface, while the IDE easily identifies

---

[14] https://github.com/insight-centre/naisc

[15] https://apitools.dev/swagger-parser/online/

[16] https://openapi.tools/

[17] https://swagger.io/tools/swagger-ui/

[18] https://openapi-generator.tech/

[19] https://rdf4j.org/

[20] https://jena.apache.org/

[21] http://owlcs.github.io/owlapi/

necessary changes to the class (e.g. new methods, changed method signatures, etc.). Currently, VocBench (see Section 3) is the only consumer of our API. In this case, we could not use the code generator precisely because of the generated domain model, which conflicted with the one already used for the communication with MAPLE: we preferred to implement the client manually, while the fact that the server was generated accordingly acted as a conformance check.

8. Related Work

Shvaiko and Euzenat (2013) analyzed the results of recent evaluation campaigns for ontology alignment[22], concluding that future growth of the field requires addressing eight challenges. Our work focuses on four of those:

- *matcher selection combination and tuning*: not explicitly addressed by MAPLE, but the *task report* is intended to help the alignment service to adapt and fine tune itself in order to fit the characteristics of the given matching scenario;
- *user involvement*: while striving to automate most of the configuration, our approach also foresees human intervention on both the task report and the configuration of the alignment service, as well as during the later validation of an alignment;
- *explanation of matching results*: in fact, our approach focuses on the visibility into the process for setting up and configuring the alignment service for a certain task;
- *alignment management: infrastructure and support*: the REST API presented in this paper and, even more, the overall integration described in Section 3 deal with the infrastructure supporting the management aspects, such as execution of alignment tasks, alignment validation and storage of links.

The Alignment Server, bundled with the Alignment API (David et al., 2011), offers a REST API[23] that can be compared to ours. In fact, the API of the Alignment Server has a wider scope: aiming at managing ontology networks, the Alignment Server supports computation, validation, storage and retrieval of alignments. Our API is focused on supporting the computation of alignments, while the rest is covered by the overall platform described in Section 3.

SEALS[24] (Semantic Evaluation At Large Scale) (Gutiérrez, García-Castro, & Gómez-Pérez, 2010) and HOBBIT[25] (Holistic Benchmarking of Big Linked Data) (Röder, Kuchelev, & Ngonga Ngomo, 2019) are two European projects whose outcome is a sustainable infrastructure for the execution of evaluation campaigns of semantic technologies in a scalable, systematic, repeatable and transparent manner. Consequently, their focus is more on i) unaided execution of heterogeneous systems against shared tests cases and ii) storage and comparison of test results. They also describe procedures to package the systems under test, and they offer a sophisticated platform to execute the resulting packages. Conversely, we don't deal

with the provisioning of computing resources to the alignment services, which are assumed to be up and running on a (remote) machine. Moreover, our approach prescribes that the alignment service is actively aided by its clients, which submit a task report and, optionally, a matcher and some configuration parameters.

The integrated architecture described in Section 3 is close to the architecture of GOMMA, a "generic infrastructure for managing and analyzing life science ontologies and their evolution" (Kirsten et al., 2011). With respect to GOMMA, our whole architecture (including VocBench) covers storing versions of ontologies and mappings, and the invocation of alignment services. We do not cover diffing of ontologies (and mappings) and their evolution yet.

9. Future Work

We represented the resources defined by our API using JSON (see Section 5), while the schema of the task submission (see Section 5.1.3) is informally based on Lime and other metadata vocabularies (i.e. by the use of property names that match the names of the metadata properties). We will investigate JSON-LD[26] to preserve the use of JSON, while making that correspondence explicit through a JSON-LD context (referenced by the responses of our API).

By disseminating our API, we hope to on-board further alignment services beyond the two mentioned in Section 6. We believe that these services shouldn't require (substantial) changes to the operations (i.e. path + HTTP verb), since these are mainly defined from the viewpoint of client systems (i.e. that invoke the alignment service). Conversely, additional alignment services will help us to better understand and improve custom configurations (both at *system level* and *matcher level*), which are specific to an alignment service. Firstly, as the diversity of custom configurations increase, we will test the adequacy of the chosen subset of JSON Schema. Problematic areas include support for complex property values (e.g. structured values, polymorphism, etc.) and complex dependencies between configuration parameters (e.g. mutual exclusiveness between properties, conditional enablement of configuration properties, etc.). More varied configuration schemas will secondly give us the opportunity to understand if there are recurring patterns that deserve being part of a (possibly optional) standard configuration.

The use case presented in Section 3 includes manual evaluation of alignments aimed at improving their quality. We will investigate automatic alignment evaluation (performances, quality etc..) as well, even though instead of reinventing the wheel it could be interesting to see if we can integrate existing solutions such as HOBBIT.

10. Conclusions

MAPLE addresses the need for robustness in alignment systems through a metadata-based approach. In this paper, we concentrated on the interface that an alignment service should implement in order to comply with MAPLE and

---

[22] Such as the ones organized by OAEI (Ontology Alignment Evaluation Initiative) http://oaei.ontologymatching.org/
[23] http://alignapi.gforge.inria.fr/rest.html
[24] http://www.seals-project.eu/
[25] https://project-hobbit.eu/
[26] https://json-ld.org/

benefit from its services. Following the API-first methodology, we started from the specifications of the API as a machine-readable artifact using the OpenAPI format. Then, we implemented the API for the alignment system GENOMA and planned the same for the system Naisc.

11. Acknowledgements

This work has been supported by the PMKI project, under the 2016.16 action of the ISA^2 Programme (https://ec.europa.eu/isa2/). ISA^2 is a programme of the European Commission for the modernization of public administrations in Europe through the eGovernment solutions.

12. Bibliographical References

Bond, F., & Paik, K. (2012). A survey of wordnets and their licenses. Proceedings of the 6th Global WordNet Conference (GWC 2012). Matsue, Japan, January, 9-13, 2012, (pp. 64-71).

Chiarcos, C., Nordhoff, S., & Hellmann, S. (Eds.). (2012). Linked Data in Linguistics. Springer. doi:10.1007/978-3-642-28249-2

Cimiano, P., McCrae, J. P., & Buitelaar, P. (2016). Lexicon Model for Ontologies: Community Report, 10 May 2016. Community Report, W3C. Retrieved from https://www.w3.org/2016/05/ontolex/

David, J., Euzenat, J., Scharffe, F., & Trojahn dos Santos, C. (2011). The Alignment API 4.0. Semantic Web Journal, 2(1), 3-10.

Enea, R., Pazienza, M. T., & Turbati, A. (2015). GENOMA: GENeric Ontology Matching Architecture. In M. Gavanelli, E. Lamma, & F. Riguzzi (A cura di), Lecture Notes in Computer Science (Vol. 9336, p. 303-315). Springer International Publishing. doi:10.1007/978-3-319-24309-2_23

Euzenat, J., & Shvaiko, P. (2013). Ontology Matching (2 ed.). Springer-Verlag Berlin Heidelberg. doi:10.1007/978-3-642-38721-0

Fielding, R. T. (2000). REST: architectural styles and the design of network-based software architectures. University of California. Retrieved from https://www.ics.uci.edu/~fielding/pubs/dissertation/fielding_dissertation.pdf

Fielding, R. T. (2008, October 20). REST APIs must be hypertext-driven. Retrieved from Untangled: https://roy.gbiv.com/untangled/2008/rest-apis-must-be-hypertext-driven

Fiorelli, M., Stellato, A., Lorenzetti, T., Schmitz, P., Francesconi, E., Hajlaoui, N., & Batouche, B. (2019). Metadata-driven Semantic Coordination. In E. Garoufallou, F. Fallucchi, & E. William De Luca (Eds.), Metadata and Semantic Research (Communications in Computer and Information Science) (Vol. 1057). Springer, Cham. doi:10.1007/978-3-030-36599-8_2

Fiorelli, M., Stellato, A., Mccrae, J. P., Cimiano, P., & Pazienza, M. T. (2015). LIME: the Metadata Module for OntoLex. In F. Gandon, M. Sabou, H. Sack, C. d'Amato, P. Cudré-Mauroux, & A. Zimmermann (Eds.), The Semantic Web. Latest Advances and New Domains (Lecture Notes in Computer Science) (Vol. 9088, pp. 321-336). Springer International Publishing. doi:10.1007/978-3-319-18818-8_20

Gutiérrez, M. E., García-Castro, R., & Gómez-Pérez, A. I. (2010). Executing evaluations over semantic technologies using the SEALS Platform. Proceedings of the International Workshop on Evaluation of Semantic Technologies (IWEST 2010). Shanghai, China: CEUR-WS.org. Retrieved from http://ceur-ws.org/Vol-666/paper11.pdf

Kirsten, T., Gross, A., Hartung, M., & Rahm, E. (2011). GOMMA: a component-based infrastructure for managing and analyzing life science ontologies and their evolution. Journal of Biomedical Semantics. doi:10.1186/2041-1480-2-6

McCrae, J. P., & Buitelaar, P. (2018). Linking Datasets Using Semantic Textual Similarity. Cybernetics and Information Technologies, 8(1), 109-123. doi:10.2478/cait-2018-0010

McCrae, J. P., Bosque-Gil, J., Gracia, J., Buitelaar, P., & Cimiano, P. (2017). The OntoLex-Lemon Model: Development and Applications. In I. Kosem, C. Tiberius, M. Jakubíček, J. Kallas, S. Krek, & V. Baisa (Ed.), Electronic lexicography in the 21st century. Proceedings of eLex 2017 conference., (pp. 587-597).

Röder, M., Kuchelev, D., & Ngonga Ngomo, A.-C. (2019). HOBBIT: A platform for benchmarking Big Linked Data. Data Science. doi:10.3233/DS-190021

Shvaiko, P., & Euzenat, J. (2013, January). Ontology Matching: State of the Art and Future Challenges. IEEE Transactions on Knowledge and Data Engineering, 25(1), 158-176. doi:10.1109/TKDE.2011.253

Stellato, A., Fiorelli, M., Turbati, A., Lorenzetti, T., van Gemert, W., Dechandon, D., . . . Costetchi, E. (in press). VocBench 3: a Collaborative Semantic Web Editor for Ontologies, Thesauri and Lexicons. Semantic Web. Accepted manuscript at http://www.semantic-web-journal.net/content/vocbench-3-collaborative-semantic-web-editor-ontologies-thesauri-and-lexicons-1

Stellato, A., Turbati, A., Fiorelli, M., Lorenzetti, T., Costetchi, E., Laaboudi, C., . . . Keizer, J. (2017). Towards VocBench 3: Pushing Collaborative Development of Thesauri and Ontologies Further Beyond. In P. Mayr, D. Tudhope, K. Golub, C. Wartena, & E. W. De Luca (Ed.), 17th European Networked Knowledge Organization Systems (NKOS) Workshop. Thessaloniki, Greece, September 21st, 2017, (pp. 39-52). Retrieved from http://ceur-ws.org/Vol-1937/paper4.pdf

Proceedings of the 7th Workshop on Linked Data in Linguistics (LDL-2020), pages 61–69
Language Resources and Evaluation Conference (LREC 2020), Marseille, 11–16 May 2020
© European Language Resources Association (ELRA), licensed under CC-BY-NC

Using Ontolex-Lemon for Representing and Interlinking Lexicographic Collections of Bavarian Dialects

Yalemisew Abgaz
Adapt Centre, School of Computing
Dublin City University Ireland
Yalemisew.abgaz@adaptcentre.ie

Abstract

This paper describes the conversion of a lexicographic collection of a non-standard German language dataset (Bavarian Dialects) into a Linguistic Linked Open Data (LLOD) format within the framework of ExploreAT! Project. The collection is divided into three parts: 1) conceptual content for unique corpus collection - questionnaire dataset (*DBÖ_questionnaires*) which contains details of the questionnaires and associated questions, 2) metadata regarding the collection framework - including collectors and hierarchical system of localisations, and 3) lexical dataset (*DBÖ_entries*) - both unique data collections as answers to the questions and unique data collections as excerpts of already published sources. In its current form, the *DBÖ_entries* dataset is available in a TEI/XML format separately from the questionnaire dataset. This paper presents the mapping of the lexical entries from the TEI/XML into an LLOD format using the Ontolex-Lemon model. We present the resulting lexicon of Bavarian Dialect and the approach used to interlink the data collection questionnaires with their corresponding answers (lexical entries). The output complements *DBÖ_questionnaires* dataset, which is already in an LLOD format, by semantically interlinking the original questions with the answers and vice-versa.

Semantic publishing, Historical data, Linguistic Linked Open Data, *exploreAT_TEI* conversion

1. Introduction

With the adoption of open access policy, public institutions that deal with a large collection of language resources have shown a growing interest in the publication of resources as linked data using machine-readable lexical models available in the LLOD cloud (Chiarcos et al., 2013). Language resources collected over a long period, with wider geographic coverage and using traditional data collection methods are still in the process of transformation to make the data available in a machine-readable, interlinked and interoperable format. The process widely involves digitisation of both original data collection methods and the collected data from a physical medium such as paper slips, cards, recordings, etc. Semantically linking the questionnaires along with the collectors, time, medium, etc., opens new doors for rich and efficient exploration and reuse to support multidimensional analysis and exploration of the data. This multidimensional analysis uses features such as the question text, authors, collectors, place, and time in addition to the features of the lexical entries such as forms, Part Of Speech (POS), grammar, etc.

The Database of Bavarian Dialects in Austria [Datenbank der Bairischen Mundarten in Österreich] (DBÖ), a digitised non-standard German language resource (Österreichische Akademie der Wissenschaften, 2018), is one of the rich linguistic and lexicographic resources collected from 1913-1998 to document the Bavarian Dialect and rural life in present-day Austria, Czech, Slovakia, Hungary and northern Italy. This collection roughly contains 762 questionnaires with a total of 24,382 questions and 3.6 million paper slips comprising answers to individual questions. There has been a long process of digitisation of the collection including the conversion of the paper-based information to a digital format initially using an old text processing tool called TUSTEP (Barabas et al., 2010), followed by the subsequent conversion of the data into a relational database (dbo@ema)(Wandl-Vogt, Eveline, 2010) and then

into TEI/XML formats (*exploreAT_TEI*) (Schopper et al., 2015; Bowers and Stöckle, 2018). A recent conversion of the dbo@ema database into an LLOD format is performed on the *DBÖ_questionnaires* including authors, collectors, places, sources and paper slips using OLDCAN ontology (Abgaz et al., 2018b; Abgaz et al., 2018a) in the framework of the project exploreAT!.

Despite several efforts made, so far the conversion did not include the *DBÖ_entries*. First efforts in dealing with LLOD were made by Wandl-Vogt and Declerck in 2014 to create a model for the conversion of the printed dictionary (Declerck and Wandl-Vogt, 2014). The *exploreAT_TEI* data efficiently supports the query and retrieval of the lexical entries, offers a well-established data model, yet is still not in a native RDF format and is not compatible with the latest *DBÖ_questionnaires* dataset. With the recent development in publishing linguistic data using widespread lexical models such as Ontolex-Lemon (Cimiano et al., 2020; Cimiano et al., 2016), several efforts are being made in curating, enriching, interlinking and publishing of the DBÖ data in the LLOD platform.

The Ontolex model is widely used to represent and publish lexical resources (Declerck, 2018; Tittel et al., 2018; McCrae et al., 2017; Tiberius and Declerck, 2017; Bosque-Gil et al., 2015). This paper presents an ongoing effort in the conversion of the current *exploreAT_TEI* entries into an LLOD format using the Ontolex-Lemon model and the OLDCAN ontology to link the entries to the corresponding questions. The core entities contained in the *exploreAT_TEI* files are identified and the relevant information is extracted for representing the lexical entries. Since the *DBÖ_entries* dataset contains diverse information extracted from the paper slips, only the relevant elements are included in the conversion.

The main contribution of this paper includes:

- the conversion of the *DBÖ_entries* dataset using the

standard Ontolex-Lemon model and the linking of the *DBÖ_entries* with *DBÖ_questionnaires* dataset which is used to collect the original data. This semantic interlinking flourishes a bi-directional exploration of the data: from lexical entries to questions and questionnaires and vice-versa using aspects including topics, authors, collectors, places, paper slips, etc.

- the analysis of the data in its current form and the mappings from the *exploreAT_TEI* into LLOD and,

- the presentation of the challenges and the lesson learned while converting the data and publishing the resulting lexicon using the Ontolex-Lemon model.

The remaining sections are organised as follows: Section 2. presents the structure and the content of the current TEI/XML format. The mapping to Ontolex-Lemon model and the major design decisions are presented in Section 3. Section 4. discusses the process of interlinking the original questions with the lexical entries, and Section 5. further presents a systematic interlinking of concepts, generated by experts at the questionnaire level, and the lexical entries. Finally, Section 6. presents some of the data quality issues that need to be addressed before publishing the dataset to the public.

2. The *exploreAT_TEI* Data

The main goal of the collection is to document the Bavarian dialects in Austria and publish it in the form of a dictionary (WBÖ) and an atlas. The digitisation of the data collection process and its various supporting materials (DBÖ) offered a knowledge base for a comprehensive, joint approach (dictionary + atlas), prototyped within dbo@ema (Scholz et al., 2008; Wandl-Vogt, 2010) and a cultural, Pan-European exploitation, prototyped within exploreAT!. The data is collected using questionnaires and paper slips distributed via mails and direct interaction with the respondents. The collection suffered several stages of evolution including the scanning and digitisation of paper slips using TUESTEP file format (Barabas et al., 2010), conversion to MySQL (Barabas et al., 2010) and TEI/XML formats (Schopper et al., 2015). The current version of the *exploreAT_TEI* data is TEI version 2 which significantly transformed the original data by reducing redundant data categories (Bowers and Stöckle, 2018). The *exploreAT_TEI* files are organised into folders with the corresponding labels from A-z matching to the physical drawers. Each file contains several elements representing lexical entries with unique identifiers.

The structure of the entries is not homogeneous. However, there are common elements shared among the majority of the entries. These major elements constitute entry, form, orthography, grammar group, POS, sense, etymology, usage, place and date. The entries further contain additional elements such as quotes, references, notes, bibliographies, etc. A snippet of the *exploreAT_TEI* file for an entry ("Oberhaus") is presented in Listing 1.

Each of the above major elements has distinct XML elements and attributes that describe the content of the elements. For keeping the discussion concise, we started from the `<entry>` element and subsequently move deep

into the `<form>` element to introduce the detail information contained in each element. An entry contained in `<entry> ... </entry>` block represents a unique lexical entry. The `<entry>` element has `<form>` representing the different forms of the lexical entry. A lexical entry could have more than one `<form>` element identified by its attribute `'type'`. The type of a form could be one of the following five categories: Hauptlemma (Main lemma), Lautung (Pronunciation), Lehnwort (Loan word), Nebenlemma (Other lemmas) and Verweislemma (Additional related form). The form with the Hauptlemma also has the `<orth>` element representing the orthography of the main lemma. A typical form has one or two `<orth>` entries identified by the type attribute. The `<orth>` could be original (as it appeared on the original paper slip) or normalised (edited by a professional). An entry further has `<gramGrp>` representing the grammar group of the entry, `<sense>` representing the sense of the form, `<ref>` representing additional data such as archive, source, questionnaire number, etc. Finally, an entry has `<usg>` element representing the usage of the lexical entry. The usage type identifies how the lexical entry is used and in the majority of the cases, it is a geographic location.

Listing 1: A snippet of the *exploreAT_TEI* file

```xml
<entry xml:id="h385_qdb-d1e386" xml:lang="bar">
 <form type="hauptlemma">
  <orth type="orig">(Ober)haus</orth>
  <orth type="normalized">Oberhaus</orth>
 </form>
 <gramGrp>
  <pos>Subst</pos>
 </gramGrp>
 <form type="lautung" n="1">
  <pron notation="tustep">s -..ow~An h&#xE2;;us
  </pron>
  <pron notation="ipa" resp="#JB" change="01">
    s -..ow~An h&#xE2;;us
  </pron>
  <gramGrp>
      <gram>[n,sg+A]</gram>
  </gramGrp>
 </form>
 <sense corresp="this:LT1">
  <def xml:lang="de">Vorhaus im ersten Stock</def>
 </sense>
 <form type="nebenlemma">
  <orth type="orig">(Obern)haus</orth>
  <gramGrp>
      <pos>Subst</pos>
  </gramGrp>
      <orth type="normalized">Obernhaus</orth>
 </form>
 <ref type="archiv">
   HK 385, h3850131.pir, korr. E.V.
 </ref>
 <ref type="quelle">Strobl Flachg. Bauer (1972)</ref>
 <ref type="quelleBearbeitet">
      {4.5d06} s&#xF6;Flachg.:
        Sa. Aufn.BAUER&#xB7; (1972) [GaFb2; chTr]
 </ref>
 <usg type="geo">
  <placeName type="orig">Strobl Sa.</placeName>
  <listPlace ref="sigle:4.5d06">
   <place type="Bundesland">
     <placeName>Sa.</placeName>
            <idno>4</idno>
            <listPlace>
                ...
   </place>
  </listPlace>
 </usg>
</entry>
```

Among these elements, the lexicographers who are working in this project have identified the elements that constitute the core of the lexicon. The following section presents a detailed discussion on how these core elements are mapped to Ontolex-Lemon model using R2RML mapping. An intermediate relational database is introduced to facilitate the conversion and to support compatibility with the *DBÖ_questionnaires* dataset. There are three user requirements that the conversion process needs to deliver.

- The use of standard, and widely used model for publishing the LLOD data. The final dataset should use existing models that are standardised and widely used by the lexicographic community.

- The resulting LLOD shall link the lexical entries with the questions used to collect the data explicitly. This will create the bridge between the questionnaire dataset and the lexical dataset.

- The selected method shall consider future semantic enrichment using resources including DBpedia [1], KBpedia [2] and BabelNet [3].

To achieve this, the prevalent Ontolex-Lemon model is used for publishing the lexical data on the LLOD platform. The OLDCAN ontology is also used to preserve the link between the entries and questions. This aspect is dealt with more detail in the following sections.

3. Mapping *exploreAT_TEI* to Ontolex-Lemon

A series of decisions are made to map the core elements of the *exploreAT_TEI* data into Ontolex-Lemon representation using an intermediate relational database and R2RML Mapping. The choice of including an intermediate relational database is to support backward compatibility with the *DBÖ_questionnaires* dataset, which is previously converted from MySQL database (dbo@ema) and also to interlink the lexical data with the questionnaire dataset which was also based on a relational data model (Abgaz et al., 2018b; Abgaz et al., 2018a).

The Ontolex-Lemon model provides a rich semantics to represent linguistic resources by presenting morphological and syntactic properties of lexical entries, which are the core classes of the model. A lexical entry is a building block of a lexicon which consists of a set of forms and their associated meanings (Cimiano et al., 2016). The lexical entry is connected to a Lexical Concept via `evokes/isEvokedby` object property. Lexical entry further relates to Lexical Sense using `sense/isSenseOf` object property. The core Ontolex module is presented in Figure 2 (Cimiano et al., 2016).

A lexical entry represents a unit of analysis of the lexicon that consists of a set of grammatically related forms and a set of base meanings that are associated with all of these forms. Thus, a lexical entry is a `Word`, `Multiword`

`Expression` or `Affix` with a single part-of-speech, morphological pattern, etymology and set of senses. WBOLexicon is created using `ontolex:Lexicon` and the following namespaces are used to be defined throughout all the listings and examples in this paper. The TURTLE syntax is used to present the resulting data snippets.

```
@prefix rdf: <http://www.w3.org/1999/02/22-rdf-
    syntax-ns#>.
@prefix dc: <http://purl.org/dc/elements/1.1/>.
@prefix dct: <http://purl.org/dc/terms/>.
@prefix foaf: <http://xmlns.com/foaf/0.1/>.
@prefix lexinfo: <http://www.lexinfo.net/ontology
    /2.0/lexinfo#>.
@prefix lime: <http://www.w3.org/ns/lemon/lime#>.
@prefix oldcan: <https://explorations4u.acdh.oeaw.
    ac.at/ontology/oldcan#>.
@prefix ontolex: <http://www.w3.org/ns/lemon/
    ontolex#>.
@prefix rdfs: <http://www.w3.org/2000/01/rdf-schema
    #>.
@prefix rr: <http://www.w3.org/ns/r2rml#>.
@prefix skos: <http://www.w3.org/2004/02/skos#>.
@prefix wbo: <https://exploreat.oeaw.ac.at/
    WBOLexicon/>.
```

3.1. Entries and Forms

Entries of the *exploreAT_TEI* dataset are the core elements of the collection. These entries are mapped to `ontolex:LexicalEntry` and are added to the WBOLexicon using `ontolex:entry`. This is a relatively simple mapping which defines all the entries as `ontolex:LexicalEntry` and lays the foundation for the rest of the elements. The following R2RML mapping creates instances of a lexical entry and associates each entry with the WBOLexicon.

```
<#LexiconEntryTriplesMap>
a rr:TriplesMap;
rr:logicalTable [ rr:sqlQuery """
Select 'WBOLexicon' as lexicon, e.id, e.lang from
    entry e; """ ];
rr:subjectMap [
  rr:template "https://exploreat.oeaw.ac.at/{
    lexicon}";
  rr:class ontolex:Lexicon ;
  rr:graph lexGraph: ;] ;
rr:predicateObjectMap [
  rr:predicate ontolex:language ;
  rr:objectMap [ rr:column "lang" ] ;
  rr:graph wbo:lexicon_graph;];
rr:predicateObjectMap [
  rr:predicate ontolex:entry;
  rr:objectMap [
    rr:template "https://exploreat.oeaw.ac.at/
      WBOLexicon/LexicalEntry/{id}" ;
  rr:graph wbo:lexicon_graph;]; ];.
```

The mapping retrieves all the entries in the database and represent them as lexical entries of the lexicon. The resulting lexicon and its lexical entries are presented below.

```
wbo:WBOLexicon a ontolex:Lexicon ;
  ontolex:entry
    <https://exploreat.oeaw.ac.at/WBOLexicon/
      LexicalEntry/h385_qdb-d1e2>,
    <https://exploreat.oeaw.ac.at/WBOLexicon/
      LexicalEntry/h385_qdb-d1e108>,
    <https://exploreat.oeaw.ac.at/WBOLexicon/
      LexicalEntry/h385_qdb-d1e129>,
    ...
```

---

[1] https://wiki.dbpedia.org/
[2] http://kbpedia.org/
[3] https://babelnet.io/

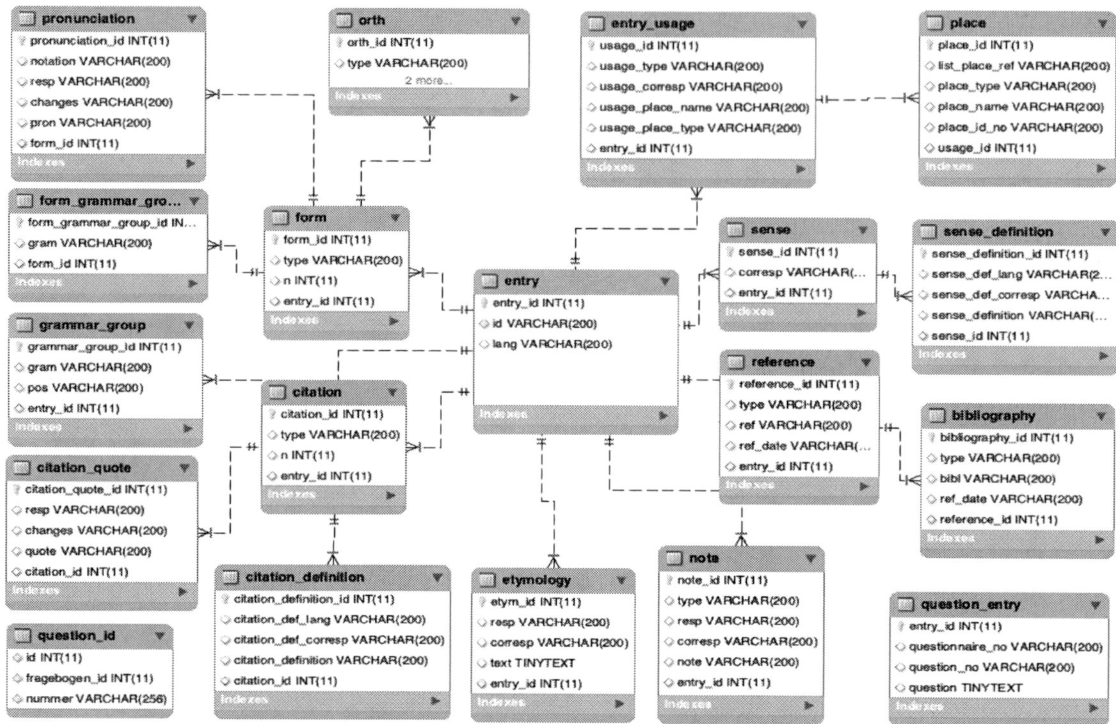

Figure 1: The *exploreAT_TEI* database schema

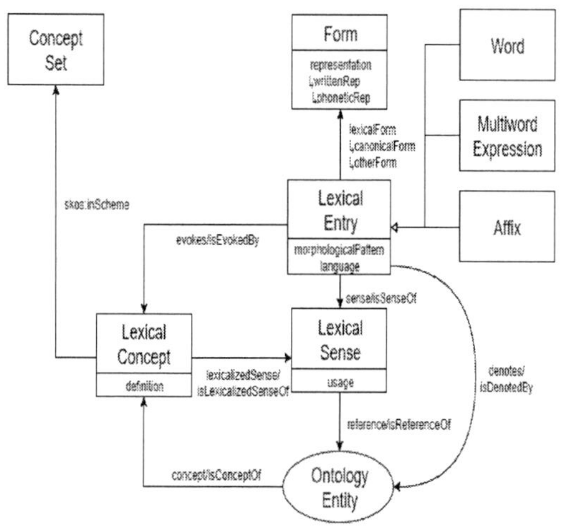

Figure 2: The Ontolex-Lemon model.

At this stage, the mapping does not distinguish between a `word` and `Multiword Expression`. However, it represents the entries using the general `LexicalEntry` class. This is done because the *exploreAT_TEI* dataset does not distinguish between `word`, `MultiwordExpression` and `Affix`. Furthermore, detecting German compound words and Affix from the dataset is complex and beyond the scope of this paper. Each lexical entry is represented using a unique URI generated from the unique id number of the entries in the

exploreAT_TEI files. To support maximum interoperability with the legacy data, we stick to the existing id numbers following trends from similar conversions (Klimek and Brümmer, 2015) use the written representation of the entries.

3.2. Form, Canonical Form and Other Forms

A form is a grammatical realisation of a lexical entry (Cimiano et al., 2016). All the entries in the *exploreAT_TEI* data have at least one form which is represented using `ontolex:Form`. The form is linked to the lexical entry using `ontolex:lexicalForm` object property. We represent the forms with further details by distinguishing between canonical form and other forms.

In the Ontolex-Lemon model, there is only one canonical form allowed per entry. However, there are five different types of forms in the *exploreAT_TEI* dataset. 'HauptLemma' is the main lemma which is selected as a `canonicalForm` and the other four forms are treated differently. The so-called "Lautung" does not represent another form of the entry, but it represents the pronunciation of the entry in Tuestep and IPA notation. Thus, this is automatically excluded but later used to add pronunciation to the entry. "Neben-lemma" is treated as `ontolex:otherForm`, however, "Verweislemma" and "Lehnwort", are not considered important at this stage due to the quality of the data and the ambiguity of the meaning of the categories. Thus, all the forms with type='Hauptlemma' are represented as `ontolex:canonicalForm`, whereas, type='Nebellemma' is represented as `ontolex:otherForm`. The mapping of the form and the `canonicalForm` is given below (Note that the mapping of the `otherForm` is also similar except the query used to extract the rows).

```
<#LexicalEntrycanonicalFormTriplesMap>
a rr:TriplesMap;
rr:logicalTable [ rr:sqlQuery """
select e.id, e.lang, f.entry_id, f.form_id from
entry e left join form f on e.entry_id =
f.entry_id where f.type ='hauptlemma'; """ ];
rr:subjectMap [
  rr:template "https://exploreat.oeaw.ac.at/
      WBOLexicon/
  LexicalEntry/{id}";
  rr:class ontolex:LexicalEntry ;
  rr:graph wbo:lexicon_graph ;] ;
rr:predicateObjectMap [
  rr:predicate ontolex:lexicalForm ;
  rr:predicate ontolex:canonicalForm ;
  rr:objectMap [
  rr:template "https://exploreat.oeaw.ac.at/
      WBOLexicon/Form/
          {form_id}";
  rr:graph wbo:lexicon_graph ;] ] ;
```

Based on the above mapping, a given form is represented using at least one `ontolex:Form` and `ontolex:canonicalForm`.

```
<https://exploreat.oeaw.ac.at/WBOLexicon/
    LexicalEntry/h385_qdb-d1e2>
  lexinfo:partOfSpeech lexinfo:noun ;
  a ontolex:LexicalEntry ;
  ontolex:lexicalForm <https://exploreat.oeaw.ac.
      at/WBOLexicon/Form/1> ;
  ontolex:canonicalForm <https://exploreat.oeaw.ac
      .at/WBOLexicon/Form/1> ;
<https://exploreat.oeaw.ac.at/WBOLexicon/
    LexicalEntry/h385_qdb-d1e108>
  lexinfo:partOfSpeech lexinfo:noun ;
  a ontolex:LexicalEntry ;
  ontolex:lexicalForm <https://exploreat.oeaw.ac.
      at/WBOLexicon/Form/4> .
  ontolex:canonicalForm <https://exploreat.oeaw.ac
      .at/WBOLexicon/Form/4> ;
```

3.3. Form Written Representation and Pronunciation

The *exploreAT_TEI* data contains the `<orth>` element embedded inside the `form` element. The `<orth>` element represents the orthography of the "Hauptlemma" or "NebenLemma".

3.3.1. Written Representation

The orthography of a lexical entry is represented by `ontolex:writtenRep`. The *exploreAT_TEI* dataset also uses a type attribute to distinguish between the original written representation and the normalised representation. The normalised representation transforms the original orthography which contains several diacritic marks and special characters into a normalised representation. I took the normalised representation as a written representation of the form. This is done for two reasons. First, the character encoding of the original representation is not human readable, and the second, search and retrieval with such representation will pose a difficulty.

The written representation is further enriched by `skos:prefLabel` and `rdfs:label`. The content of the original written representation is also captured using `skos:altlabel` which will serve as an alternate label for the form and enable the representation of the standard form.

```
<#FormTriplesMapNormalised>
a rr:TriplesMap;
rr:logicalTable [ rr:sqlQuery """
Select o.orth_id, o.type, o.orth, f.form_id from
form f inner join orth o on f.form_id =o.form_id
where o.type<>'orig'; """ ];
rr:subjectMap [
  rr:template "https://exploreat.oeaw.ac.at/
      WBOLexicon/Form/
  {form_id}";
  rr:class ontolex:Form ;
  rr:graph wbo:lexicon_graph ;] ;
rr:predicateObjectMap [
  rr:predicate ontolex:writtenRep ;
  rr:objectMap [ rr:column "orth" ;rr:language "bar
      ";];
  rr:graph wbo:lexicon_graph ;];
rr:predicateObjectMap [
  rr:predicate rdfs:label;
  rr:predicate skos:preflabel;
  rr:objectMap [ rr:column "orth" ;rr:language "bar
      ";];
  rr:graph wbo:lexicon_graph ;] ;
----------------------------------------------
<#FormTriplesMapPronunciationIPA>
a rr:TriplesMap;
rr:logicalTable [ rr:sqlQuery """
SELECT pron,notation, form_id FROM pronunciation
where notation='ipa'; """ ];
rr:subjectMap [
    rr:template "https://exploreat.oeaw.ac.at/
        WBOLexicon/Form/
    {form_id}" ,
    rr:class ontolex:Form ;
    rr:graph wbo:lexicon_graph ;] ;

rr:predicateObjectMap [
    rr:predicate ontolex:phoneticRep ;
    rr:objectMap [ rr:column "pron";
    rr:language "ipa"; ] ;
    rr:graph wbo:lexicon_graph ;];
```

3.3.2. Pronunciation

The pronunciation of the "Hauptlemma" is included in a separate form element with type "Lautung". All the variant pronunciations with IPA notation and the so called Tustep notation are also included inside `<pron>` element with notation attribute. This information about the pronunciation is represented using `ontolex:phoneticRepresentation`. Below, We demonstrate the result of the mapping of both Tustep and IPA notations.

```
<https://exploreat.oeaw.ac.at/WBOLexicon/Form/1>
    a ontolex:Form ;
    ontolex: rdfs:label "Oberhaus"@bar ;
    skos:altlabel " (Ober)haus"@bar ;
    skos:preflabel "Oberhaus"@bar ;
    ontolex:phoneticRep "'s Oberhaus"@ipa,
            s"'s Oberhaus"@tustep ;
    ontolex:writtenRep "Oberhaus"@bar .
```

3.4. Part of Speech (POS) and Grammatical Groups

The POS of an entry which applies to all the forms within an entry is provided inside the `<gramgrp>` element. This POS applies to all the forms except those forms which have their grammar group. If a form has its grammar group and if the POS is defined there, this form will get its POS instead of inheriting the entry-level POS. Whenever a POS

TEI	Lexinfo	TEI	Lexinfo
Verb	verb	Verb Verb	verb
Subst	noun	Subst Subst	noun
Pron	pronoun	Adj Adj	adjective
Adv	adverb	Adv Adv	adverb
Adj	adjective	Adj Subst	?
Interj	interjection	Verb Subst	?
Num	numeral	Subst Prep	?
Conj	conjunction	Affix	?
Prep	fusedPreposition		

Table 1: Mapping of POS between *exploreAT_TEI* and Lexinfo.

Gram	Gram	Gram	Gram
[P2/1+A]	[sg3+5P3]	[sg3]	[D1,n+A]
[P2/1]	[pl1+5P1]	[pl2+5P2]	[I/1,n+A]
[P1/1,n+A]	[imp,sg2]	[kj,pl3+5P3]	[P1/1,f+A]
[P2]	[pl3+5P3]	[+7]	[P1/1,f]
[P2/1+U]	[kj]	[pl3]	[sg3+0]
[sg+U]	[P1]	[sg3+5P3]	
[sg2+5P2]	[kj,sg1+5P1]	[kj,sg3+5P3]	[m+A]
[sg1+5P1]	[imp]	[kj,sg2+5P2]	[m+U]
[sg2]	[+5P1]	[kj,pl1+5P1]	[il] [m+A]
[D1]	[sg1]	[kj,pl2+5P2]	[+A]

Table 2: Sample grammar group observed in the dataset

information is identified inside the `<form>` element, it is mapped to `lexinfo:pos` in addition to the POS associated with the entry. In the *exploreAT_TEI*, there are 17 different POS used whereas in lexinfo there are only 13 (Buitelaar et al., 2011). A partial mapping of the POS from the *exploreAT_TEI* to lexinfo is implemented during the mapping process shown in Table 1. There are also POS instances (with question marks) which are not mapped to lexinfo due to ambiguous POS elements.

```
<https://exploreat.oeaw.ac.at/WBOLexicon/
    LexicalEntry/h385_qdb-d1e2>
   lexinfo:partOfSpeech lexinfo:noun ;
<https://exploreat.oeaw.ac.at/WBOLexicon/
    LexicalEntry/h385_qdb-d1e689>
   lexinfo:partOfSpeech lexinfo:noun ;
<https://exploreat.oeaw.ac.at/WBOLexicon/
    LexicalEntry/h385_qdb-d1e72>
   lexinfo:partOfSpeech lexinfo:adverb ;
```

This work looks into the grammar group represented at the form level. The grammar group identifies between gender, number and case. Here again, an attempt is made to map the grammar groups at the form level using `lexinfo:gender`, `lexinfo:number` and `lexinfo:case`. However, in the collection, there are more than one million rows of data related to the grammar group. What makes it worse is that there are 5,720 unique combinations of pos, number, gender and case. Supporting a mapping of this grammatical information to the respective representation required significant effort and knowledge. Some of the complexity of the data is shown in the following table where the possible combinations are presented. Due to this complexity, this work does not include details of the form in the current conversion process and this task is left for future work (see the lexinfo entries with "?" in Table 1).

3.5. Sense, Definition, and Etymology

The entry has `ontolex:Sense` information which specifies the context in which the given entry is used. The `<sense>` element also has the `<def>` element which provides the definition of the word. The sense further contains the ISO 639-21 language tag which specifies the language of the definition. Whenever the entry has more than one sense, additional `<sense>` element containing the definition is added. These elements are identified using a number attribute @n.

```
<#SenseTriplesMap>
a rr:TriplesMap;
rr:logicalTable [ rr:sqlQuery """

select s.sense_id, sense_definition from Sense s
left join sense_definition sd
on s.sense_id =sd.sense_id; """ ];
rr:subjectMap [
  rr:template "https://exploreat.oeaw.ac.at/
      WBOLexicon/Sense/
  {sense_id}" ;
  rr:class ontolex:LexicalSense ;
  rr:graph wbo:lexicon_graph ;] ;
rr:predicateObjectMap [
  rr:predicate dct:description ;
  rr:objectMap [ rr:column "sense_definition";
  rr:language "de"; ] ;
  rr:graph wbo:lexicon_graph ;];
```

At this stage, sense is mapped to `ontolex:Sense` and is associated the definition of the sense using `skos:definition` and `dct:description` together with the language in which the definition is given.

```
<https://exploreat.oeaw.ac.at/WBOLexicon/Sense/1>
   dct:description "das obere Stockwerk"@de ;
   a ontolex:LexicalSense ;
   skos:definition "das obere Stockwerk"@de .
<https://exploreat.oeaw.ac.at/WBOLexicon/Sense/10>
   dct:description "Dachbodenraum; Dachboden"@de ;
   a ontolex:LexicalSense ;
   skos:definition "Dachbodenraum; Dachboden"@de .
<https://exploreat.oeaw.ac.at/WBOLexicon/Sense/11>
   dct:description "Vorhaus im ersten Stock"@de ;
   a ontolex:LexicalSense ;
   skos:definition "Vorhaus im ersten Stock"@de .
<https://exploreat.oeaw.ac.at/WBOLexicon/Sense/12>
   dct:description "Husl bei Strengberg"@de ;
   a ontolex:LexicalSense ;
   skos:definition "Husl bei Strengberg"@de .
```

This paper further presents the etymology of the lexical entries whenever they are available. The etymology of the lexical entries represents the origin of the word and a proposed module for representing details of the etymology is presented in (Khan, 2018). Since our etymology collection is not complex, it is represented using the `lexinfo:etymology` object property linked to the lexical entry. A careful investigation of the etymology data in the collection shows that a further expert analysis of the content of the etymological data is crucial for the efficient utilisation by non-expert users.

```
https://exploreat.oeaw.ac.at/WBOLexicon/
    LexicalEntry/h385_qdb-d1e2>
  lexinfo:etymology "s.a. TSA 3,53"@de ;
  lexinfo:partOfSpeech lexinfo:noun ;
  a ontolex:LexicalEntry ;
  ontolex:canonicalForm <https://exploreat.oeaw.ac
      .at/WBOLexicon/Form/1>;
  ontolex:lexicalForm <https://exploreat.oeaw.ac.
      at/WBOLexicon/Form/1>;
  ontolex:sense <https://exploreat.oeaw.ac.at/
      WBOLexicon/Sense/1>.
```

4. Interlinking Lexical Entries to the Original Questions

One of the requirements is to create a meaningful relationship between the different stages of the collection. In (Abgaz et al., 2018b), the data collection method is represented with OLDCAN ontology. The subsequent task which interlinks the original questions used to collect the data to the answers is also covered included in the model. OLDCAN models the answers initially as lemma and subsequently, they are represented as lexical entries using Ontolex-Lemon. This has not been done initially due to the absence of information to represent the answers in a detailed form. However, once the *exploreAT_TEI* data is converted into LOD, the next step is to link the questionnaire with the lexical entries.

Each entry in the *exploreAT TEI* file contains a `<ref>` element with a pointer to the question number (fragebogen-Nummer) that combines the questionnaire and the question number to identify the corresponding question for the lexical entry. This provides crucial information, however, the raw data itself is not represented accurately and it poses a challenge to directly create the required link. To address this problem, the scope is narrowed down to the Systematic, Additional and Dialectographic questionnaires (1-120)(Abgaz et al., 2018b) and link the questions of these questionnaires with the lexical entries. For the rest of the questionnaire, currently, it is not possible to resolve the links from the data provided in the *exploreAT_TEI* dataset.

```
<https://exploreat.oeaw.ac.at/WBOLexicon/
    LexicalEntry/h385_qdb-d1e108>
  lexinfo:partOfSpeech lexinfo:noun ;
  a ontolex:LexicalEntry ;
  ontolex:canonicalForm <https://exploreat.oeaw.ac
      .at/WBOLexicon/Form/4> ;
  ontolex:lexicalForm <https://exploreat.oeaw.ac.
      at/WBOLexicon/Form/4> ;
  oldcan:isAnswerOf <https://exploreat-
      questionnaireexplorer.hephaistos.arz.oeaw.
      ac.at/Question/13225>.

<https://exploreat-questionnaireexplorer.
    hephaistos.arz.oeaw.ac.at/Question/13225>
  oldcan:isQuestionOf <https://exploreat-
      questionnaireexplorer.hephaistos.arz.oeaw.
      ac.at/Questionnaire/92> ;
  oldcan:originalQuestion "Wohnhaus/Dachboden:
      Dachboden (Speicher, Unterdach, Diele); Ra.
      wie: auf der hoh' Diel'"@de ;
  a oldcan:SyntacticQuestion ;
  oldcan:number "F13";
  oldcan:shortQuestion "Dachboden (Speicher,
      Unterdach, Diele); Fg./Ra.*"@de .
```

Thus, this work implements the link using the `oldcan:hasAnswer` object properties with the question as a domain and the lexical entry as a range of the object property along with its inverse oldcan:isAnswerOf property. The Previous example shows the details of a question linked with its answers.

5. Interlinking of Questionnaire Concepts to Lexical Entries

In previous efforts, the questionnaires were linked to DBpedia concepts via a semi-automatic extraction of fine-grained questionnaire topics. These topics in combination with the questionnaire titles were used to extract potential concepts using DBpedia Spotlight[4]. Further, the suggested concepts with greater than 99% accuracy were evaluated and selected by subject matter experts. Even if these concepts are a bit generic, they are very useful in representing the main concepts that are covered by the questionnaires. This gives us the starting point to link the lexical entries to DBpedia concepts using `ontolex:denotes` relationship. At this stage, an experiment is conducted on some selected questionnaire concepts to see whether it is appropriate to use these suggested DBpedia concepts for lexical entries. The result shows that the concepts at the questionnaire level are too generic and can not be used meaningfully to represent the concepts of the lexical entries. As the assumption is evaluated, the topics in the questionnaires provide only high-level concepts, whereas the lexical entries provide very detailed concepts. The gap is created because the concepts in the questionnaires are further specialised in the questions and subquestions. The lexical entries are collected in response to the questions and due to this, they represent very specific concepts. To effectively resolve this problem, both bottom-up and top-down approach should be used. The bottom-up approach seeks to retrieve a matching concept for the lexical entry from DBpedia and the top-down approach will provide a mechanism to disambiguate the results of the bottom-up approach. With this idea in mind, this paper demonstrates the potential of the interlinking process to support further enrichment to the collection. Thus, we decide to relate these questionnaire concepts indirectly via `oldcan:isAnswerOf` relation (Section 4.), which link the lexical entries with the questions.

6. Data Quality Issues for Further Improvement

The resulting LLOD data represents the lexicographic collection with rich information using the standard ontolex model. Sample *exploreAT_TEI* file, the database structure, the R2RML mapping and some resulting dataset in a TTL format is available at github[5]. Since the final data size is large, it not available for public use at this stage. The entries are represented using the core classes defined in the Ontolex-Lemon model. The dataset in its current form, however, needs further quality checks before it is made available to the public. Some of the data quality issues and potential remedies are outlined below.

---

[4]https://www.dbpedia-spotlight.org/
[5]https://github.com/yalemisewAbgaz/
TEI-XML_Mapping.git

6.1. Word, MultiwordExpression and Affix

The current conversion of the lexical entries does not use the subclasses of the `ontolex:LexicalEntry`. The entries are not classified as Word, MultiwordExpression or Affix. In its current form, it is not a trivial task to classify the lexical entries into the subclasses. However, by combining the grammatical information with external resources such as GermaNet, BabelNet and DBPedia entries, it is possible to classify the entries with their respective subclasses. This will improve the quality of the final dataset by incorporating useful details about the entries.

6.2. Part of speech, Grammar and Etymology

The conversion represents a significant portion of the POS of the lexical entries. However, there are some POS entries that are not mapped to `lexinfo:partOfSpeech`. There are two options to address this problem. First, involving experts to map the parts of speech that are not mapped to `lexinfo:partOfSpeech` and provide the complete mapping. The second option is to use the parts of speech in the *exploreAT_TEI* files and include them in the OLD-CAN ontology to represent them, which is a less preferable option. The first option will keep the data compatible by using standardised POS used elsewhere, however, it requires a deeper expert analysis of the cases. This will improve the quality of the resulting LLOD data.

The grammar group is also another area of investigation to deliver a rich lexicon with the grammatical information already available in the *exploreAT_TEI* file. It requires a deeper analysis of the combinations of the grammar groups and a method to decipher the grammatical data and map it to the standard grammatical groups, for example, `lexinfo:case`, `lexinfo:number`, `lexinfo:gender`, etc.

The etymology data and other related data also needs some improvement. There are several abbreviations, mnemonics and acronyms that are included in the data. The presence of such data without the corresponding interpretation will make the data less usable both by humans and machines. To address this problem, a scripting language with some expert assistance can be used to transform the abbreviations, mnemonics and acronyms into their corresponding definitions.

7. Conclusion

This paper presents the results of ongoing conversion of a huge lexicographic dataset from *exploreAT_TEI* format to a LLOD format to digitally publish the RDF version of the dictionary of the Bavarian dialects. In the conversion process, the core elements of the *exploreAT_TEI* data are transformed into Ontolex-Lemon classes and properties. As the data is not homogeneous, the mapping process is not always straightforward, however, the implementation tries to identify the best mappings for each of the selected data. This is the first stage of the transformation of the *exploreAT_TEI* data by focusing on the core elements of the dataset. Future work will include the enrichment of the LOD data with additional information including fine-grained DBpedia concepts for each lexical entry, enrichment of the lexical entries into Word, Multiword Expression and Affix and integration of the resulting data into the visualisation system (Rodríguez Díaz et al., 2019) developed for the exploreAT! project.

Acknowledgements: This research is funded by the Nationalstiftung of the Austrian Academy of Sciences under the funding scheme: Digitales kulturelles Erbe, No. DH2014/22. as part of the exploreAT! and the ADAPT SFI Research Centre at Dublin City University. The ADAPT SFI Centre for Digital Media Technology is funded by Science Foundation Ireland through the SFI Research Centres Programme and is co-funded under the European Regional Development Fund (ERDF) through Grant # 13/RC/2106.

8. Bibliographical References

Abgaz, Y., Dorn, A., Piringer, B., Wandl-Vogt, E., and Way, A. (2018a). A semantic model for traditional data collection questionnaires enabling cultural analysis. In John P. McCrae, et al., editors, *Proceedings of the Eleventh International Conference on Language Resources and Evaluation (LREC 2018)*, Paris, France, may. European Language Resources Association (ELRA).

Abgaz, Y., Dorn, A., Piringer, B., Wandl-Vogt, E., and Way, A. (2018b). Semantic modelling and publishing of traditional data collection questionnaires and answers. *Information*, 9(12).

Barabas, B., Hareter-Kroiss, C., Hofstetter, B., Mayer, L., Piringer, B., and Schwaiger, S. (2010). *Digitalisierung handschriftlicher Mundartbelege. Herausforderungen einer Datenbank. In Fokus Dialekt.* Analysieren-Dokumentieren-Kommunizieren; Olms Verlag, Hildesheim, Germany.

Bosque-Gil, J., Gracia, J., Aguado-de Cea, G., and Montiel-Ponsoda, E. (2015). Applying the ontolex model to a multilingual terminological resource. In Fabien Gandon, et al., editors, *The Semantic Web: ESWC 2015 Satellite Events*, pages 283–294, Cham. Springer International Publishing.

Bowers, J. and Stöckle, P. (2018). Tei and bavarian dialect resources in Austria: updates from the DBÖ and WBÖ. In Andrew U. Frank, et al., editors, *Proceedings of the Second Workshop on Corpus-Based Research in the Humanities (CRH-2)*, pages 45–54. Gerastree proceedings.

Buitelaar, P., McCrae, J., and Sintek, M. (2011). Lexinfo: A declarative model for the lexicon-ontology interface. *Web Semantics: Science, Services and Agents on the World Wide Web*, 9:29–51, 03.

Chiarcos, C., Cimiano, P., Declerck, T., and McCrae, J. P. (2013). Linguistic linked open data (LLOD). introduction and overview. In *Proceedings of the 2nd Workshop on Linked Data in Linguistics (LDL-2013): Representing and linking lexicons, terminologies and other language data*, pages i – xi, Pisa, Italy, September. Association for Computational Linguistics.

Cimiano, P., McCrae, J. P., and Buitelaar, P. (2016). Lexicon model for ontologies: Community report. Technical report, W3C Ontology-Lexicon Community Group.

Cimiano, P., Chiarcos, C., McCrae, J. P., and Gracia, J.,

(2020). *Modelling Lexical Resources as Linked Data*, pages 45–59. Springer International Publishing, Cham.

Declerck, T. and Wandl-Vogt, E. (2014). Cross-linking Austrian dialectal dictionaries through formalized meanings. In Andrea Abel, et al., editors, *Proceedings of the XVI EURALEX International Congress*. EURAC research, July.

Declerck, T. (2018). Towards a linked lexical data cloud based on ontolex-lemon. In *Proceedings of the Eleventh International Conference on Language Resources and Evaluation (LREC 2018)*, page 7–12, Miyazaki, Japan.

Khan, A. F. (2018). Towards the representation of etymological data on the semantic web. *Information*, 9(12).

Klimek, B. and Brümmer, M. (2015). Enhancing lexicography with semantic language databases. *Kernerman DICTIONARY News*.

McCrae, J., Bosque-Gil, J., Gracia, J., Buitelaar, P., and Cimiano, P. (2017). The ontolex-lemon model: Development and applications. In *Proceedings of the 5th Biennial Conference on Electronic Lexicography (eLex 2017)*, page 587–597, Leiden, The Netherlands.

Rodríguez Díaz, A., Benito-Santos, A., Dorn, A., Abgaz, Y., Wandl-Vogt, E., and Therón, R. (2019). Intuitive ontology-based sparql queries for rdf data exploration. *IEEE Access*, 7:156272–156286.

Scholz, J., Bartelme, N., Fliedl, G., Hassler, M., Kop, C., Mayr, H., Nickel, J., Vöhringer, J., and Wandl-Vogt, E. (2008). dbo@ema. a system for archiving, handling and mapping of heterogeneous dialect data for dialect dictionaries. In *Proceedings of the XIII euralex International Congress*, pages 1467–1472. Documenta Universitaria.

Schopper, D., Bowers, J., and Wandl-Vogt, E. (2015). dboe@tei: Remodelling a data-base of dialects into a rich lod resource. In *Proceedings of the 9th International Conference on Tangible, Embedded, and Embodied Interaction (TEI 2015)*, Stanford, CA, USA.

Tiberius, C. and Declerck, T. (2017). A lemon model for the ANW dictionary. In Iztok Kosem, et al., editors, *Proceedings of the eLex 2017 conference. Biennial Conference on Electronic Lexicography (eLex-17), Lexicography from scratch, September 19-21, Leiden, Netherlands*, pages 237–251. INT, Trojína and Lexical Computing, Lexical Computing CZ s.r.o., 9.

Tittel, S., Bermúdez-Sabel, H., and Chiarcos, C. (2018). Using rdfa to link text and dictionary data for medieval french. In *Proceedings of the Eleventh International Conference on Language Resources and Evaluation (LREC 2018)*, page 7–12, Miyazaki, Japan.

Wandl-Vogt, E. (2010). Point and find: the intuitive user experience in accessing spatially structured dialect dictionaries. *Slavia Centralis*, pages 35–53, 02.

9. Language Resource References

Wandl-Vogt, Eveline. (2010). *Datenbank der bairischen Mundarten in Österreich electronically mapped [Database of the Bavarian Dialects in Austria electronically mapped] (dbo@ema)*. Österreichische Akademie der Wissenschaften.

Österreichische Akademie der Wissenschaften. (2018). *Datenbank der bairischen Mundarten in Österreich [Database of Bavarian Dialects in Austria] (DBÖ)*. Österreichische Akademie der Wissenschaften.

Proceedings of the 7th Workshop on Linked Data in Linguistics (LDL-2020), pages 70–74
Language Resources and Evaluation Conference (LREC 2020), Marseille, 11–16 May 2020
© European Language Resources Association (ELRA), licensed under CC-BY-NC

Involving Lexicographers in the LLOD Cloud with LexO, an Easy-to-use Editor of Lemon Lexical Resources

Andrea Bellandi, Emiliano Giovannetti
Institute of Computational Linguistics
Via G. Moruzzi, 1 - Pisa, Italy
{name.surname}@ilc.cnr.it

Abstract

In this contribution we show LexO, a user-friendly web collaborative editor of lexical resources based on the *lemon* model. LexO has been developed in the context of Digital Humanities projects, in which a key point in the design of an editor was the ease of use by lexicographers with no skill in Linked Data or Semantic Web technologies. Though the tool already allows to create a *lemon* lexicon from scratch and lets a team of users work on it collaboratively, many developments are possible. The involvement of the LLOD community appears now crucial both to find new users and application fields where to test it, and, even more importantly, to understand in which way it should evolve.

Keywords: Semantic Web, tools for E-Lexicography, lemon model

1. Introduction

The increasing growth of the Linguistic Linked Open Data Cloud[1] (LLOD) witnesses the liveliness of activities carried out by the relative community (in which the Open Linguistics Working Group[2] stands out) in the last few years. In this context, the availability of models and tools can be crucial to attract people (such as linguists, lexicographers, terminologists) willing to be involved but who feel worried by the lack of standards and, at the same time, by the technological skills required to face the construction of a resource as a linked data.

A solution to the first issue has come from the definition of *lemon*, a model developed to create resources formally describing lexicalizations of ontological concepts (McCrae et al., 2012b). The *lemon* model has been designed to compensate for the way in which the Web Ontology Language (OWL) (McGuinness and Harmelen, 2004) allows to denote a concept, i.e. by simply labelling it with a string and not, as it can be desired, with a complex lexical unit. Today, *lemon* can be considered a *de facto* standard for the representation of computational lexicons in the Semantic Web (SW). The number of users potentially interested in editing or consuming *lemon* data is large (McCrae et al., 2017). However, the construction of a lexicon based on *lemon* can be a tedious process, due to the complexity of the model (constituted by a number of different modules) and on the need of relying on complex patterns, such as reification, to represent certain phenomena.

In order to face the second issue, relative to the aforementioned "technical bottleneck", we have developed LexO[3] (Bellandi et al., 2019; Bellandi and Khan, 2019), a collaborative, easy to use, web editor of lexical resources based on the *lemon* model. In the context of Semantic Web (SW), very few editors of lexicons exist, and just two of them (at

least to the best of our knowledge) handle the *lemon* model. The first one is "*lemon* source", a Wiki-like web interface to manipulate and publish *lemon* data in a collaborative way (McCrae et al., 2012a). *lemon* source allows a user to upload a lexicon and share it with others. This tool was developed as an open-source project, based on the *lemon* API, and it is freely available for use online. However, it can only manage older versions of the *lemon* model, and it doesn't seem to be updated anymore.

The tool that appears to be the most similar to LexO is VocBench (Stellato et al., 2017) a web-based, multilingual, collaborative development platform born to manage OWL ontologies and SKOS(/XL) thesauri and more recently updated to manage also Ontolex-Lemon lexicons and generic RDF datasets. VocBench is a very well engineered tool, conceived for users with experience in SW technologies and vocabularies. Indeed, the main difference between VocBench and LexO lies in target users and the required expertise to use the tool. As a matter of fact, LexO is aimed at lexicographers who have no (or very limited) skills in representing lexica using the OntoLex-Lemon model and, more in general, in using SW and LD related technologies. However, the ease with which a user can create a lemon lexical resource in LexO is counterbalanced by the little flexibility it currently offers, for example to extend the underlying lexical model with custom classes or relations, as VocBench allows to do.

2. An Overview of LexO

LexO[4] is a collaborative web editor for easily building and managing *lemon* resources. The features of LexO were defined on the basis of our experience gained in the creation of lexical and terminological resources in the framework of several projects in the field of Digital Humanities. The context in which the first version of LexO was devel-

---

[1] https://linguistic-lod.org/

[2] http://linguistics.okfn.org

[3] It is fully compatible with the latest version of lemon, developed by the Ontology Lexicon (Ontolex) community group. Please, see https://www.w3.org/2016/05/ontolex/

[4] The source code is available at https://github.com/andreabellandi/LexO-lite. You can find a demo at http://klab.ilc.cnr.it/talmud/LexO

oped is DiTMAO[5], a project aimed at producing a digital-born multilingual medico-botanical terminology pivoting on Old Occitan and developed by philologists (Bellandi et al., 2018b). Then, a team of lexicographers applied LexO to create FdS[6], a multilingual diachronic lexicon of Saussurean terminology in the framework of an Italian PRIN project (Bellandi et al., 2018a). Finally, a bilingual Chinese-Italian resource was created with LexO on the basis of Matteo Ricci's Atlas in the context of Totus Mundus[7] project (Piccini et al., 2018).

Currently LexO is being used in the context of the Babylonian Talmud Translation Project in Italian[8], to create a multilingual Aramaic/Hebrew/Italian terminological resources of the talmudic domain. The examples that will follow are based on this work. During the development of LexO we have also been influenced by some of the latest works taking place in the European H2020 project ELEXIS (in which the Institute of Computational Linguistics of Pisa is involved as a partner). In particular, our work has been closely informed by the survey of lexicographic users' needs conducted as part of the project and recently published as a deliverable[9]. The main aim of LexO is to encourage the involvement of lexicographers in the LLOD community by i) spreading the use of the *lemon* model also in communities of lexicographers new to the modelling of resources as linked data ii) make the model available to lexicographers already involved in LD and SW but who do not have the skills to handle the required technologies.

In this sense, LexO acts as a filter between the formal representation language encoding the lexicon and the user, allowing the latter to focus on the lexicographic work without having to take care of the underlying modeling technology. To bring an example, to establish a translation relation between two lexical senses the user does not have to know which properties are to be involved and how to instantiate the reification pattern required by the "variation and translation" (vartrans) module of *lemon*. Another key feature of LexO is its collaborative nature. As a web application, it allows a team of users with different roles (administrators, editors, viewers, etc.) to work on the same resource at the same time. The issue of concurrent access has been faced by implementing locking mechanisms. As soon as a user starts editing a certain lexical entry, the system locks it and all the related entities, avoiding the concurrent editing of other users.

Finally, LexO provides a set of services implemented with RESTful protocols that give software agents access to the resources managed by the tool. The REST interface implemented in the system allows to query individual resources and get information about lexical entries in JSON format.

In the current version, a first set of basic REST services is available, though which it is possible to list all the lexicon languages, the lexicon lemmas, the lemma metadata, the lemmas involved in a specific lexico-semantic relation with a given lemma, and some basic statistics.

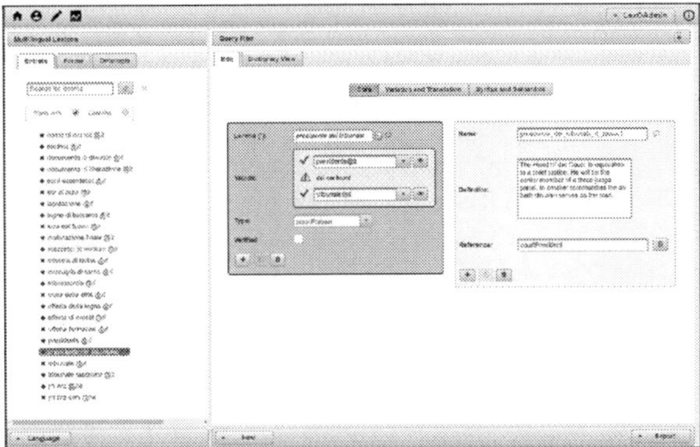

Figure 1: The main interface of LexO showing the core module.

The system interface has been conceptually designed on the basis of the *lemon* model[10]. As shown in figure 1, the linguistic information is organized in 3 modules[11]:

- the core module, to define the structure of each entry, e.g., lemma, other forms, senses;

- the variation and translation module, to represent the variation of relations across entries in the same or different languages (e.g., dialectal, register, and translation relations, or morphological and orthographic ones);

- the syntactic and semantics module, to describe the syntactic behavior of an entry, its valence (the syntactic arguments involved by the situation the word refers to) and the link to the ontological structures representing the meaning of the entry.

A particular consideration has to be made regarding the core module (OntoLex). As already said, LexO is based on the lemon model, which was designed to lexicalize ontologies in an onomasiological perspective (i.e. from the concept to the word). LexO, on the contrary, aims at supporting in the construction of lexical resources by starting from text, in a more semasiological perspective (i.e. from the word to the concept), without requiring that an ontology must be available from the beginning. As a matter of fact, the system does not force the user to link each lexical sense to a concept. However, to stay compliant to the lemon model, it links an *OWL:Nothing* class to each new lexical sense, though in a transparent way to the user. If a user does want to specify the conceptual reference of a lexical sense, LexO provides a way to import an OWL ontology and link

---

a sense to any of its ontological entities (class, instance or property).

2.1. Working Examples

The main interface of LexO, as shown in Figure 1, is designed for the editing of a multilingual lexicon. It is mainly composed of 2 parts. The leftmost column allows a user to browse lemmas, forms and senses, according to the OntoLex-Lemon core model. If the resource is multilingual, a lexicographer can filter lemmas, forms and senses by language. Information related to the selected entry is shown in the central panel where the system shows the lexical entry of reference, alongside the lemma (red box), its forms (blue boxes) and the relative lexical senses (yellow boxes). By means of the plus button it is possible to add other forms and other senses. Figure 1 shows the entry "presidente del tribunale" (court president) modeled with the decomp[12] module. LexO automatically tries to link each multiword component to the correspondent lexical entry, if already available in the lexicon.

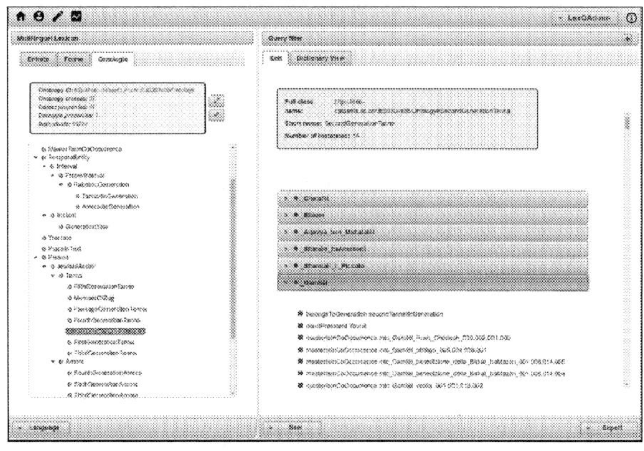

Figure 2: The management of the imported ontology.

As figure 2 depicts, LexO gives users the possibility to import an existing domain ontology, visualize its hierarchical structure, its properties and instances, and allows the association of an ontological entity to a lexical sense. In our example of figure 2, the Talmud domain ontology, which is being developed within the project, is shown. The sense of the term "presidente del tribunale" is linked to the object property *talmud:courtPresident* binding Jewish Rabbis to geographical places.

Through the select button at the top center of the interface of figure 1, a lexicographer can switch to the "variation and translation" or the "syntax and semantics" part. The former (figure 3) consists of two kinds of relations: i) the semantic relations holding between senses and including terminological relations (dialectal, register, chronological, discursive, and dimensional variation) and the translation relation; ii) the relations linking lexical entries and/or forms, which describe, for example, the morphological and orthographic variations of the word. Figure 3 shows an example of relation between lexical entries, i.e. "presidente" is the head of

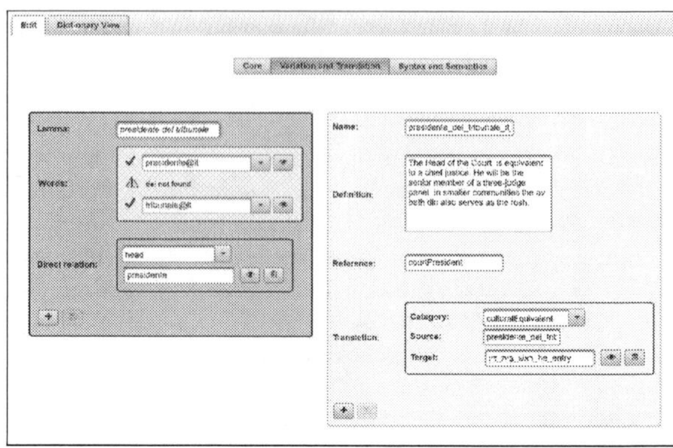

Figure 3: The interface to the variation and translation module.

"presidente del tribunale", and a relation between senses, i.e. the cultural Italian translation[13] with the original sense associated with the Hebrew term. The encoding generated by LexO is the following:

```
:presidente_del_tribunale_it_entry a
    ontolex:LexicalEntry,
    ontolex:MultiwordExpression ;
    lexinfo:partOfSpeech lexinfo:NounPhrase ;
    decomp:constituent :presidente_it_comp0,
        :del_it_comp1, :tribunale_it_comp2 ;
    ontolex:canonicalForm
        :presidente_del_tribunale_it_lemma ;
    ontolex:sense
        :presidente_del_tribunale_it_sense1 .

:presidente_del_tribunale_it_lemma a ontolex:Form ;
    ontolex:writtenRep "presidente del tribunale"@it .

:presidente_it_entry lexinfo:head
    :presidente_del_tribunale_it_entry .

:presidente_del_tribunale_it_sense1 a
    ontolex:LexicalSense ;
    skos:definition "The Head of the Court ..."@en ;
    ontolex:reference talmud:courtPresident .

:rosh_beit_din_heb_sense1 a
    ontolex:LexicalSense ;

:trans a vartrans:Translation ;
    vartrans:source
        :presidente_del_tribunale_it_sense1 ;
    vartrans:target :rosh_beit_din_heb_sense1 ;
    vartrans:category transcat:culturalEquivalent .
```

Figure 4 shows the syntactic behavior of a word and its government pattern, namely the actants introduced by the word, their syntactic functions and their morpho-syntactic realization. These syntactic frames need also to be bound to the ontological structures representing their meaning. As a consequence, LexO makes it possible to map the argument of a predicate defined in an ontology and the syntactic argument introduced in a given syntactic frame.

Figure 4 depicts an example of noun frame of the term having a subject and an (optional) object that has the preposition "di" (of) as marker. An example of frame instance in the Italian translation of the Babylonian Talmud is: "Ma quando giunsero presso il tribunale a Yavnè, rabbàn Gamlièl, che era il presidente del tribunale, accettò la loro

---

[12]https://www.w3.org/2016/05/ontolex/ #decomposition-decomp

[13]LexO also uses the vocabulary *transcat* defined at http:// purl.org/net/translation-categories

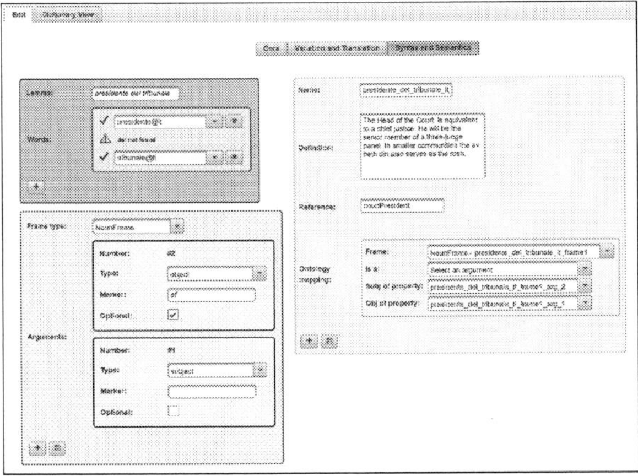

Figure 4: The interface to the syntax and semantics module.

testimonianza" ("But when they arrived at the court in Yavnè, rabbàn Gamlièl, who was the president of the court, accepted their testimony"). Basically, the term verbalizes the property *talmud:courtPresident* where the subject corresponds to the first argument of the property (i.e., the property domain class), and the object corresponds to the second argument of the property (i.e., the property range class). The encoding generated by LexO is the following.

```
:presidente_del_tribunale_it_entry a
    ontolex:LexicalEntry,
    ontolex:MultiwordExpression ,
    synsem:synBehavior
    :presidente_del_tribunale_it_frame1 .

:presidente_del_tribunale_it_frame1 a
    synsem:SyntacticFrame, lexinfo:NounFrame ;
    lexinfo:subject
        :presidente_del_tribunale_it_frame1_arg1 ;
    lexinfo:object
        :presidente_del_tribunale_it_frame1_arg2 .

:presidente_del_tribunale_it_frame1_arg1 a
    synsem:SyntacticArgument .

:presidente_del_tribunale_it_frame1_arg2 a
    synsem:SyntacticArgument ;
    synsem:marker "of" ;
    synsem:optional "true"^^xsd:boolean .

:presidente_del_tribunale_it_sense1 a
    synsem:OntoMap, ontolex:LexicalSense ;
    synsem:ontoMapping
        :presidente_del_tribunale_it_sense1 ;
    ontolex:reference talmud:courtPresident ;
    synsem:subjOfProp
        :presidente_del_tribunale_it_frame1_arg2 ;
    synsem:objOfProp
        :presidente_del_tribunale_it_frame1_arg1 .
```

Finally, by selecting the "dictionary view" tab, a dictionary-like rendering of all the information related to the selected entry is shown in the central panel of LexO. The rendering layout can be modified by replacing the relative CSS files[14].

3. Next Steps

In this work we have introduced LexO, a web collaborative tool for the construction of lexicographic resources based on the *lemon* model. LexO does not require any knowledge on Linked Data and Semantic Web technologies to be used by a lexicographer. Though similar tools already exist (in primis the cited VocBench), we intend to specialize LexO in the ease with which it makes it possible to create lexical LLOD resources, though at the expense of flexibility and generality.

Regarding further developments of LexO, a number of upgrades have already been planned, among which we list the following: i) the integration of a module for the management of text, to allow a user to import a corpus of texts and use them as a source of lexicographic data; ii) the integration of tools for text processing to support in the construction of the lexicographic resource (for example, given a lemma, by automatically suggesting candidate forms), similarly to what Lexonomy (Měchura, 2017) and Sketch Engine (Kilgarriff et al., 2014) allow to do; iii) the possibility of easily extending the underlying lexical model by the user, through high level interfaces hiding properties and classes; iv) the integration of an importing module, to enable a user to upload an existing lexical resource encoded in other models, such as TEI-Lex0 (Bański et al., 2017), or LMF; v) the enhancement of LexO's REST APIs for allowing users to get the lexical data in either JSON-LD, LMF, or TEI-Lex0[15]; vi) the possibility to manage the module for lexicography (Bosque-Gil et al., 2017) targeted at the representation of dictionaries[16].

To figure out where to start from and to what extent we should reassess our planned activities we would like to have feedback from the LLOD community and from lexicographers willing to create resources in this field. As a matter of fact, it is now crucial both to find new users and application fields where to test it, and, even more importantly, to understand in which way LexO should evolve.

Finally, we are planning to perform an evaluation of LexO focused on its usability by involving some potential users coming from the LLD community.

4. Acknowledgements

This work was supported by the TALMUD project and carried out within the scientific collaboration between S.c.a r.l. PTTB and ILC-CNR (09/11/2017).

5. Bibliographical References

Bański, P., Bowers, J., and Erjavec, T. (2017). Tei-lex0 guidelines for the encoding of dictionary information on written and spoken forms. In *Proceedings of Electronic Lexicography in the 21st Century*, pages 485–494.

Bellandi, A. and Khan, A. F. (2019). Lexicography and the semantic web: A demo with lexo. In *Proceedings of Electronic Lexicography in the 21st Century*, pages 53–56.

Bellandi, A., Giovannetti, E., , and Piccini, S. (2018a). Collaborative editing of lexical and termino-ontological resources: a quick introduction to lexo. In *XVIII EU-RALEX International Congress Lexicography in Global*

---

[14]This operation requires the skills for editing the Java project, substituting the CSS files, and recompiling the LexO project.

[15]Considerations and results coming from ELEXIS project will take into account. See for example `https://elex.is/wp-content/uploads/2019/02/ELEXIS_D2_1_Interface_for_Interoperable_Resources.pdf`

[16]`https://www.w3.org/2019/09/lexicog/`

Contexts – Book of Abstracts, pages 23–27, Ljubljana, Slovenia.

Bellandi, A., Giovannetti, E., , and Weingart, A. (2018b). Multilingual and multiword phenomena in a lemon old occitan medico-botanical lexicon. *Information*, 9(3) 52.

Bellandi, A., Khan, A. F., and Monachini, M. (2019). Enhancing lexicography by means of the linked data paradigm: Lexo for clarin. In Kirl Simov et al., editors, *Proceedings of the CLARIN Annual Conference 2019*, pages 134–137, Leipzig.

Bosque-Gil, J., Gracia, J., and Montiel-Ponsoda, E. (2017). Towards a module for lexicography in ontolex. In *Proceedings of the LDK 2017 Workshops: 1st Workshop on the OntoLex Model*, pages 74–84.

Kilgarriff, A., Baisa, V., Bušta, J., Jakubíček, M., Kovář, V., Michelfeit, J., Rychlý, P., and Suchomel, V. (2014). The sketch engine: Ten years on. *Lexicography*, 1(1).

McCrae, J., Montiel-Ponsoda, E., and Cimiano, P. (2012a). Collaborative semantic editing of linked data lexica. In *In the Proceedings of the Language Resources and Evaluation*, pages 2619–2625, Instanbul.

McCrae, J. P., Aguado de Cea, G., Buitelaar, P., Cimiano, P., Declerck, T., Gómez-Pérez, A., Gracia, J., Hollink, L., Montiel-Ponsoda, E., Spohr, D., and Wunner, T., (2012b). *Interchanging Lexical Resources on the Semantic Web*, pages 701–709. Language Resources and Evaluation. Springer Netherlands.

McCrae, J. P., Bosque-Gil, J., Gracia, J., Buitelaar, P., and Cimiano, P. (2017). The ontolex-lemon model: Development and applications. In *Proceedings of Electronic Lexicography in the 21st Century*, pages 19–21.

McGuinness, D. L. and Harmelen, F. V. (2004). Owl web ontology language overview. W3C recommendation 10.

Měchura, M. (2017). Introducing lexonomy: an open-source dictionary writing and publishing system. In *Proceedings of Electronic Lexicography in the 21st Century*, pages 19–21.

Piccini, S., Bellandi, A., and Giovannetti, E. (2018). A semantic web approach to modelling and building a bilingual chinese-italian termino-ontological resource. In *XVIII EURALEX International Congress Lexicography in Global Contexts – Book of Abstracts*, pages 87–90, Ljubljana, Slovenia.

Stellato, A., Turbati, A., Fiorelli, M., Lorenzetti, T., Costetchi, E., Laaboudi, C., Gemert, W. V., and Keizer, J. T. (2017). Vocbench 3: Pushing collaborative development of thesauri and ontologies further beyond. In *Proceedings of 17th European Networked Knowledge Organization Systems Workshop*, pages 39–52.

Proceedings of the 7th Workshop on Linked Data in Linguistics (LDL-2020), pages 75–81
Language Resources and Evaluation Conference (LREC 2020), Marseille, 11–16 May 2020
© European Language Resources Association (ELRA), licensed under CC-BY-NC

Supervised Hypernymy Detection in Spanish through Order Embeddings

Gun Woo Lee, Mathias Etcheverry, Daniel Fernández Sánchez, Dina Wonsever
InCo, Fing, Universidad de la República
Montevideo, Uruguay
{gun.woo.lee, mathiase, daniel.fernandez.sanchez, wonsever}@fing.edu.uy

Abstract

This paper addresses the task of supervised hypernymy detection in Spanish through an order embedding and using pretrained word vectors as input. Although the task has been widely addressed in English, there is not much work in Spanish, and according to our knowledge there is not any available dataset for supervised hypernymy detection in Spanish. We built a supervised hypernymy dataset for Spanish using WordNet and corpus statistics, with different versions according to the lexical intersection between its partitions: random and lexical split. We show the results of using the resulting dataset within an order embedding consuming pretrained word vectors as input. We show the ability of pretrained word vectors to transfer learning to unseen lexical units according to the results in the lexical split dataset. To finish, we study the results of giving additional information in training time, such as, co-hyponymy links and instances extracted through lexico-syntactic patterns.

Keywords: Hypernymy Detection in Spanish, Order Embedding, Word Embedding

1. Introduction

Hierarchical organizations are key in language semantics. Hypernymy refers to the general-specific relationship between two lexical terms. Such is the case of biology taxonomies (e.g. mammal-vertebrate, pangolin-mammal), seasons (e.g. spring-season) and colors (e.g. green-color), among many others. The general term is called the hypernym and the specific one the hyponym. In natural language processing, automatic hypernymy detection (or taxonomy learning) is an active NLP research area, that has applications in several tasks such as question answering (Clark et al., 2007), textual entailment (Chen et al., 2017) and image detection (Marszalek and Schmid, 2007).

A well known hand-crafted resource is WordNet (Miller, 1995). It is a large lexical database that contains semantic relations, including hypernymy among them. Manual resources consume a considerable human effort for its creation and maintenance, and suffer from incompleteness and inadequacies. Furthermore, different applications require the expansion of the hypernymy relationship to particular instances like celebrities, song names, movies, and so on. Hence, it is clear the importance of automatic mechanisms to overcome or assist manual ones.

Regarding Spanish, the resources available for supervised hypernymy detection are quite scarce. WordNet was originally created for English and later translated into other languages, among which is Spanish (Atserias et al., 2004). This consists in the main source of hypernyms for Spanish. *Hypernymy detection* has been evaluated mainly through binary classification relying on datasets that contain a number of pairs of terms and a label for each pair indicating if hypernymy relation is held between the terms (Shwartz et al., 2016).

A complementary evaluation benchmark for modeling hypernymy is given by *hypernymy discovery* (Espinosa-Anke et al., 2016). It consists on given a domain's vocabulary and an input term, discover its hypernyms. This formulation is beneficial to avoid the lexical memorization phenomena (Levy et al., 2015). Regarding to hypernymy discovery,

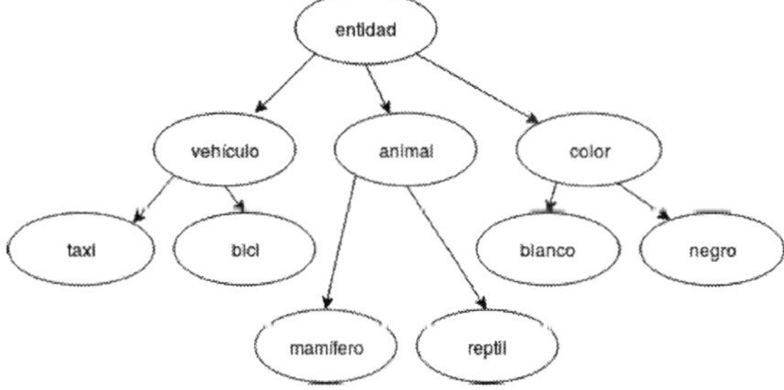

Figure 1: Example of a very simplified taxonomy in Spanish.

a dataset in Spanish (among other languages) was introduced for the task 9 of SemEval-2018 (Camacho-Collados et al., 2018).

In this work we does not pursuit hypernymy discovery and we are aware that it is not clear how realistic hypernymy detection is, since in many scenarios the potential pairs may not be given and need to be discovered. However, we believe that a dataset for hypernymy detection in Spanish can be useful for model comparisons, and according to our knowledge there is no such resource available for Spanish at the time of this work.

We introduce a dataset for supervised hypernymy detection for Spanish built using Spanish WordNet and corpus statistics. We describe its creation process and we made it available to the NLP community as a complementary benchmark for hypernymy detection in Spanish. In addition, we train and evaluate using the created dataset an order embedding (Vendrov et al., 2015) based model using pretrained word embeddings as input, and we report the obtained results for future comparisons. Also, we show that this model, disregarding the use of Hearst patterns, outperforms other distributional approaches and the much more complex hybrid LSTM-based model, that combines distributional and path-based information, proposed by Shwartz et al. (2016).

2. Related Works

Hypernymy detection in NLP can be focused as a supervised or an unsupervised learning task. Supervised approaches relies on pairs annotated with the information of whether they belong to the relationship or not. On the contrary, unsupervised approaches do not use annotated instances, they rely solely in the distributional inclusion hypothesis (Zhitomirsky-Geffet and Dagan, 2005) or entropy based measures (Santus et al., 2014).

Supervised approaches have been addressed mainly using two types of information: paths and contexts distributions (or word embeddings). Path-based (or pattern-based) approaches use the paths of words that connect instances of the relationship. Hearst (1992) presents the first path-based approach where hand-crafted patterns were used for hypernymy extraction. For example, the path "is a type of" would match cases like "tuna is a type of fish" allowing to detect that "tuna" is an hyponym of "fish", etc. Also, paths of joint occurrences in syntactic dependency trees result useful for hypernymy detection (Snow et al., 2004). Path patterns were generalized using part-of-speech tags and ontology types by Nakashole et al. (2012). A different kind of pattern-based approach is proposed in the work of Navigli and Velardi (2010), they consider word lattices to extract definitional sentences in texts and then extract hypernymy related pairs from them, or learning lexical taxonomies (Navigli et al., 2011). The main disadvantage of path-based approaches is that both candidates must occur simultaneously in the same context.

In the other hand, the distributional approaches relies in the contexts of each word independently. Many methods propose supervised classification after applying a binary vector operation on the pair of representations, such as vector concatenation (Baroni et al., 2012) and difference (Roller et al., 2014; Fu et al., 2014; Weeds et al., 2014). Vylomova et al. (2016) studied vector difference behavior in a wider set of lexical relations and they remarked the importance of negative training data to improve the results. Ustalov et al. (2017) performed hypernyms extraction based on projection learning. Instead of classifying the pair of representations, they learned a mapping to project hyponyms embeddings to their respective hypernyms, remarking also the importance of negative sampling. A related approach is presented by Dash et al. (2019), where a neural network architecture is designed to enforce asymmetry and transitivity through non-linearities and residual connection. These last two approaches present some overlap with the work of Vendrov et al. (2015), that its order embedding approach is the one considered in this work.

Shwartz et al. (2016) combined path-based and distributional information in supervised hypernymy detection, concatenating the embedding of each term independently with a distributional representation of all paths between the terms in a dependency parsed corpus. The representation was built with the average of the LSTM resulting representation of each path. Additionally, they introduced a dataset for lexical entailment where they tested their model.

LEAR (Lexical Entailment Attract-Repel) (Vulic and Mrksic, 2017) gives great performance on hypernymy detection specializing word embeddings based on WordNet constraints. The direction of the asymmetric relation was encoded in the resulting vector norms while cosine distance jointly enforces synonyms semantic similarity. The resulting vectors were specialized simultaneously for lexical relatedness and entailment.

3. Hypernymy Dataset for Spanish

In this section we describe the dataset construction process. The dataset consists of pairs of words and a boolean label associated to each pair that is true when the first element is an hyponym of the second and false otherwise. We will refer as positive instances to those pairs that are labelled as true (e.g. summer-season) and as negative instances to those that are labelled as false (e.g. cat-fish).

In the dataset construction process we use a variety of sources to obtain positive and negative instances. In the following we describe each source and technique used; and we give a measure of the quality of the dataset based on a random sampling.

In addition and based on the dataset built by Shwartz et al. (2016), we performed a random split (in train, validation and test) and a split without terms occurring in more than one partition to deal with the lexical memorization (Levy et al., 2015). The latter is referred as lexical split.

3.1. Related Pairs

The extraction of positive pairs was performed using Spanish WordNet, patterns against a Spanish Corpus, and Shwartz dataset translation.

In addition to these sources, it is possible to consider the transitive links as positive instances, since the hypernym relation fulfills the transitive property. However, this assumption may not be satisfied when different senses are faced in the transitive link. So, we decided to not consider inferred transitive instances in this work, and the dataset discard word sense information.

In the following we describe how we use each source:

- Spanish WordNet:
  The main source of positive instances of our dataset is the Spanish version of the WordNet of the Open Multilingual Wordnet (OMW). We consider the hypernymy relation defined in WordNet between synsets, and then we perform a selection of pairs, taking one word of each synset, to obtain hypernymic pairs that will belong to the dataset.

  We considered the following two heuristics:

  1. We choose from each synset those words that are most frequently used according to its frequency in the corpus of Cardellino (2016)[1].

  2. Based on Santus et al. (2014) work, we filtered the resulting candidate pairs that the hyponyms has a frequency greater than the frequency of it proposed hypernym.

---

[1]Spanish Billion Word Corpus and Embeddings by Cristian Cardellino: `https://crscardellino.github.io/SBWCE/`

k	Size (# pairs)	% Correct
1	15695 / 10103	83.9 / 84.3
2	29180 / 19258	82.2 / 83.3
3	35103 / 22851	77.6 / 83.5

Table 1: Size and percentage of correct hypernyms of a sample of the resulting pairs considering 1, 2 and 3 most frequent words of each synset. We show the results applying (right) and without applying (left) the second heuristic filtering.

Regarding the first heuristic, we observe the result of considering the pairs from an all-vs-all of the k most frequent lemmas of each synset. In table 1 we report the respective sizes and percentage of correct pairs of a 0.5% random sample, where can be observed that taking into account more than the two most frequent words of each synset the results degrade considerably.

We filter the output of the first heuristic using the second heuristic and we observe a quality improvement in the resulting pairs. The values on the right in table 1 details the obtained results. According to this minimal evaluation criterion we decide to consider the most three frequent words of each synset filtering the pairs where the hyponym is more frequent than the hypernym.

To finish with WordNet extracted hypernyms, we eliminate the cycles that are generated due to the multiple senses of certain words and the transitivity of the hypernym relation. The resulting pairs are the final set of the WordNet positve instances of the dataset.

- Pattern-based:
Relying on the well known importance of the pattern (or path) based approaches to detect and discover hypernyms, originated by Hearst (1992), we consider to include in our dataset positive instances extracted using high confidence patterns. We consider the following two patterns for Spanish built by Ortega et al. (2011) they found to present a high confidence in their experiments (confidence value near to 1):

1. "el <hyponym> es el único <hyperonym>"
2. "de <hyponym> y otras <hyperonym>"

We use these patterns to extract candidate pairs from the corpus of Cardellino (2016). Unfortunately, the quality of the resulting pairs was poor. Subsequently, we achieve a little improvement filtering the obtained candidates using the part of speech. Even so, we did not obtain good enough results to be included in the final dataset. However, we consider that despite the poor quality the extracted instances, it may become useful to study the behavior of including them as training data. For that purpose it is available along with the dataset.

- Shwartz dataset translation:
In the dataset built by Shwartz et al. (2016), they obtained the hypernymy relation instances from English WordNet, DBPedia, Wikidata and Yago. Their

dataset contains a considerable number of instances like shakespeare-writer. Therefore, we consider to select those pairs that contain proper names as hyponym candidate. We limit our selection to the instances of: "village", "city", "company", "town", "place", "river" and "person"; and we translate the instances through Google's translation library. We include the resulting candidates as positive instances in our dataset.

3.2. Unrelated Pairs

The unrelated pairs, or negative instances, are those pairs that does not hold an hypernymic relation between them. We consider for the procurement of unrelated pairs the following approaches:

- Random sampling:
Since most of the words are not hypernym between them, we can randomly pick two words from a given vocabulary and we probably will get a non hypernymic pair. So, we obtain the noun words from the Cardellino's Corpus, with at least 4 characters and a frequency greater than to 200, jointly with the vocabulary of the positive part, above mentioned, of the dataset. Then we proceed to generate tuples, that were not already included in the dataset, till complete the desired ratio of 1:3 of positive:negative instances.

The dataset resulting of WordNet, Shwartz translation and random pairs is what we refer as our base dataset, presented in its two versions: random and lexical split, as we will detail later.

- Cohyponyms:
Cohyponymy is the relation between hyponyms that share the same hypernym. They are words that have properties in common, but which in turn have their own characteristics that differentiate them well from each other. Cohyponymy can be seen as words belonging to a same class (e.g male-female, march-november). Given a pair of cohponyms it is highly probably that an hypernymy relation is not fullfilled between them. Therefore, it is possible to obtain negative pairs from cohyponymic relations entailed from the positive instances.

- Inverted links:
The hypernym relation is asymmetric. Therefore, if a tuple satisfies the hypernym relation, its inverse not. Then, having our positive dataset already, a simple way to build negative dataset is exchanging the order of the pairs of the positive dataset. However, synonyms may become a problem in this assumption. We can think between some synonyms that an hypernymic relation is fulfilled in both directions (e.g. neat-tidy). For this reason we does not include inverted links in the distributed dataset.

- Antonymy:
Words that have an opposite meaning are called Antonyms. We assume that if there is an antonymy relationship, the hypernym relationship is not satisfied. Therefore, we include the antonyms extracted from WordNet as negative instances.

Positive Pairs		
WordNet	Pattern-based	Shwartz
27861	2731	3798

Negative Pairs			
Random	Cohyponym	Antonym	Meronym
~ 90000	~ 45000	1107	5940

Table 2: Total amount of positive and negative instances from where each version of the dataset is built.

3.3. Dataset Splits

As usual in supervised training, we split the whole dataset (positive and negative pairs) into train, validation and test partitions. Following the work of Shwartz et al. (2016), we consider two splits of the data: random and lexical split. While the random split is performed randomly, the lexical split does not allow lexical intersection between the partitions. In the following section we describe each one.

3.3.1. Random Split

The random split consists in splitting the dataset randomly, without taking into account any consideration. We perform a random split with the following ratio: 70 % for training set, 25 % for test set and 5 % for validation set. This splitting process has the advantage that any tuple is discarded, leading to a larger dataset, but may suffer of the phenomena of lexical memorization (Levy et al., 2015). The lexical memorization phenomenon occurs when different pairs of hypernym, instead of learning the semantic relationship between words, learn a specific word independently as a strong indicator of the label. For example, given the positive pairs such as: (cat, animal), (dog, animal), (horse, animal), the algorithm tends to learn that the word "animal" is a "prototype" and given any new (x, animal) classifies it as a positive pair.

3.3.2. Lexical Split

To avoid the phenomenon of lexical memorization, the training, validation, and test sets are split with different vocabularies. We split the dataset with the same methodology of (Shwartz et al., 2016). The approximate division ratio was 70-25-5. The respective sizes of the random and lexical splits of our base dataset are shown in Table 3.

		Train	Val	Test	Total
Rnd.	P	18654	1332	6662	106592
Split	N	55962	3996	19986	
Lex.	P	8221	513	2506	44960
Split	N	24663	1539	7518	

Table 3: Spanish dataset sizes for each split: lexical and random. The sizes are discriminated in terms of positive (P) and negative (N) instance. This sizes does not contain cohyponyms or pattern extracted positive instances.

4. Experiments using Order Embeddings

To automatically detect hypernymy we consider a simple feed forward network trained as an order embeddings (Vendrov et al., 2015). This network takes the word embedding to a non negative vector with a partial order relation defined and trained to take hypernym pairs to related vectors.

In this work we show that without path or any additional information than the proper word embedding of each word, and a feed forward network trained as above mentioned, fairly good results can be achieved.

We first give an introduction to the order embedding proposal and our experiments configuration.

4.1. Order Embedding Model

An order embedding is a function between two partially ordered sets $f : (X, \preceq_X) \rightarrow (Y, \preceq_Y)$ that preserves and reflects its order relationships. That is to say, $x_1 \preceq_X x_2$ if and only if $f(x_1) \preceq_Y f(x_2)$.

Vendrov et al. (2015) introduce a method to train an order embedding into $\Re_{\geq 0}^m$ considering the *reversed product order*, defined as follows:

$$x \preceq y \iff \bigwedge_{i=1}^{m} x_i \geq y_i, \tag{1}$$

where $x, y \in \Re_{\geq 0}^m$ and x_i and y_i correspond to the i-th component of x and y, respectively. By definition this relationship is antisymmetric and transitive, being $\vec{0}$ the top element of the hierarchy.

4.1.1. Contrastive Loss Function

The partial order relation $(\preceq, \Re_{\geq 0}^m)$ defined above allows to define measures to quantify the degree to which a pair of two elements does not satisfy the relationship. Let us consider

$$E_p(\vec{x}, \vec{y}) = ||max(\vec{0}, \vec{y} - \vec{x})||^2, \tag{2}$$

where $\vec{x}, \vec{y} \in \Re_+^m$ and max is the maximum function element-wise. Note that E_p indicates the relation satisfaction degree and $E_p(x, y) = 0$ iff $\vec{x} \preceq \vec{y}$.

Then, E_p can be forced to be higher than a threshold α for unrelated terms through the max-margin loss as follows:

$$E_n(\vec{x}, \vec{y}) = max\{0, \alpha - E_p(\vec{x}, \vec{y})\}, \tag{3}$$

guaranteeing that $E_n(\vec{x'}, \vec{y'})$ is 0 when $E_p(\vec{x'}, \vec{y'}) \geq \alpha$ and therefor $\vec{x'}\vec{y'}$.

Then, summing (2) and (3) the resulting contrastive loss function, which consists of minimizing E_p and E_n jointly, stands as follows:

$$L = \sum_{(x,y)\in P} E_p(\vec{x}, \vec{y}) + \sum_{(x',y')\in N} E_n(\vec{x'}, \vec{y'}), \tag{4}$$

where P and N are sets of positive and negative examples, respectively. Note that L is differentiable allowing to fit a mapping to an order embedding through gradient descent based techniques.

4.2. Hyperparameter Configuration

We search for a good hyperparameter configuration through random search. We search for an hyperparameter configuration according to the validation set and report the evaluation results on the test set partition. We consider feed

		P_{rand}	R_{rand}	F_{rand}	P_{lex}	R_{lex}	F_{lex}
(a)	OrdEmb	0.855	0.904	0.879	**0.823**	0.674	0.741
	OrdEmb +cohyp	0.857	**0.932**	**0.893**	0.809	**0.827**	**0.818**
	OrdEmb +pattern	**0.860**	0.885	0.872	0.798	0.766	0.782
	OrdEmb +pattern +cohyp	0.859	0.930	0.893	0.802	0.821	0.811

		P_{rand}	R_{rand}	F_{rand}	P_{lex}	R_{lex}	F_{lex}
(b)	OrdEmb	0.719	**0.946**	0.817	0.744	0.841	**0.789**
	OrdEmb +cohyp	0.847	0.869	0.858	**0.781**	0.716	0.747
	OrdEmb +pattern	0.742	0.931	0.826	0.666	**0.857**	0.749
	OrdEmb +pattern +cohyp	**0.848**	0.870	**0.859**	0.759	0.678	0.716

Table 4: Results on test set on Spanish. The upper table (a) shows the result of evaluating without introducing inferred cohyponymy instances in the test partition and the lower table (b) shows the results including cohyponymy instances in the test partition. The labels +cohyp and +pattern stand for cohyponymy and pattern-extracted instances in the training data.

	P_{rand}	R_{rand}	F_{rand}	P_{lex}	R_{lex}	F_{lex}
Best Distributional (Shwartz et al., 2016)	0.901	0.637	0.746	0.754	0.551	0.637
HypeNET Integrated (Shwartz et al., 2016)	0.913	**0.890**	0.901	0.809	0.617	0.700
OrdEmb ReLU	0.936	0.876	**0.905**	**0.958**	0.615	0.749
OrdEmb SELU-ReLU	0.932	0.845	0.887	0.740	**0.872**	**0.801**
OrdEmb tanh-sigm	**0.967**	0.836	0.897	0.788	0.756	0.771

Table 5: Order embedding results with different activation functions on test of Shwartz English dataset, and we include HypeNET and Best Distributional results reported by Shwartz.

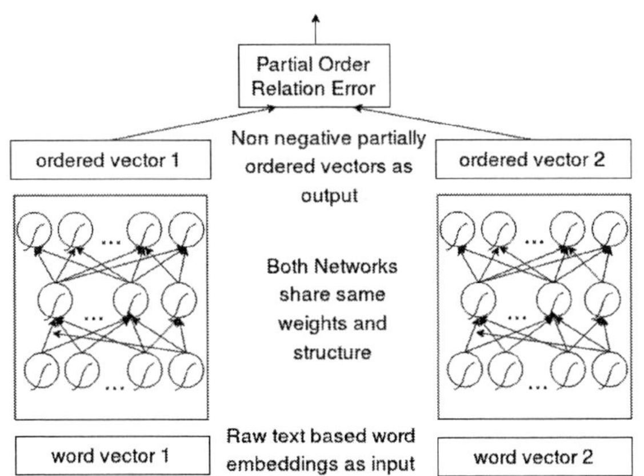

Figure 2: Order embedding diagram.

forward networks using pretrained fastText (Joulin et al., 2016) word vectors for Spanish and English.

We evaluate our models using precision, recall and F measures. The best configuration consisted on a three layered feed forward networks, with 150 neurons and SELU activation function on the first two layers and 100 ReLU units for the output layer. For the training we consider Adam (Kingma and Ba, 2014), with a learning rate of 0.005, and we conclude the training by early stopping, with a patience of 5. We checkout the best performing model against the validation set along the whole training.

4.3. Results for English

We include for comparison the results of the best distributional model reported by Shwartz et al. (Shwartz et al., 2016) and HypeNET integrated mdoel. In the Table 5 can be seen how the order embedding achieves considerable good results in comparison to the best distributional model reported by Shwartz and also in comparison to HypeNET, that is a pattern-based and distributional combined model. We found interesting the good performance of the order embedding model taking as input general purpose word embeddings and without considering any explicit paths information on a corpus.

4.3.1. Results for Spanish

In this section we show the results obtained with the above described model in the introduced dataset for Spanish. We report order embedding results as a baseline in the dataset for future comparisons.

In order to show the behavior of pattern-extracted and cohyponymy instances we consider the following different variants of the training data:

- As base, the positive instances from WordNet and the translated instances of Shwartz dataset, and the negative instances randomly, sampling words from the vocabularies of Cardellino and WordNet. (OrdEmb)

- The base dataset adding cohyponyms as negative instances for training. (OrdEmb +cohyp)

- The base dataset adding positive instances extracted by patterns. (OrdEmb +pattern)

- The base dataset adding for training cohyponyms as negative instances and pattern extracted pairs as positive. (OrdEmb +pattern+cohyp)

We show the obtained results in the table 4. We evaluate the model against the base test partition and including cohyponymy instances on the test data. In the results can be observed that both cohyponyms and pattern-extracted instances during the training give some improvement in most cases, where cohyponyms are most beneficial, with the exception of the lexical split evaluating with cohyponyms addition in test partition.

5. Conclusion

In this paper we show the results obtained on supervised hypernymy detection in Spanish. Given the lack of resources in Spanish for hypernymy detection we build a dataset based on previous work for English. We included two versions of the dataset according to its train, validation and test partitions, and the lexical intersection between them: random and lexical split. The former is done randomly while the lexical split does not contain lexical intersection between the partitions, tackling the lexical memorization problem of the hypernymy detection. We train an order embedding using general purpose word vectors and we obtain that considerable good results. We show the behavior of including cohyponyms pairs for the training considerably improves the overall result.

6. Bibliographical References

Atserias, J., Villarejo, L., and Rigau, G. (2004). Spanish wordnet 1.6: Porting the spanish wordnet across princeton versions. In *LREC*.

Baroni, M., Bernardi, R., Do, N., and Shan, C. (2012). Entailment above the word level in distributional semantics. In *EACL*, pages 23–32. The Association for Computer Linguistics.

Camacho-Collados, J., Delli Bovi, C., Espinosa-Anke, L., Oramas, S., Pasini, T., Santus, E., Shwartz, V., Navigli, R., and Saggion, H. (2018). Semeval-2018 task 9: Hypernym discovery. In *Proceedings of the 12th International Workshop on Semantic Evaluation (SemEval-2018); 2018 Jun 5-6; New Orleans, LA. Stroudsburg (PA): ACL; 2018. p. 712–24.* ACL (Association for Computational Linguistics).

Cardellino, C. (2016). Spanish billion words corpus and embeddings. *Spanish Billion Words Corpus and Embeddings*.

Chen, Q., Zhu, X., Ling, Z., Inkpen, D., and Wei, S. (2017). Natural language inference with external knowledge. *CoRR*, abs/1711.04289.

Clark, P., Fellbaum, C., and Hobbs, J. (2007). Using and extending wordnet to support question-answering. 01.

Dash, S., Chowdhury, M. F. M., Gliozzo, A., Mihindukulasooriya, N., and Fauceglia, N. R. (2019). Hypernym detection using strict partial order networks.

Espinosa-Anke, L., Camacho-Collados, J., Delli Bovi, C., and Saggion, H. (2016). Supervised distributional hypernym discovery via domain adaptation. In *Conference on Empirical Methods in Natural Language Processing; 2016 Nov 1-5; Austin, TX. Red Hook (NY): ACL; 2016. p. 424-35.* ACL (Association for Computational Linguistics).

Fu, R., Guo, J., Qin, B., Che, W., Wang, H., and Liu, T. (2014). Learning semantic hierarchies via word embeddings. In *ACL (1)*, pages 1199–1209. The Association for Computer Linguistics.

Hearst, M. A. (1992). Automatic acquisition of hyponyms from large text corpora. In *14th International Conference on Computational Linguistics, COLING 1992, Nantes, France, August 23-28, 1992*, pages 539–545.

Joulin, A., Grave, E., Bojanowski, P., Douze, M., Jégou, H., and Mikolov, T. (2016). Fasttext.zip: Compressing text classification models. *arXiv preprint arXiv:1612.03651*.

Kingma, D. P. and Ba, J. (2014). Adam: A method for stochastic optimization. *CoRR*, abs/1412.6980.

Levy, O., Remus, S., Biemann, C., and Dagan, I. (2015). Do supervised distributional methods really learn lexical inference relations? In Rada Mihalcea, et al., editors, *NAACL HLT 2015, The 2015 Conference of the North American Chapter of the Association for Computational Linguistics: Human Language Technologies, Denver, Colorado, USA, May 31 - June 5, 2015*, pages 970–976. The Association for Computational Linguistics.

Marszalek, M. and Schmid, C. (2007). Semantic hierarchies for visual object recognition. *Computer Vision and Pattern Recognition, 2007. CVPR '07. IEEE Conference*, pages 1–7, June.

Miller, G. A. (1995). Wordnet: A lexical database for english. *Commun. ACM*, 38(11):39–41.

Nakashole, N., Weikum, G., and Suchanek, F. M. (2012). PATTY: A taxonomy of relational patterns with semantic types. In *EMNLP-CoNLL*, pages 1135–1145. ACL.

Navigli, R. and Velardi, P. (2010). Learning word-class lattices for definition and hypernym extraction. In *Proceedings of the 48th Annual Meeting of the Association for Computational Linguistics*, pages 1318–1327, Uppsala, Sweden, July. Association for Computational Linguistics.

Navigli, R., Velardi, P., and Faralli, S. (2011). A graph-based algorithm for inducing lexical taxonomies from scratch. In *Twenty-Second International Joint Conference on Artificial Intelligence*.

Ortega, R. M. A.-a., Aguilar, C. A., Villaseã, L., Montes, M., and Sierra, G. (2011). Hacia la identificaciÃde relaciones de hiponimia/hiperonimia en Internet. *Revista signos*, 44:68 – 84, 03.

Roller, S., Erk, K., and Boleda, G. (2014). Inclusive yet selective: Supervised distributional hypernymy detection. In *Proceedings of the 25th International Conference on Computational Linguistics (COLING 2014)*, pages 1025–1036, Dublin, Ireland, August.

Santus, E., Lenci, A., Lu, Q., and Schulte im Walde, S. (2014). Chasing hypernyms in vector spaces with entropy. In *Proceedings of the 14th Conference of the European Chapter of the Association for Computational Linguistics, EACL 2014, April 26-30, 2014, Gothenburg, Sweden*, pages 38–42.

Shwartz, V., Goldberg, Y., and Dagan, I. (2016). Improving hypernymy detection with an integrated path-based and distributional method. *CoRR*, abs/1603.06076.

Snow, R., Jurafsky, D., and Ng, A. Y. (2004). Learning syntactic patterns for automatic hypernym discovery. In *Advances in Neural Information Processing Systems 17 [Neural Information Processing Systems, NIPS 2004, December 13-18, 2004, Vancouver, British Columbia, Canada]*, pages 1297–1304.

Ustalov, D., Arefyev, N., Biemann, C., and Panchenko, A. (2017). Negative sampling improves hypernymy extraction based on projection learning. In *EACL (2)*, pages 543–550. Association for Computational Linguistics.

Vendrov, I., Kiros, R., Fidler, S., and Urtasun, R. (2015). Order-embeddings of images and language. *CoRR*, abs/1511.06361.

Vulic, I. and Mrksic, N. (2017). Specialising word vectors for lexical entailment. *CoRR*, abs/1710.06371.

Vylomova, E., Rimell, L., Cohn, T., and Baldwin, T. (2016). Take and took, gaggle and goose, book and read: Evaluating the utility of vector differences for lexical relation learning. In *ACL (1)*. The Association for Computer Linguistics.

Weeds, J., Clarke, D., Reffin, J., Weir, D. J., and Keller, B. (2014). Learning to distinguish hypernyms and co-hyponyms. In *COLING*, pages 2249–2259. ACL.

Zhitomirsky-Geffet, M. and Dagan, I. (2005). The distributional inclusion hypotheses and lexical entailment. In *ACL*.

Proceedings of the 7th Workshop on Linked Data in Linguistics (LDL-2020), pages 82–86
Language Resources and Evaluation Conference (LREC 2020), Marseille, 11–16 May 2020
© European Language Resources Association (ELRA), licensed under CC-BY-NC

Lexemes in Wikidata: 2020 status

Finn Årup Nielsen
DTU Compute, Technical University of Denmark
Richard Petersens Plads, Kongens Lyngby, Denmark
faan@dtu.dk

Abstract

Wikidata now records data about lexemes, senses and lexical forms and exposes them as Linguistic Linked Open Data. Since lexemes in Wikidata was first established in 2018, this data has grown considerably in size. Links between lexemes in different languages can be made, e.g., through a derivation property or senses. We present some descriptive statistics about the lexemes of Wikidata, focusing on the multilingual aspects and show that there are still relatively few multilingual links.

Keywords: Wikidata, lexicographic data, Linguistic Linked Open Data

1. Introduction

Wikidata is the structured data sister of Wikipedia where users can collaboratively edit a knowledge graph (Vrandečić and Krötzsch, 2014). Wikidata does not only support the different language versions of Wikipedia but also the other Wikimedia wikis such Wikisource, Wikimedia Commons, Wikiquote, etc. as well as describe many items without any equivalent article in the other wikis. For instance, Wikidata describes tens of millions of scientific articles (Nielsen et al., 2017). The data in Wikidata is converted to a Semantic Web representation (Erxleben et al., 2014) and a public and continuously updated SPARQL endpoint—*Wikidata Query Service* (WDQS)—is set up at `https://query.wikidata.org`.

Since 2018, Wikidata has included special pages for lexicographic data distinguished from the usual Wikidata "Q-items" with a new namespace for lexemes. Each page represents one lexeme, its sense(s) and its lexical form(s) together with annotation about them and links between them, both within and between lexemes as well as to the Q-items. The lexicographic data is also converted to a Semantic Web representation and available in WDQS. For the RDFication of the lexeme data, Wikidata uses a combination of classical Wikidata URIs and URIs from (Linguistic) Linked Open Data ontologies (Cimiano et al., 2016; McCrae et al., 2017): `ontolex:lexicalForm`, `ontolex:sense`, `ontolex:LexicalEntry`, `ontolex:LexicalSense`, `ontolex:Form` and `dct:language` as well as other URIs, e.g., `dct:langauage` and `wikibase:lemma`.

We have described the lexicographic information on Wikidata before focusing on the Danish lexemes (Nielsen, 2019a) and also described our SPARQL-based Web application *Ordia* for aggregating and visualizing the Wikidata lexicographic data (Nielsen, 2019b). Here we will make an update of the work on lexemes in Wikidata and focus on the multilingual aspects.

2. Descriptions

In February 2020, Wikidata had more than 77 million Q-items.[1] Over 250,000 lexemes are in February 2020 avail-

Chains	Count	Between-language count
1	3897	1453
2	1158	333
3	443	127
4	141	33
5	47	9
6	12	3

Table 1: Counts of level of etymological derivations (chains) per 23 February 2020. The last result is available in WDQS from `https://w.wiki/Htz`.

able in Wikidata.[2] This is up from 43,816 we reported in 2019 (Nielsen, 2019a). In February 2020, there were over 3 million lexical forms and over 55,000 senses.

2.1. Languages

Lexemes from 668 languages are recorded in Wikidata.[3] However, many languages have only a single lexeme. The top language with most lexemes is Russian (101,137 lexemes), followed by English (38,122), Hebrew (28,278), Swedish (21,790), Basque (18,519), French (10,520) and Danish (4,565). Russian is also the language with more forms than any other language (1,236,456), followed by Basque (956,473), Hebrew (446,795), Swedish (148,980), Czech (77,747) and English (64,798). For senses, the languages from the top are Basque (20,272), English (12,911), Hebrew (3,845), Russian (2,292) and Danish (2,217).

2.2. Etymology

Etymological information may be described through the *derived from* property (P5191) corresponding to `lemonet:derivedFrom` from (Chiarcos et al., 2016). It has been used over 3,800 times, see Table 1. Apart from tracking derivations between different languages, the property may also be used to record intralanguage derivations. Table 1 shows statistics for the total number of derivations and the cross-language derivations by the derivation chain

---

[1] `https://www.wikidata.org/wiki/Special:Statistics`

[2] `https://tools.wmflabs.org/ordia/statistics/`

[3] `https://tools.wmflabs.org/ordia/language/`

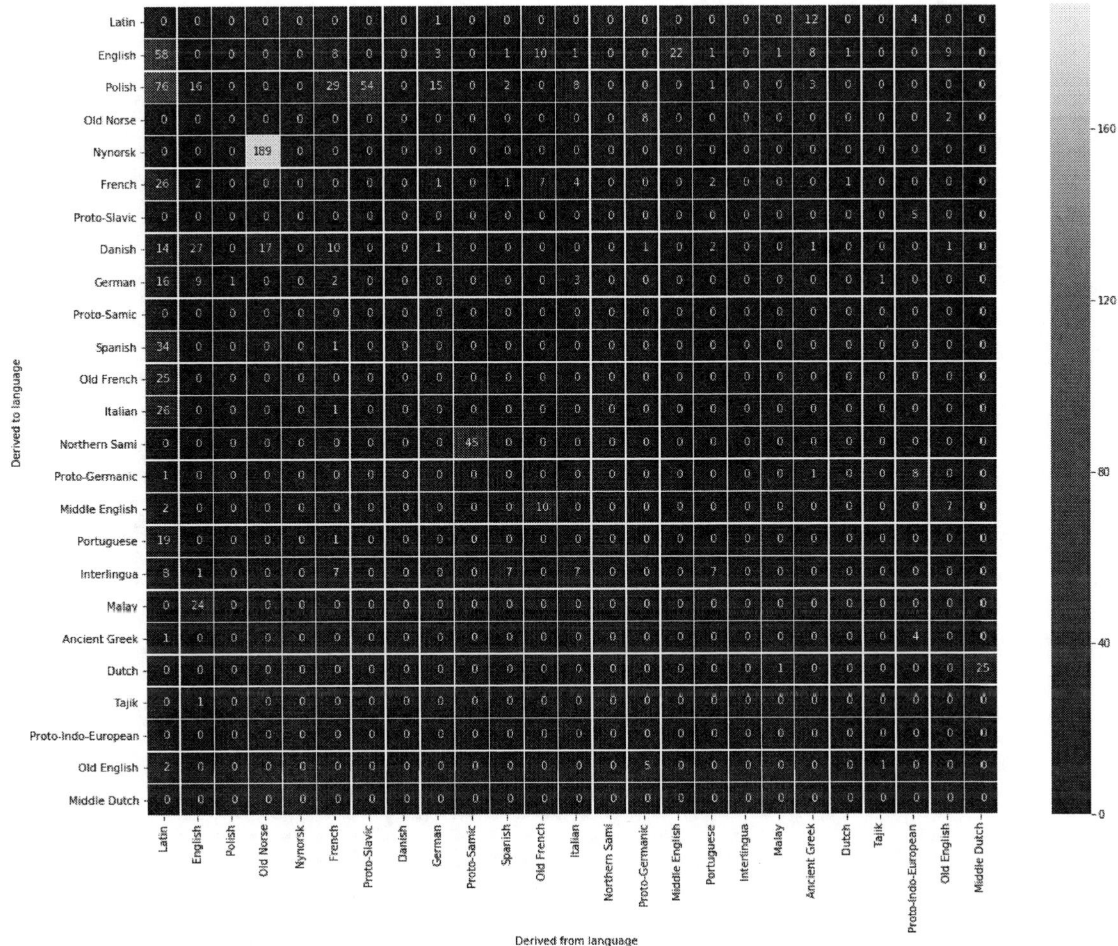

Figure 1: Derivation matrix: Count of the number of derived lexemes between languages as recorded in Wikidata.

length. The currently longest derivation chain is 6, and an example of a long between-language derivation is from the Afrikaans word *hond* (dog) through Dutch, Middle Dutch, Old Dutch, Proto-Germanic to Proto-Indo-European.

The etymological derivation matrix in Figure 1 shows the yet sparse between-language derivation data among the 25 languages with the most derivations. Most of the languages are Indoeuropean, though among the 25 are also Samic languages, Malay and Interlingua. The largest number of recorded (direct) derivations is from Old Norse to Nynorsk, — but with just 189 links. Latin is the source language with the most derivations. A PageRank analysis in NetworkX of the directed and count-weighted derivation graph with $\alpha = 0.9$ presents Proto-Indo-European on the top, followed by Latin, Ancient Greek and English.

Derivations and compounding may also be described by the compound property (P5238). As of 25 February 2020, Dan-

ish (1,735), French (320), Polish (245) and English (197) are the languages which have used the property the most.[4] The etymological data in Wikidata is dwarfed by the amount that can be extracted from Wiktionary (de Melo, 2014).

2.3. Senses

Lexemes link to senses and a sense can link to senses in other languages. The two primary means are through the *translated to* property (P5972) that links to other senses or by the *item for this sense* (P5137) that links to a Q-item. As of 26 February 2020, the former property has been used 3,633 times, while the latter property has been used 25,891 times. Figure 2 shows the number of translations

---

[4]Counting distinct lexemes with WDQS with the SPARQL `?lexeme dct:language ?language ; wdt:P5238 [] .` with the result at `https://w.wiki/J5x`.

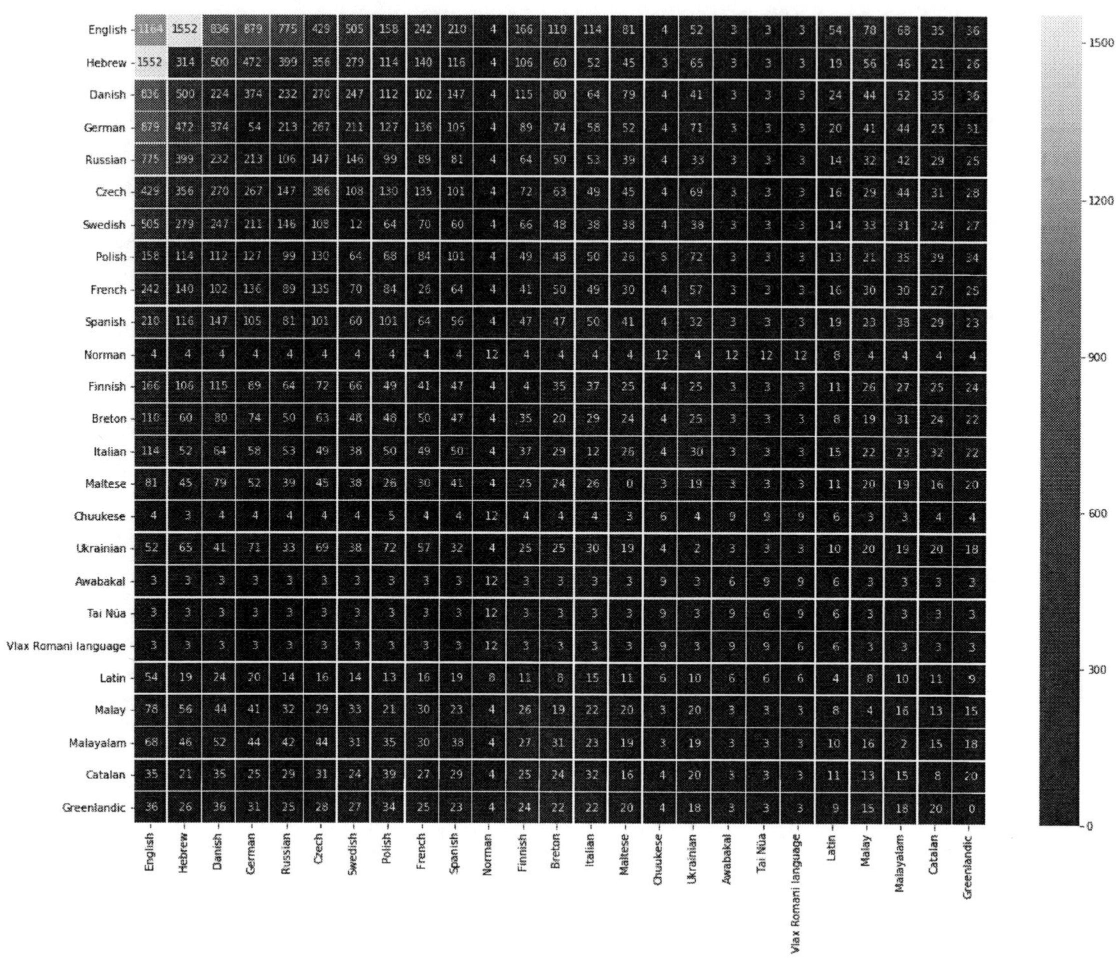

Figure 2: Sense-Q-item links between languages among lexemes in Wikidata. The diagonal shows twice the number of synonym combinations for lexemes within each languages. The data has been extracted with a SPARQL query that contains the following fragment: `?lexeme1 dct:language ?language1 ; ontolex:sense / wdt:P5137 ?item . ?lexeme2 dct:language ?language2 ; ontolex:sense / wdt:P5137 ?item.`

via the *item for this sense* property for the 25 languages with the most translation links. The diagonal shows twice the number of synonym combinations for lexemes within each language. The current number of translations is much lower than what can be extracted from Wiktionary, see, e.g., (Sérasset, 2014, Table 4). Only the combination English-Hebrew has over 1,000 translations. While Basque is the language with the most senses defined, the senses of the language do not in a sufficient degree link further on to the Q-items to get among the 25 most linked languages that is shown in Figure 2.

A different way to link senses to Q-items is by the *demonym of* (P6271) property that is only relevant to use for demonyms. It does not link to the sense of the demonym, but rather to the sense of the region associated with demonym, e.g., from the French lexeme *parisienne* (L25620) to the Q-item for Paris (Q90). Figure 3 shows the demonym matrix where the Spanish-Danish language pair has the largest number of links between demonyms.

There are several other properties that link sense-to-sense within language, e.g., *hypernym*, *troponym of* and a seldomly used *periphrastic definition* property.

2.4. External identifiers

Wikidata has numerous deep links to items in external databases through the properties with the *external identifier* datatype. There are currently 4.789 recorded prop-

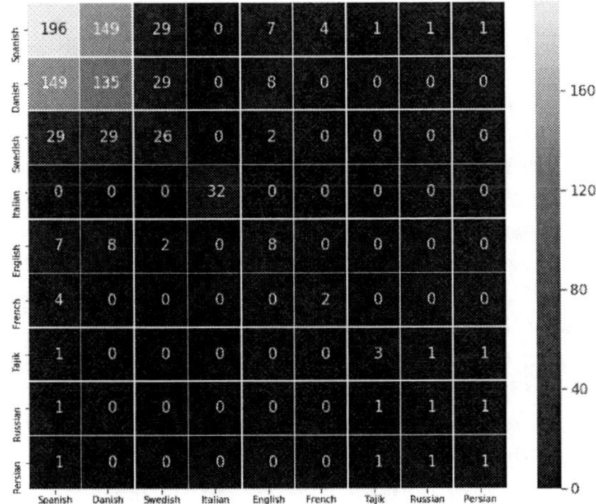

Figure 3: Sense-Q-item links between languages among lexemes in Wikidata with the *demonym for* property. The diagonal counts the number of distinct lexemes per language with demonym senses.

Count	Identifier	Language(s)
14440	Elhuyar	Basque
2878	DanNet word	Danish
1688	WSO Online	Polish
1353	SJP Online	Polish
1288	Doroszewski	Polish
1027	Dobry słownik	Polish
1009	WSJP	Polish
388	Oqaasileriffik	Greenlandic, Danish, English
216	Vocabolario Treccani	Italian
212	OED Online	English
160	Kopaliński	Polish

Table 2: External identifiers in Wikidata sorted according to usage per 22 February 2020. Updated statistics is available at `https://tools.wmflabs.org/ordia/statistics/`

erties of this type.[5] A few of these relate to the lexicographic items, potentially making Wikidata a multilingual hub for lexicographic resources. The statistics page in *Ordia* at `https://tools.wmflabs.org/ordia/statistics/` shows statistics on 19 linguistics external identifiers. Only 11 of these have currently more than 100 links and they are shown in Table 2. The Elhuyar identifier for a Basque online dictionary has by far the most identifiers. The second most frequent identifier is for words within the Danish wordnet DanNet (Pedersen et al., 2009), and then follows several identifiers for the Polish language. The Greenlandic Oqaasileriffik online dictionary records both Greenlandic, Danish and English lexemes.

[5]`https://www.wikidata.org/wiki/Category:Properties_with_external-id-datatype`

Apart from these identifiers, Wikidata has identifiers to link its Q-items to BabelNet (P2581) and for the Interlingual Index Identifier (P5063) (Navigli and Ponzetto, 2010; Bond et al., 2016). They receive 61,378 and 31 links, respectively.

2.5. Other linguistic data in Wikidata

Wikidata can describe linguistic resources and use them to annotate lexemes. Datasets, corpora and dictionaries may have entries in Wikidata. *Ordia* shows resources that have been used in the usage examples for the lexemes of Wikidata.[6] The *National Corpus of Polish* (Q6971865) and the *Europarl* (Q5412081) corpus (Koehn, 2005) are the two resources that have been used the most.

Wikidata's Q-items may link to lexeme items with the *subject lexeme* (P6254). 824 distinct Q-items makes 831 links in total. Most of these Q-items describe Wiktionary pages for French conjugations. A few other items describe scientific papers that focus on particular lexemes, e.g., the new Swedish pronoun *hen* discussed in (Tavits and Pérez, 2019).

3. Discussion

The amount of lexeme data in Wikidata continues to grow, but in many aspects the extent is still low and the annotation for etymology and senses is meager. Russian lexemes and forms are exceptions. They have been automatically set up from the Russian Wiktionary with the Lexicator tool.[7] Wikidata requires the permissive Creative Commons Zero license for its data and this may have prohibited the set up of lexicographic data from other resources, including sharealike-licensed Wiktionary.

What might also have held the sense data growth back is the unresolved issue of linking non-noun lexemes. Q-items in Wikidata usually correspond to common or proper nouns, — at least their labels are usually nouns. The question is how lexemes corresponding to verbs, adjectives and adverbs should be linked. Take the example of the English adjective *little*: Should a Q-item for *smallness* be created and the *little* lexeme linked to that item by the P5137 property, should there be a separate Q-item for *little* linked by P5137, or should the *little* lexeme be linked to a *smallness* by some other means? Wordnets may link lexicographic items across part-of-speech classes with, e.g., *derivationally related form* or *pertainym*.

The tool *Wikidata Lexeme Forms*,[8] that works for several languages, helps Wikidata lexeme editors create lexemes and their forms. We have set up several ShEx expression to detect errors of omission and commission or diversions from normal use for Danish lexemes (Nielsen et al., 2019). Such tools help Wikidata editors maintain a form of consistency and comprehensiveness within each language.

[6]`https://tools.wmflabs.org/ordia/reference`

[7]`https://github.com/nyurik/lexicator`. Issues about what is copyrightable lexicographical data in the context of Wikidata has been discussed, see, e.g., `https://meta.wikimedia.org/wiki/Wikilegal/Lexicographical_Data`.

[8]`https://tools.wmflabs.org/lexeme-forms/`

4. Conclusion

The lexicographic data in the lexeme part of Wikidata is yet not extensive in most aspects, but continuously growing. The most represented languages are Indoeuropean, particularly Slavic, Germanic and Romance languages. Links between lexemes of different languages can be established by an etymological property as well as through senses and the Q-items of Wikidata and links to external lexicographic resources can be established by several external identifier properties in Wikidata.

5. Acknowledgements

This work is funded by the Innovation Fund Denmark through the projects DAnish Center for Big Data Analytics driven Innovation (DABAI) and Teaching platform for developing and automatically tracking early stage literacy skills (ATEL).

6. Bibliographical References

Bond, F., Vossen, P., McCrae, J. P., and Fellbaum, C. (2016). CILI: the Collaborative Interlingual Index. *Proceedings of the Eighth Global WordNet Conference*, pages 50–57, January.

Chiarcos, C., Abromeit, F., Fäth, C., and Ionov, M. (2016). Etymology Meets Linked Data. A Case Study In Turkic. *Digital Humanities 2016: Conference Abstracts*, pages 458–460.

Cimiano, P., McCrae, J. P., and Buitelaar, P. (2016). Lexicon Model for Ontologies: Community Report, 10 May 2016. May.

de Melo, G. (2014). Etymological Wordnet: Tracing The History of Words. *Proceedings of the Ninth International Conference on Language Resources and Evaluation*, pages 1148–1154, May.

Erxleben, F., Günther, M., Mendez, J., Krötzsch, M., and Vrandečić, D. (2014). Introducing Wikidata to the Linked Data Web. *The Semantic Web – ISWC 2014*, pages 50–65.

Koehn, P. (2005). Europarl: A Parallel Corpus for Statistical Machine Translation. *The Tenth Machine Translation Summit: Proceedings of Conference*, pages 79–86.

McCrae, J. P., Bosque-Gil, J., del Río, J. G., Buitelaar, P., and Cimiano, P. (2017). The OntoLex-Lemon Model: Development and Application. *Electronic lexicography in the 21st century. Proceedings of eLex 2017 conference.*, pages 587–597.

Navigli, R. and Ponzetto, S. P. (2010). BabelNet: building a very large multilingual semantic network. *Proceedings of the 48th Annual Meeting of the Association for Computational Linguistics*, pages 216–225, July.

Nielsen, F. Å., Mietchen, D., and Willighagen, E. (2017). Scholia, Scientometrics and Wikidata. *The Semantic Web: ESWC 2017 Satellite Events*, pages 237–259, October.

Nielsen, F. Å., Thornton, K., and Gayo, J. E. L. (2019). Validating Danish Wikidata lexemes. *Proceedings of the Posters and Demo Track of the 15th International Conference on Semantic Systems*, June.

Nielsen, F. Å. (2019a). Danish in Wikidata lexemes. *Proceedings of the Tenth Global Wordnet Conference*, pages 33–38.

Nielsen, F. Å. (2019b). Ordia: A Web application for Wikidata lexemes. *The Semantic Web: ESWC 2019 Satellite Events*, pages 141–146, May.

Pedersen, B. S., Nimb, S., Asmussen, J., Sørensen, N. H., Trap-Jensen, L., and Lorentzen, H. (2009). DanNet: the challenge of compiling a wordnet for Danish by reusing a monolingual dictionary. *Language Resources and Evaluation*, 43:269–299, August.

Sérasset, G. (2014). DBnary: Wiktionary as a Lemon-Based Multilingual Lexical Resource in RDF. *Semantic Web: interoperability, usability, applicability*.

Tavits, M. and Pérez, E. O. (2019). Language influences mass opinion toward gender and LGBT equality. *Proceedings of the National Academy of Sciences of the United States of America*, 116:16781–16786, August.

Vrandečić, D. and Krötzsch, M. (2014). Wikidata: a free collaborative knowledgebase. *Communications of the ACM*, 57:78–85, October.